EV Charging Systems for Apartments

DiscoverNet Publishing
1000 North Main Street, Suite 102
Fuquay Varina, NC 27526 USA
Telephone: +1.919.301.0109
email: info@DiscoverNet.com
web: www.DiscoverNet.com

International Standard Book Number: 9781932813463

DiscoverNet

First Printing

Printed and Bound by Lightning Source, TN.

Some of the materials in this book were created by or with the assistance of AI tools including ChatGPT, Gemini and others.

Every effort has been made to make this manual as complete and as accurate as possible. However, there may be mistakes both typographical and in content. Therefore, this text should be used only as a general guide and not as the ultimate source of book publishing industry information. Furthermore, this manual contains information on publishing and marketing that is accurate only up to the printing date. The purpose of this manual is to educate. The authors and DiscoverNet Publishing shall have neither liability nor responsibility to any person or entity with respect to any loss or damage caused, or alleged to be caused, directly or indirectly by the information contained in this book.

International Standard Book Number (ISBN): 9781932813463

This book is available in other formats:

eBook - ISBN: 9781932813333

Audio Book - ISBN: 9781932813654

About the Expert Contributors

Lawrence Harte

Lawrence Harte is the publisher and editor-in-chief of EV Business Magazine and host of the EV Business Podcast and publisher of EV Industry Directory. He has authored over 151 books including EV Charging Systems for Apartments and Businesses and Connected EVs Explained. Mr. Harte has conducted more than 4,100 interviews with EV, media, and communications industry leaders. His background includes work with Ericsson/General Electric, Audiovox/Toshiba, communications integration projects with BMW, Ford, and Delphi. Mr. Harte has been an expert consultant for Samsung, Google TV, and other top companies. He is also the inventor of multiple communication patents and holds an Executive MBA from Wake Forest University and a BSET from the University of the State of New York.

Mike Battaglia

Mike Battaglia is the President and CEO of Blink Charging. He has over 30 years of leadership and development experience with growth strategy, global operations, and EV infrastructure expansion and has overseen Blink's rapid global expansion and service and product launches. He previously worked at J.D. Power, Toyota Motor Sales, U.S.A., and SmartDisk. In 2020 he joined Blink and was promoted to President and CEO in early 2025. He has led Blink's revenue growth, has overseen the global rollout of EV chargers in multifamily residences, workplaces, fleets and public venues, and has been recognized among industry leaders, driving EV adoption and sustainability in transport.

Omar Riahi

Omar Riahi is the Global EV Enablement & Sales Development Manager at Percepta, specializing in innovative customer support strategies for the EV industry. With over 15 years of expertise in customer service operations, process optimization, and EV support technologies, Omar has driven initiatives that enhance satisfaction, streamline workflows, and reduce costs. A Lean Six Sigma Black Belt, he is known for implementing data-driven solutions that elevate EV customer experiences while creating new value for automotive clients.

Nas Jafari

Nas Jafari is a specialist in EV chargers for multi-unit residences and commercial properties, focusing on making electric vehicle charging accessible and efficient for apartment communities and businesses. With over 10 years of experience in renewable energy, EV infrastructure, and sustainable technology, Nas combines hands-on expertise with strategic vision to deliver practical, future-ready solutions that work for both residents and property managers.

Her leadership and innovation were recognized when Future Charging Solutions won the 2025 Australian Women's Small Business Champion Award in the Environmental Business category, celebrating the quality, impact, and influence of her work in the EV and sustainability space. Passionate about driving adoption of clean technology, Nas continues to design scalable charging networks, optimize energy efficiency, and educate

Ben Prochazka

Ben Prochazka is the Executive Director of the Electrification Coalition, leading national efforts to advance transportation electrification across public and private sectors. He has over 25 years of leadership and development experience in environmental advocacy, human rights, and voter engagement. Ben's career includes roles as Vice President at FieldWorks, Campaign Director for the Save Darfur Coalition, and Legislative Director for the Colorado Environmental Coalition. He has spearheaded landmark initiatives such as establishing one of the nation's first EV deployment communities in Northern Colorado, launching the first electric rental car program in Orlando, driving the Smart City Challenge with USDOT.

Jeff Allen

Jeff Allen is the Executive Director of Forth and a transportation electrification expert. He works closely with charging providers, utilities, automakers, policymakers, and site hosts to turn EV charging policy and technology into practical, deployable solutions. Jeff understands the real-world challenges EV charging system owners face—from infrastructure planning and grid coordination to incentives, operations, and long-term adoption. Previously, Jeff served as an Executive Director and organizational development consultant for nonprofit conservation organizations. He holds a Master's degree in Public Policy from UC Berkeley's Goldman School of Public Policy and graduated Phi Beta Kappa from the University of Michigan.

Willie Moore

Willie Moore is an EV funding, rebates, and incentive specialist at Resound Energy, where he helps organizations navigate the complex landscape of grants, utility incentives, and clean-energy funding programs that support EV charging and electrification projects. He brings leadership and project-development experience across energy efficiency, renewable energy, and transportation electrification, with a focus on helping commercial and multifamily property owners reduce upfront costs and improve project ROI. Willie has worked with public and private stakeholders to identify eligible funding sources, prepare incentive documentation, and align EV charging projects with utility and government program requirements. His work supports faster deployment of EV infrastructure while minimizing financial and compliance risk for site hosts and developers.

Pravin Sankhwar

Pravin Sankhwar, PE, LEED AP (BD+C) is a Licensed Professional Engineer and Electrical Engineer at a leading engineering and project management services firm, specializing in electrical design, inspections, commissioning, and quality assurance for residential, commercial, and renewable energy projects. He brings over 14 years of experience across power distribution systems, NEC code compliance, electrical safety, and grid-connected solar and wind energy systems. Pravin holds a Professional Engineer (PE) license, LEED AP credential, and ICC Commercial Electrical Inspector certification, along with a Master's degree and graduate studies in advanced power systems engineering and business. His expertise includes distribution planning, relay testing, load analysis, and power flow optimization, and he is known for delivering high-quality, compliant engineering solutions that support reliable infrastructure and sustainable energy development.

Tim Meyer

Tim Meyer is EV Technology expert specializing in renewable energy solutions and sector coupling. With over 27 years of experience in technology and management within the renewable energy and energy industries, Tim has held executive positions, including Chief Technology Officer at DirectNu Energy and board member at Inductive Robotics. He has been instrumental in developing and commercializing EV technology, contributing to the advancement of sustainable transportation. Tim is also a frequent speaker at industry events, sharing insights on the integration of renewable energy and electric mobility. His passion for innovation drives his mission to create a more sustainable future.

Anup Parikh

Anup Parikh is the Founder of Pangea Charging which is focused on solving the challenges of advancing EV charging infrastructure solutions in multifamily buildings. He has over 12 years of experience and thought leadership in electric mobility. Anup Parikh has worked for startups and established organizations, like ChargePoint, and now operates his own business. He is also a content creator (check out The Fast and The Curious on YouTube) covering the electric vehicle and charging infrastructure ecosystem, showing the successes and gaps of the market as they exist today.

Massimo Lagrutta

Massimo (Max) Lagrutta is the Founder and Director of Charge N Go Australia, a company focused on building and operating EV charging infrastructure for apartments, businesses, fleets, and commercial properties. He began developing EV charging infrastructure in 2018 when he established Charge N Go in Malaysia, deploying charging solutions for high-end apartments and condominium developments. Working in dense multi-resident environments gave him experience addressing the challenges of access control, billing automation, and electrical load balancing for shared charging systems. Massimo later expanded Charge N Go into Australia, where the company delivers end-to-end EV charging solutions including charger installation, charging network operation, cloud-based management platforms, and Charging-as-a-Service models. He works with property developers, strata managers, electrical contractors, and businesses to deploy scalable EV charging infrastructure that supports reliable operation, fair billing, and efficient electrical capacity management.

Kim Gray

Kim Gray is an EV charging services and infrastructure expert known in the industry for helping to build the industry's first underwritten warranty on charging equipment. She has extensive leadership and development experience supporting EV charging manufacturers, warranty providers and servicing companies with a strong focus on preventative maintenance and scalable charging infrastructure deployment. Kim works closely with charging network operators, site hosts, and service providers to improve charger uptime, service workflows, and customer experience across public and commercial charging locations. Her background includes property management, commercial real estate, hands-on experience performing thousands of inspections on charging equipment across the country, O&M strategy, and vendor coordination.

Foreword

In the decade since I first began building out and supporting nationwide charging networks, I've come across one question frequently brought up by property developers and owners, and it isn't whether or not they should install chargers, but rather how to do it in a way that is practical, scalable, and financially sound.

As President and CEO of Blink Charging, I've watched EV charging evolve in the real estate industry from a niche, early-adopter trend into a fundamental requirement of modern real estate. We are witnessing a defining shift in consumer behavior. The traditional refueling paradigm of the gas station is being replaced by charging meeting EV drivers where they live and work. For the millions of people living in multifamily communities, the availability of reliable, on-site charging is no longer a luxury; it is the deciding factor in where they choose to live and sign a lease.

While demand has escalated, the path to installation execution has a few bumps in the road. Navigating the intersection of aging electrical grids, evolving software requirements, and compliance with local regulatory codes can make the prospect of integrating EV charging infrastructure seem overwhelming, even the most seasoned property manager. I've come across, and had to support, property owners who rushed into poorly planned installations that result in underutilized equipment, frustrated tenants, and systems that simply don't deliver.

This is why "EV Charging Systems for Apartments and Businesses" fills such an important gap to further EV charging infrastructure development in real estate.

What sets this book apart is its foundation in collective intelligence. It's real-world expertise over theoretical text; it is grounded in tacit knowledge from the professionals who live this work every day. By distilling the practical lessons learned by the experiences of 12 contributing authors and over 100 industry experts—from manufacturers and installers to utility directors and property owners—this book provides a comprehensive view of the charging ecosystem. I'm proud to have contributed to this important collaboration.

In this guide, you will find the same principles we rely on at scale:

The Business of Charging: Understanding charging beyond an immediate cost and seeing it as a long-term asset, enhancing property value and creating revenue opportunities.

The Logic of Feasibility: Using data-driven forecasting to ensure your infrastructure grows alongside tenant demand.

The Reality of Operations: Recognizing that the success of an EV charging installation depends on reliability, uptime, and software to consistently deliver a seamless charging experience.

We are at a pivotal point in the evolution of electric mobility. The infrastructure we build today will define the urban landscape for decades. Whether you are a property owner looking to strengthen your portfolio, or a professional looking to master the operational side of this new trade, this book provides the practical, step-by-step clarity needed to turn a complex technical challenge into a seamless business advantage.

The future of transport is electric, and for the multifamily industry, that future starts at the parking stall.

Mike Battaglia,
President & CEO, Blink Charging

Acknowledgements

Many smart people have helped to create and make this book possible. Some of them gave substantial amounts of time to share their experience and answer questions, while others contributed through their media platforms, professional expertise, or industry leadership.

We would like to recognize the organizations and professionals leading the development, deployment, and operation of EV charging infrastructure and energy systems. Their work is foundational to the growth of electric mobility and the advancement of reliable, scalable charging solutions. We thank Raul Arredondo (eMobility Strategy & Marketing LLC), Brandon Barry (Block Harbor Cybersecurity), Jason Barton (Ford Motor Company), Paul DiBenedetto (PSEG Long Island), Tom DelViscio (Duke Energy), Paul Glenney (InCharge Energy), Frank Gilligan (EVoke Systems), Brendan Jones (EnviroSpark Energy Solutions), Rob Minton (Geotab), Joseph Nagle (Pando Electric), Paul Nijssen (Evcharge4u), Ahmad Nsour (EagleTC), Kurt Regerm (Act2EV), Andrei Stsiapanau (ChargePoint), Mike Weseloh (GoPowerEV), Ken Williams (Ford Motor Company), Ubaldo Rodriguez (Ford Motor Company), and Eric Zeng (Future Digital Energy Co., Ltd).

We also extend our appreciation to consultants, service providers, and industry professionals who bring expertise in strategy, operations, and business development across the EV ecosystem. Their insights help shape practical solutions and accelerate adoption. We thank Tony Abraham (Lighthouse Ethics & Risk P/L, Australia), Liz Allan (Full Circle), Jim Burness (National Car Charging), Jeremy Carter (Rapport Leadership, Australia), Allie Dennis, Mike Dull (EV Universe), Merideth Evans (Percepta), James Goldberg (Percepta), Quenita Marshall (TriNet), Pete Rodriguez (Percepta), and Yasemin Selvi (Alchemy Charge).

We acknowledge the contributions of professionals working within government, energy, and industrial organizations who play a critical role in enabling infrastructure, policy, and large-scale deployment. We thank Surendra Sankhwar (Qatar Petroleum) for his contributions to the broader energy and mobility landscape.

We recognize the important role of academic and research institutions in advancing knowledge, innovation, and workforce development within the EV industry. Their work supports long-term progress and technical excellence. We thank Nikhil Aryan (Graphic Era), Pritam Biswas (Engineers India Limited), Dr. Biswajit Roy Chowdhury (South Asian Institute for Advanced Research & Development – SAIARD), and Dr. Narendra Gariya (Graphic Era).

We also appreciate the contributions of individuals and organizations serving communities and the public sector, helping to expand awareness and accessibility of emerging technologies. We thank Ivy West (Howard County Library System), Khushbu Sankhwar (Kanpur, India), and Kim Thore (Gryphon House Inc).

Deep thanks go to those representing EV associations, whose advocacy and thought leadership are shaping industry standards and policy: Sara Baldwin, Genevieve Cullen, Cliff Fietzek, Joel Levin, Scott McCormick, and Ben Prochazka. Their efforts have laid a strong foundation for EV adoption and sustainability. We're also thankful for our EV regulation contributors, Thomas Boylan and Sture Portvik, for their efforts to align innovation with public policy.

We also want to recognize the influential voices in the EV media landscape who help educate and inspire professionals and consumers alike. Thank you to Sam Evans (Electric Viking), Tom Moloughney (InsideEVs), Laycee Schmidtke (Mss GoElectric), and Gill Nowell (Green.TV Media) for spreading awareness and sparking curiosity.

Special thanks to the family and friends of the contributing experts. You helped and inspired us to learn, do and achieve great things. Thank you to Allie Dennis, Virginia Harte, Douglas Harte, Buddy Howard, Mum and Dad Jafari, Denis McDuff, Tara Ramos, Liliana Riahi, and Shahla Talebi.

Table of Contents

Chapter 1

EV Charging at Apartments

EV Charging Systems at Apartments allow residents to conveniently charge their electric vehicles while helping property owners turn rising EV demand into a high-value amenity that enhances occupancy, generates new revenue, strengthens property performance, and supports sustainability goals. Apartment complexes worldwide are under increasing pressure to provide EV charging access, yet only a small fraction of multi-dwelling properties currently offer it—even as urban populations and EV adoption continue to rise. Property owners and operators must balance high installation costs, limited parking, grid-capacity constraints, and billing complexities while meeting safety standards and pursuing funding or revenue opportunities.

Installing EV-charging infrastructure is not simply a logistical exercise—it is a value creation strategy. By offering transparent, reliable EV-charging access to tenants, owners align with shifting resident priorities: convenience, cost-savings, and sustainability. The proposition is clear: when you install EV chargers, you're not just meeting demand—you're unlocking an up-lift in property performance.

Electric Vehicles and Apartments

The literature specifies, electric vehicle essentially consists of an electric motor irrespective of whether it's capable of being charged by an external power source. This results in categorizing all types of EVs under this umbrella starting from hybrid, plug-in hybrid, battery, and extended range

EVs. However, based on wider adoption and trends for residential apartment application, mainly plug-in hybrid and battery EV are the most viable options. This book mainly focuses on plug-in and battery EVs for apartments defined and categorized under local building codes.

Based on local building codes, an apartment usually consists of a separate set of rooms dedicated for a permanent or non-transient dwelling. Cooking and bathroom facilities are available for independent units. The apartment building usually comprises three or more such units and are categorized as a commercial property for investment and zoning purposes, even though its use is residential. They are either categorized: garden , low/mid/high-rise, lofts, duplex, triplex, penthouse, and many more.

Transforming Apartments Through EV Charging Systems

EV Charging Systems for Apartments are transforming multifamily properties by creating new benefits for both owners and tenants. For residents, convenient charging access delivers modern mobility, cost savings, and sustainability—all increasingly important factors in leasing decisions. For owners, EV charging enhances property value, attracts higher-quality tenants, and opens opportunities for new revenue streams through usage fees, subscriptions, and energy incentives. The result is a powerful amenity that strengthens tenant retention, supports environmental goals, and differentiates properties in competitive markets.

Behind every EV charging system is a combination of advanced hardware, software, and connectivity that work together to deliver reliable service. Chargers vary by level, speed, and network capability, while management platforms handle scheduling, access control, and billing. Successful implementation begins with careful planning—evaluating site infrastructure, electrical capacity, and parking layouts to determine the most feasible and cost-effective design. The installation phase integrates electrical upgrades, chargers, and secure data networks, ensuring that the system meets code requirements and supports future scalability.

Apartment Complex with EV Chargers

Once operational, effective management is key to maximizing performance and user satisfaction. Access control systems, billing automation, and remote monitoring simplify day-to-day operation and enhance the tenant experience. On the business side, clear models for revenues, costs, and return on investment (ROI) guide ownership decisions and long-term financial planning. Funding sources such as grants, tax credits, and partnerships help reduce capital costs, while adherence to regulations ensures safety and compliance. Looking forward, properties can use industry codes and standardsto integrate batteries, solar energy, and expansion options to increase resilience, optimize energy use, and position themselves for the evolving electric mobility future.

EV Charging Value for Apartment Complex Owners

EV charging systems are transforming apartment complexes into more attractive, profitable, and sustainable properties by meeting growing tenant demand for convenient charging access. They enhance occupancy by attracting higher-value residents, generate recurring revenue through usage fees and partnerships, and can be largely funded through grants, rebates, and tax incentives. With automated management tools and reliable support, these systems operate efficiently with minimal staff involvement—delivering long-term value, boosting property performance, and positioning apartment communities as leaders in modern mobility and sustainability.

Amenity Value

EV charging systems have become an essential amenity for apartment complexes, offering a strategic way to attract and retain residents while boosting property value. As more tenants drive electric vehicles, properties that provide reliable charging access stand out in competitive rental markets. Beyond convenience, EV charging aligns with sustainability goals and helps properties qualify for green certifications, enhancing their reputation and appeal to eco-conscious renters and investors.

Higher Occupancy

Occupancy performance improves significantly when EV charging is available on-site. Studies show that properties offering this amenity attract higher-income residents, experience lower turnover, and command premium rents. Tenants increasingly view charging access as a must-have feature—similar to Wi-Fi or parking—making it a key factor in leasing decisions. By meeting this growing demand early, property owners can increase tenant satisfaction, improve retention rates, and position their communities as forward-thinking and future-ready.

New Revenues

Revenue generation is another major advantage. EV charging systems create consistent, high-margin income through per-use fees, subscriptions, or

Whey EV Charging Matters for Apartment Complex Ownersf

time-based billing. Many operators also partner with charging networks or service providers that share revenue or manage billing on behalf of the property. When combined with energy-efficient load management, these systems not only cover their operating costs but can also become steady profit centers that increase net operating income (NOI).

Grants and Incentives

Funding opportunities further improve the financial case for installing EV chargers. Federal, state, and utility programs offer grants, rebates, and tax credits that can offset 30–80% of installation costs. Apartment owners who actively pursue these incentives often find that EV charging projects can be cash-flow positive within a few years. Understanding how to identify, apply for, and manage these incentives is critical to maximizing returns while minimizing upfront investment.

Automated Operation

Smart automation and reliability make smart EV charging systems easy to operate with minimal staff involvement. Cloud-based management platforms handle user access, billing, and monitoring automatically, reducing administrative work. Selecting dependable equipment backed by responsive support ensures long-term uptime and tenant satisfaction. With proper planning and the right partners, apartment communities can seamlessly integrate EV charging into daily operations—creating a sustainable, profitable amenity that serves residents and strengthens property value for years to come.

Surprising Facts – *Apartment complex owners and operators that provide EV charging services to their tenants see a 31% higher tenant retention rate compared to properties without chargers (JLL Research). Properties with EV chargers can command 5–10% higher rents per unit (IREM/Urban Land Institute), and operators report earning $1,200–$2,500 in new annual revenues per charger through usage fees and energy cost pass-throughs (National Multifamily Housing Council).*

Apartment Tenant EV Charging Needs

Electric vehicles offer apartment tenants significant benefits in cost savings, convenience, and sustainability. EVs provide reliable transportation with far lower maintenance needs than traditional gas vehicles, thanks to simpler drivetrains and fewer mechanical parts. Charging at home within the apartment complex can cut fueling expenses by more than half, delivering both economic and environmental advantages. Additionally, the ability to charge overnight allows tenants to refuel effortlessly while they sleep, eliminating the time and inconvenience of visiting public stations and ensuring their vehicles are always ready for daily use.
Electric Vehicle Tenant Benefits

Electric vehicles (EVs) are transforming how apartment tenants think about daily transportation. For residents, EVs provide a dependable and efficient mode of travel with substantially lower maintenance costs compared to

Tenant EV Charging Needs - Low Vehicle Cost, Low Energy Cost, Save Time.

gasoline vehicles. The simplicity of electric drivetrains—fewer moving parts, no oil changes, and less wear on brakes—translates into long-term savings and reliability that appeal to modern renters looking for convenience and sustainability.

EV Charging Costs

When it comes to fueling, EV charging offers tenants a major financial advantage. Home-based charging at apartment complexes can reduce fueling costs by more than half compared to relying on public charging stations or gasoline. This cost difference can translate into hundreds or thousands of dollars in annual savings, making properties with EV charging access far more attractive to current and prospective tenants who prioritize affordability and value.

EV Charging Time

Equally important is the convenience of EV charging time. Overnight charging at home allows tenants to "refuel" while they sleep, eliminating trips to

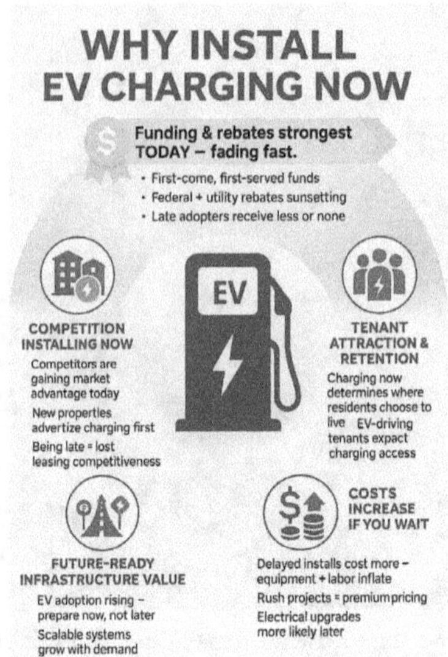

EV Charging System Installation Urgency

gas stations or waiting for a public charger to become available. This effortless routine enhances the quality of life for EV drivers, giving them the confidence that their vehicle is ready every morning—fully charged and waiting in their parking space.

Why Properties Need EV Charging Now

Delaying the installation of EV charging systems at apartment properties poses growing financial and competitive risks as tenant expectations, market adoption, and regulatory requirements accelerate. Early adoption allows property owners to attract and retain sustainability-minded residents, benefit from limited-time grants, rebates, and tax credits, and avoid higher future installation and compliance costs. With competing properties already adding chargers and government mandates expanding, proactive investment not only safeguards long-term property value but also positions communities as modern, future-ready, and aligned with the fast-evolving electric mobility landscape.

Delayed Adoption Risks

Waiting too long to install EV charging can lead to growing frustration among current and prospective tenants who already own or plan to purchase electric vehicles. As EV adoption increases, tenants expect convenient charging access as a standard amenity, similar to Wi-Fi or fitness centers. Properties that delay implementation risk losing tenants to competitors who offer this capability, while also missing out on limited-time incentives and rebates that make installation more affordable today.

Incentives are Time-Sensitive

Federal, state, and utility programs offering grants, rebates, and tax credits are helping early adopters offset a large portion of EV charging installation costs. However, these funds are often awarded on a first-come, first-served basis or within limited funding windows. Acting quickly allows property owners to secure these financial advantages and position their properties as forward-thinking leaders in sustainability and modern living—strengthening brand appeal and long-term asset value.

Competing Properties Are Installing Now

Apartment communities and commercial real estate operators across the country are already adding EV charging stations to attract and retain tenants. Properties that delay installation risk falling behind market trends, losing competitiveness, and being perceived as outdated or less accommodating to modern lifestyles. Early movers are also learning operational best practices, giving them an edge in managing demand, billing, and maintenance.

Tenant Acquisition and Retention

EV ownership is growing rapidly, and tenants increasingly view charging access as a deciding factor when choosing where to live. Offering EV charging not only helps attract these new tenants but also retains existing residents who might otherwise move to properties that better support their evolving transportation needs. Investing in charging infrastructure demonstrates commitment to convenience, sustainability, and tenant satisfaction—all key drivers of long-term occupancy and profitability.

EV Charging Requirements Coming

Government mandates for EV-ready infrastructure are expanding at both state and local levels. Many jurisdictions are updating building codes to require a percentage of parking spaces to be EV-capable, and future legislation may require retrofit compliance. Properties that install EV infrastructure now can stay ahead of these mandates, avoid compliance penalties, and plan upgrades in a cost-effective and phased manner.

Grants and Incentives May Decline

Public and private funding programs are designed to accelerate early adoption, not to subsidize long-term laggards. As EV adoption becomes mainstream, these generous grants and rebates are likely to taper off or disappear entirely. Taking advantage of available funding now ensures properties benefit from maximum cost savings before programs phase down or become more competitive.

Avoid Higher Costs Later

Deferring EV charging installations often results in significantly higher future expenses. As more tenants demand access, rushed or reactive installations can lead to higher equipment costs, increased labor rates, and the need for expensive electrical upgrades. Planning and implementing EV charging systems today allows property owners to spread costs strategically, leverage available incentives, and future-proof their properties against inevitable infrastructure demands.

EV Charging System at Apartment Complex

EV Charging Systems at Apartments

EV charging systems at apartment complexes combine hardware, electrical infrastructure, and intelligent software to deliver safe, efficient, and convenient charging for residents. Properties can choose from Level 1, Level 2, or DC fast chargers, with networked options offering added features like remote monitoring and payment integration. A well-designed electrical system ensures efficient power distribution, scalability, and cost control, while reliable communication networks enable real-time data exchange for monitoring and maintenance. Centralized management platforms automate user

access, billing, and energy optimization—simplifying operations and maximizing long-term value for property owners and tenants alike.
EV Charger Types

Apartment charging systems begin with understanding the types of EV chargers available. These range from basic plug-in Level 1 units suitable for overnight charging to more advanced Level 2 chargers that can fully recharge most vehicles in just a few hours. Some properties are also exploring DC fast chargers that provide rapid energy delivery for public or shared-access parking areas. Networked smart chargers enhance the user experience by offering features such as remote monitoring, payment options, and integration with energy management systems, making them ideal for multi-tenant environments.

Electrical System

Behind every successful EV charging installation is a well-designed electrical system to support EV slow and fast charging solutions. In apartment settings, this can vary from simple dedicated circuits serving a few parking spaces to complex, load-managed systems that optimize power use across dozens of chargers. Smart electrical designs distribute available capacity efficiently, reducing the need for costly utility upgrades while ensuring safety and reliability. Proper planning also allows for scalability—accommodating future tenant demand as EV ownership continues to grow.

EV Charger Communication

Smart EV charging systems rely on data communication to connect each charger to a central network. These systems use Wi-Fi, cellular, or Ethernet connections to enable real-time monitoring, usage reporting, and remote diagnostics. Communication capabilities are critical for ensuring uptime, managing billing, and supporting software updates. For property owners and operators, this connectivity allows them to view usage trends, detect problems early, and provide a seamless charging experience for residents.

EV Charger Management System

At the heart of apartment EV infrastructure is the charger management system—typically a cloud-based platform that automates user access, billing, and system performance. These platforms allow property managers to control who can charge, track electricity usage per tenant, set pricing models, and receive maintenance alerts automatically. Advanced management systems also integrate with utility programs and smart building platforms, enabling load balancing and energy optimization. This centralized control simplifies operations and enhances the long-term value of the charging investment.

EV Charging System Feasibility and Planning

Evaluating the feasibility of EV charging at an apartment complex begins with a comprehensive assessment of the property's readiness. This process includes analyzing tenant demand, existing electrical capacity, available parking, and long-term operational goals. A well-structured feasibility plan

EV Charging Systems for Apartments Feasibility Planning

helps property owners understand costs, identify potential incentives or rebates, and define a scalable roadmap for deployment. It ensures that decisions made early in the project—such as charger type, placement, and management strategy—align with both current needs and future growth.

Tenant Requirements

Understanding tenant needs is the foundation of successful EV charging implementation. Property owners should survey residents to determine how many currently own or plan to purchase EVs, how often they drive, and when they typically charge. This data helps design a charging system that matches real usage patterns—whether tenants need overnight access, shared-use chargers, or dedicated stations. Anticipating future growth in EV ownership ensures that the system remains relevant and avoids costly retrofits as adoption increases.

Electrical Capacity

Before any installation, it is critical to evaluate the property's electrical capacity and infrastructure. This includes assessing the available power from the utility, existing panels and transformers, and potential limitations in wiring or conduit space. A professional load analysis can determine how many chargers can be supported without upgrades and whether smart load management is needed to balance power distribution. Proper electrical planning allows for cost-effective installation and helps avoid unexpected utility or construction expenses.

Surprising Fact - *Many apartment complexes can add EV chargers without upgrading electrical panels or transformers. Smart EV charger load management dramatically caps daytime charging speeds while prioritizing off-peak nighttime charging—when most residents plug in and rates are lowest. Since the average EV requires only about 7 kWh per day, dynamic load management ensures total charging demand stays within the property's existing electrical capacity, avoiding costly infrastructure upgrades.*
Equipment

Selecting the right mix of EV chargers and management software is key to balancing cost, performance, and future flexibility. Property owners should consider the types of chargers—Level 1, Level 2, or DC fast chargers—along with connectivity features, payment systems, and scalability options. Networked chargers with cloud-based management capabilities provide long-term value by supporting usage tracking, energy management, and software updates. Investing in adaptable equipment today ensures the system can evolve with technology and tenant demand.

Installation

A successful installation requires detailed planning and coordination. This involves creating an efficient site layout, obtaining the necessary permits, and scheduling licensed contractors familiar with EV charging systems. Clear communication between electricians, property managers, and tenants helps minimize disruption during construction. Ensuring compliance with local codes, ADA accessibility, and safety standards not only prevents delays but also establishes a foundation for reliable, long-term operation.

Operations & Support

Once installed, maintaining a reliable and user-friendly EV charging system is essential. Property owners should implement management systems that automate access control, billing, and reporting while providing real-time monitoring for maintenance alerts. Regular inspections, software updates, and customer support protocols keep the network running efficiently. A proactive operations plan transforms the charging system from a basic amenity into a managed asset that enhances tenant satisfaction and generates ongoing revenue.

EV Charging System for Apartments Installation

Installing EV charging systems at apartment complexes requires meticulous planning and coordination among multiple specialized contractors. The process involves aligning construction, electrical, network, and utility tasks to ensure safety, efficiency, and regulatory compliance. Because apartment properties often have shared infrastructure and limited parking availability, installations must be designed to minimize disruption for residents while achieving maximum accessibility and long-term reliability. Successful installations rely on clear communication, documented procedures, and adherence to both electrical codes and local permitting requirements.

Project Management

Effective project management is the backbone of a smooth EV charging installation. Property owners or project leads must oversee scheduling, task assignments, progress tracking, and budget control. Coordinating timelines among contractors—such as electricians, general contractors, and utility providers—ensures that each phase proceeds efficiently. Regular progress meetings and inspections help identify potential delays early, while maintaining proper documentation keeps the project compliant with municipal and financial requirements, especially if incentives or grants are being utilized.

Construction Contractors

Construction teams prepare the physical environment for EV charger installation. Their responsibilities include trenching for conduit runs, pouring new concrete pads, painting and striping parking spaces, and installing signage to meet accessibility and safety standards. Proper site preparation ensures chargers are positioned conveniently for users while maintaining compliance with ADA and fire-safety regulations. Coordinating this work before electrical installation prevents rework and keeps the project timeline on track.

Installation Steps for EV Charging Systems at Apartment Complexes

Electricians

Licensed electricians play a critical role in ensuring safe and functional EV charging installations. They handle all aspects of electrical infrastructure, including wiring, conduit placement, breaker panel setup, grounding, and connection of charging equipment. Electricians must verify that the property's electrical load capacity aligns with the planned number of chargers and incorporate smart load management systems if needed. Their work directly impacts reliability, safety, and long-term maintenance, making it essential to use experienced EV-certified professionals.

Utility Coordination

Close coordination with the local utility company is often required to ensure adequate power supply for new EV charging systems. Utilities may need to upgrade transformers, service panels, or meters to accommodate additional electrical load. Early engagement helps avoid project delays and ensures compliance with interconnection and metering requirements. Some utilities also offer make-ready programs that cover part of the infrastructure costs, making collaboration beneficial both technically and financially.

Network Setup

Modern EV chargers rely on reliable data network and internet connections to communicate with management platforms. Network setup involves configuring wired Ethernet, Wi-Fi, or cellular connectivity depending on site conditions. A strong, secure network connection enables real-time monitoring, billing, and software updates. Proper network configuration during installation prevents connectivity issues later and ensures that residents and property managers can depend on uninterrupted charging service.

Software Configuration

Once the hardware and network are in place, software configuration ensures that the system operates smoothly. Technicians or platform administrators set up user access controls, payment options, and maintenance alerts within the charging management system. Testing is performed to verify communication between the chargers, cloud platform, and user applications. Proper configuration enables automated reporting, accurate billing, and data-driven insights, ensuring the property's EV charging infrastructure delivers both convenience for tenants and operational efficiency for management.

EV Charging Systems at Apartments Revenues

EV charging systems at apartment complexes are no longer just sustainability features—they're emerging as valuable revenue-generating assets with some surprising new services. By strategically managing access, pricing, and usage, property owners can transform EV charging from a cost center into a profitable amenity that enhances property value and tenant satisfaction. When properly implemented, charging infrastructure can yield multiple income streams, improve tenant retention, and position the property as a modern, future-ready community that supports eco-conscious living.

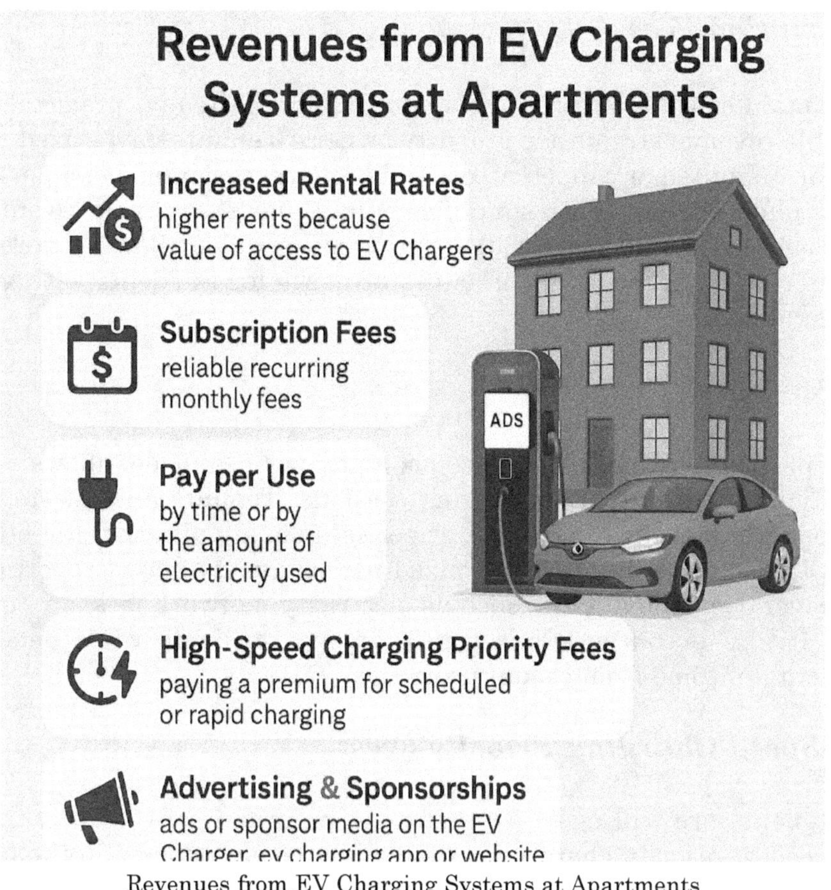

Revenues from EV Charging Systems at Apartments

Increased Rental Rates

Installing EV charging stations allows property owners to offer a premium amenity that justifies higher rent rates. Tenants are increasingly willing to pay more for the convenience of charging at home rather than relying on public stations. This perceived value also attracts sustainability-minded renters who view EV charging as part of a forward-thinking lifestyle. By marketing EV-ready parking spaces as a premium feature, properties can enhance both their competitiveness and long-term revenue potential.

Subscription Fees

Subscription-based charging plans can provide a steady, predictable and profitable revenue stream for property owners. Tenants pay a fixed monthly fee for unlimited or capped access to EV chargers, similar to a parking or utilities plan. This approach simplifies billing, ensures reliable revenue, and encourages consistent usage. Subscription models also allow for tiered pricing—offering different levels of access or perks for residents with varying charging needs.

Pay-Per-Use

For properties seeking flexible income, a pay-per-use model allows revenue generation based on actual charging sessions. Tenants and guests can be billed per kilowatt-hour, per hour, or per session, aligning fees directly with usage. This method is ideal for mixed-use or guest-access properties and helps cover operational costs such as electricity, network fees, and maintenance. It also encourages fair access among residents while generating incremental income from casual users.

High-Speed Charging Priority Fees

Some tenants are willing to pay extra for premium convenience. Offering high-speed or priority charging options provides an opportunity to capture additional revenue from those who value faster turnaround times. This model can include dedicated fast chargers, priority access reservations, or tiered pricing for peak charging speeds. By catering to diverse tenant needs, properties can increase satisfaction while optimizing charger utilization and profitability.

Advertising & Sponsorships

EV charging stations and their associated software platforms open new doors for advertising and sponsorship revenue. Chargers equipped with digital displays or mobile app integrations can showcase paid ads, local promotions, or corporate sponsorships. Partnerships with nearby businesses, automakers, or sustainability brands can also create mutually beneficial marketing opportunities. This additional income stream not only offsets operational costs but also positions the property as a hub for modern, connected living experiences.

Surprising Fact *– Advertising revenue from EV charger displays and their mobile apps can actually exceed the income from selling electricity. Standard EV charger screens typically earn $10–$22 CPM (cost per thousand impressions), compared to just $2–$15 CPM for most digital out-of-home (DOOH) advertising. This means the typical advertising revenue earned per EV Charger display is roughly $1–$3 per hour. The potential grows dramatically with interactive displays, which can generate 10x or more when drivers engage directly with ads. For instance, a streaming subscription sign-up can deliver $5–$20 per customer, while auto test drive bookings can return $25–$75 per qualified lead.*

EV Charging Systems at Apartments Costs

The total cost of installing EV charging systems at apartment complexes includes several interconnected components—equipment, installation, management software, permitting, and ongoing operational expenses. Together, these form a comprehensive investment that balances upfront setup with long-term reliability and revenue generation. While initial costs can seem substantial, EV charging systems can enhance property value, attract tenants, and create recurring income streams that offset expenditures over time. Understanding each cost category helps property owners budget effectively and take advantage of available grants or incentives.

Equipment

Equipment costs for EV charging systems at apartment complexes typically range from $2,000 to $7,000 per Level 2 charger installed, depending on the brand, connectivity features, and charging speed. Networked smart chargers generally cost more than basic plug-in units but offer greater flexibility for user management, billing, and data analytics. Selecting the right charger type ensures the system matches tenant needs and supports future technology upgrades such as load management or vehicle-to-grid capabilities.

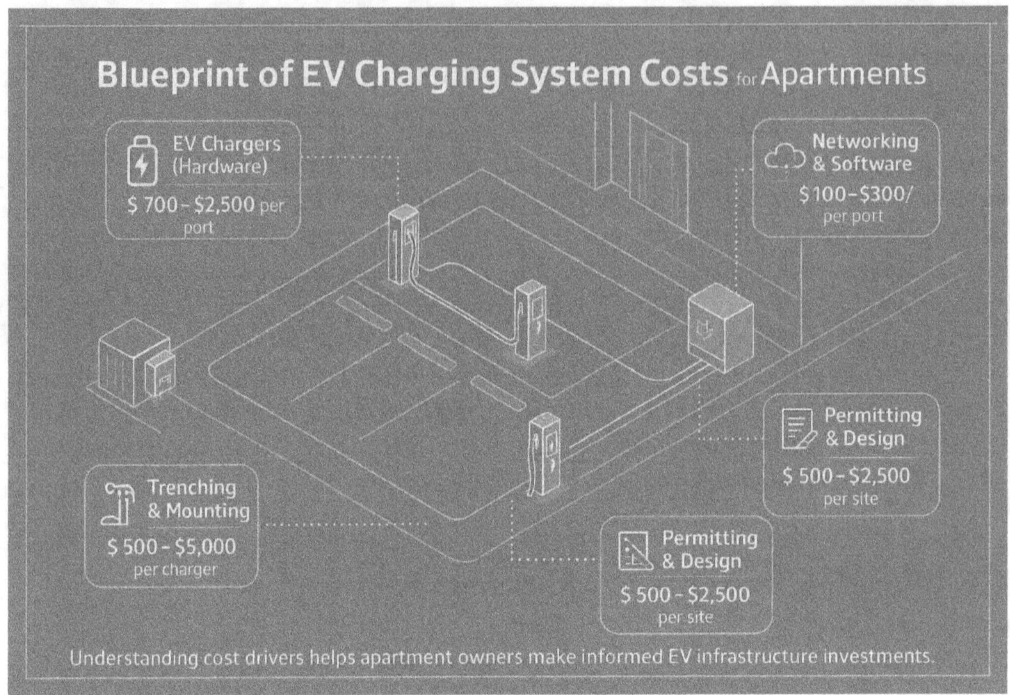

Key EV Charging Systems Costs at Apartments

Installation

Installation represents one of the most variable costs in an EV charging project, typically ranging from $3,000 to $12,000 per charger. The final price depends on site-specific factors such as distance from electrical panels, the need for new conduit or trenching, electrical service upgrades, and local permitting or inspection requirements. Projects requiring concrete work, bollards, or signage may incur additional costs. Choosing experienced contractors and completing a feasibility assessment early in the process helps reduce installation surprises and ensures code compliance.

Management System

The management system provides the digital backbone for operating and maintaining the charging network. Costs typically range from $5 to $25 per charger per month, covering cloud-based monitoring, access control, billing, reporting, and software support. A robust management platform enables property owners to automate user access, track usage, and generate revenue while maintaining visibility into performance and maintenance needs. Many platforms also integrate with utility demand response and incentive programs, offering potential cost offsets over time.

Permits & Inspections

Permitting and inspection fees vary by jurisdiction but are an essential component of any compliant EV charging installation. Local building departments may require electrical, structural, and accessibility reviews before and after installation. These processes ensure safety, adherence to electrical codes, and compliance with ADA and fire regulations. Costs can range from a few hundred to several thousand dollars per project depending on the complexity and size of the installation. Early coordination with local authorities can streamline approvals and prevent costly delays.

Operations & Support

Ongoing operations and support are key to ensuring the reliability and long-term success of the charging system. This includes technical support, periodic maintenance, customer service, and software updates. Property managers should budget for professional service agreements that provide regular inspections, warranty management, and 24/7 help desk access for users. Well-managed support programs minimize downtime, enhance tenant satisfaction, and protect the investment throughout its lifecycle.

Additional Costs

Beyond the major categories, several additional costs contribute to total ownership expenses. These can include electricity usage, network connectivity fees, insurance, signage, and administrative overhead. Such costs typically add $300 to $800 per charger per year, depending on utilization rates and service agreements. Factoring these operational costs into financial planning helps property owners set appropriate charging fees or subscription rates to maintain profitability while delivering a dependable and user-friendly charging experience.

EV Charging System Grants & Incentives

Grants, incentives, and tax credits can significantly reduce the cost of installing EV charging systems at apartment properties. By strategically combining multiple funding sources, property owners can minimize upfront capital investment and lower ongoing operational expenses. These financial tools not only make projects more affordable but also accelerate implementation timelines and improve long-term returns. Understanding how to layer programs effectively—federal, state, local, and utility-based—can make the difference between a costly capital project and a profitable long-term amenity.

Grants

Federal, state, and local governments, as well as utility providers, offer grants designed to make multifamily EV charging more accessible and equitable. These programs can take the form of rebates, cost-sharing agreements, or direct funding allocations to help offset installation and equipment costs. Popular examples include the federal NEVI program, state-level initiatives such as CALeVIP in California, and utility-sponsored EV infrastructure grants. Apartment property owners can often stack these opportunities, provided they meet eligibility and reporting requirements, to substantially reduce out-of-pocket costs.

Incentives

Utilities, manufacturers, or local agencies may provide rebates, discounts, or bill credit incentives to reduce the installation and operating costs. These incentive programs can play a vital role in making EV charging projects financially viable. Many utilities now offer "make-ready" programs that cover a portion of the electrical infrastructure work needed to support chargers, while others provide per-port rebates that help offset hardware and labor expenses. Special EV rate plans can further reduce operational costs by lowering electricity prices during off-peak hours. These incentives are

EV Charging System Budget Proposal – Apartment Complex

Project overview and estimated funding structure for installation of 10 Level 2 EV chargers.

Item Description	Qty	Unit Cost (USD)	Total (USD)
Level 2 Smart EV Chargers (7.6kW, OCPP 1.6J compatible, Wi-Fi + RFID)	10	1250	12500
Installation & Electrical Work (wiring, conduit, breakers, permits)	10	900	9000
EV Charging Management Software Setup	1	2500	2500
System Testing & Commissioning	1	1200	1200
Onsite Staff Training	1	1000	1000
Project Management & Documentation	1	750	750
Miscellaneous Supplies (mounting hardware, signage, labels, protective covers)	1	550	550

Budget Summary

Category	Amount (USD)
Total Project Cost	27500
Grants	-22500
Incentives	-7800
Tax Credits	-10250
Net Project Cost (After Funding)	-13050

Estimated grants, incentives, and tax credits are subject to eligibility and approval by respective agencies.

Key EV Charging Systems at Apartments Grants and Incentives

typically time-sensitive and region-specific, so early engagement with local utilities and energy agencies ensures that property owners capture the most value available.

Tax Credits

Tax-based benefits offer another layer of financial relief for property owners investing in EV infrastructure. Federal programs like the Alternative Fuel Infrastructure Tax Credit (AFITC) can reimburse up to 30% of eligible costs, while accelerated depreciation and energy-efficiency deductions further enhance return on investment. Property owners should consult with tax professionals familiar with renewable energy incentives to ensure full compliance and maximize available savings. By leveraging these credits strategically, apartment communities can transform EV charging into a cost-effective, revenue-generating asset.

Partnerships

Collaborative EV Charging system partnerships can amplify the impact of funding programs while spreading costs and risks. Working with utilities, EV service providers, or municipal agencies can open access to shared resources such as equipment procurement, technical expertise, or co-branded marketing support. In some cases, utilities or private partners may even install and operate charging systems at little to no cost in exchange for long-term service agreements. These partnerships strengthen community sustainability goals and make it easier for property owners to scale EV infrastructure efficiently.

Bartering

Beyond traditional funding models, creative cost-sharing or barter arrangements can further reduce project costs. For example, property owners may allow an EV charging company to display branding, advertisements, or public-access rights in exchange for discounted hardware, installation services, or revenue sharing. These agreements can be especially beneficial for properties with high-visibility locations or mixed-use developments where public access supports both residents and visitors. By thinking beyond conventional financing, apartment communities can unlock new opportunities to make EV charging both affordable and profitable.

EV Charging Systems for Apartments Solar & Battery Options

Combining solar power, battery storage, and Vehicle-to-Grid (V2G) technologies offers apartment communities a powerful way to enhance both the sustainability and economics of EV charging systems. By integrating these energy solutions, properties can lower electricity costs, reduce demand charges, and improve resilience during outages or peak pricing events. The

EV Charging Systems for Apartments Solar & Battery Storage Options

combination transforms charging infrastructure from a passive utility service into an active energy management system—one that supports renewable energy adoption, increases energy independence, and contributes to a cleaner, more stable grid.

Solar for Apartments

Solar power provides apartment complexes with an immediate opportunity to generate clean electricity for EV charging. Installing rooftop or carport-mounted solar panels allows properties to offset grid energy consumption and lower utility bills while reducing their carbon footprint. Solar energy can directly power EV chargers during daylight hours or feed stored energy into batteries for use at night. In addition to the environmental benefits, solar installations can qualify for federal tax credits, depreciation benefits, and local renewable energy incentives, making them a financially attractive upgrade for multifamily properties.

Batteries for Apartments

Battery energy storage systems complement both solar power and EV charging by storing excess energy for later use. Apartments can use batteries to capture surplus solar energy or charge them during off-peak utility hours when rates are lower, then discharge the stored power during high-demand periods. This strategy helps flatten energy peaks, reduce demand charges, and enhance overall grid stability. Battery storage also provides backup power in case of outages, ensuring residents can still charge vehicles when grid power is unavailable—a valuable resilience feature for modern communities.

Vehicle-to-Grid (V2G)

Vehicle-to-Grid technology allows electric vehicles to not only consume energy but also supply it back to the grid or building during peak demand times. In apartment environments, V2G-enabled chargers can turn residents' EVs into distributed energy resources, collectively acting as a flexible energy storage network. This bidirectional capability helps stabilize power systems, reduce peak load costs, and generate potential revenue for the apartment complex and tenants through grid participation programs. As V2G technology continues to mature, it presents a forward-looking strategy for properties aiming to maximize both sustainability and return on investment.

Smart Energy Management

Smart energy management systems serve as the central intelligence for integrating solar, battery, and EV charging operations. These automated platforms use sensors, data analytics, and predictive algorithms to monitor and balance energy flow between chargers, batteries, and the grid. By optimizing when and how power is used or stored, these systems reduce costs, enhance reliability, and extend the lifespan of equipment. They can also communicate with utility programs for demand response participation, allowing apartment properties to earn incentives for reducing energy use during peak periods—all while maintaining a seamless charging experience for tenants.

Regulations for EV Charging Systems at Apartments

Regulations governing EV charging systems at apartment complexes are designed to ensure that installations are safe, accessible, and compliant with national, state, and local standards. These requirements typically include minimum EV-ready parking mandates, adherence to electrical and safety codes, proper permitting and inspections, and coordination with utilities. Compliance not only protects residents and property owners but also helps qualify installations for public funding and incentive programs. Understanding these regulations early in the planning process helps prevent costly redesigns or delays during installation and approval.

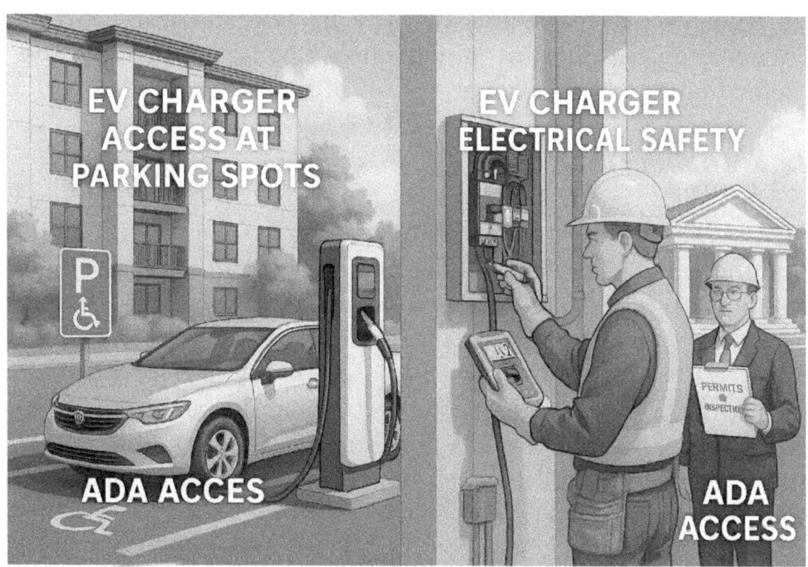

EV Charger Regulations and Requirements at Apartments

Required EV Charger Access

Many jurisdictions now require new or renovated multifamily properties to include a specific number or percentage of EV-ready or fully equipped EV charging spaces. These mandates aim to future-proof residential developments and ensure equitable access to charging infrastructure. EV-ready standards typically require that electrical capacity, conduit, and wiring be installed during construction—even if chargers themselves are not immediately added. These rules also ensure that accessibility standards, electrical load requirements, and space designations meet both tenant and regulatory expectations for long-term functionality.

Electrical & Safety

Electrical and safety regulations are central to every EV charging system installation. Compliance with national and local electrical codes—such as the National Electrical Code (NEC)—is mandatory, along with the use of certified equipment that meets recognized safety standards. Proper grounding, circuit protection, and load balancing are required to prevent electrical faults, overloads, or fire hazards. Additionally, all installations must be performed by licensed electricians trained in EV charging infrastructure. Regular inspections and maintenance ensure continued safety and reliable operation for residents and property staff alike.

Permits & Inspections

Before any EV charger can be activated, property owners must obtain local building and electrical permits. This process typically involves submitting detailed installation plans for review, securing approval from building departments, and passing final inspections. Inspectors verify that chargers are correctly wired, grounded, and installed using certified components in compliance with all applicable codes. Accessibility, safety, and labeling requirements must also be met. Completing these steps ensures legal operation, protects against liability, and establishes eligibility for rebates or tax credits tied to regulatory compliance.

Additional Requirements

Beyond core safety and electrical codes, additional regulations often apply to ensure efficient and equitable operation of EV charging systems. These may include utility interconnection approvals for load management and demand response programs, ADA accessibility standards for charger placement, signage for designated parking spaces, and parking enforcement policies. Some jurisdictions also require data reporting on charger usage and energy consumption to track progress toward sustainability goals. Meeting these evolving standards helps property owners maintain compliance while providing residents with reliable, safe, and accessible charging options.

Chapter 2

EV Charging Systems

EV charging systems at apartments combine hardware, software, power infrastructure, and user experience into a unified, scalable ecosystem that improves operations and resident satisfaction. This chapter summarizes key elements such as charger selection, connector types, smart features, access control, and data networks. It also covers automated billing, app-based scheduling, load balancing, cybersecurity, and OCPP standards. Additional topics include reservation systems, performance monitoring, revenue models, advertising, and public-network integration—designing charging as a profitable, future-ready amenity for modern EV-driving tenants.

EV Charging System at Apartment Complexes

EV charging systems at an apartment property are more than just the chargers themselves—they are an integrated ecosystem where EV chargers, electrical power, data networks, software platforms, and user support all work together to provide a seamless experience for residents and property managers. Proper planning and management of these components ensure reliability, efficiency, and a positive tenant experience while preparing the property for future growth in EV adoption.

EV Charging Stations

EV chargers are devices that safely deliver electricity to an EV's battery, available in three main types: Level 1 (slow), Level 2 (faster) and DC Fast

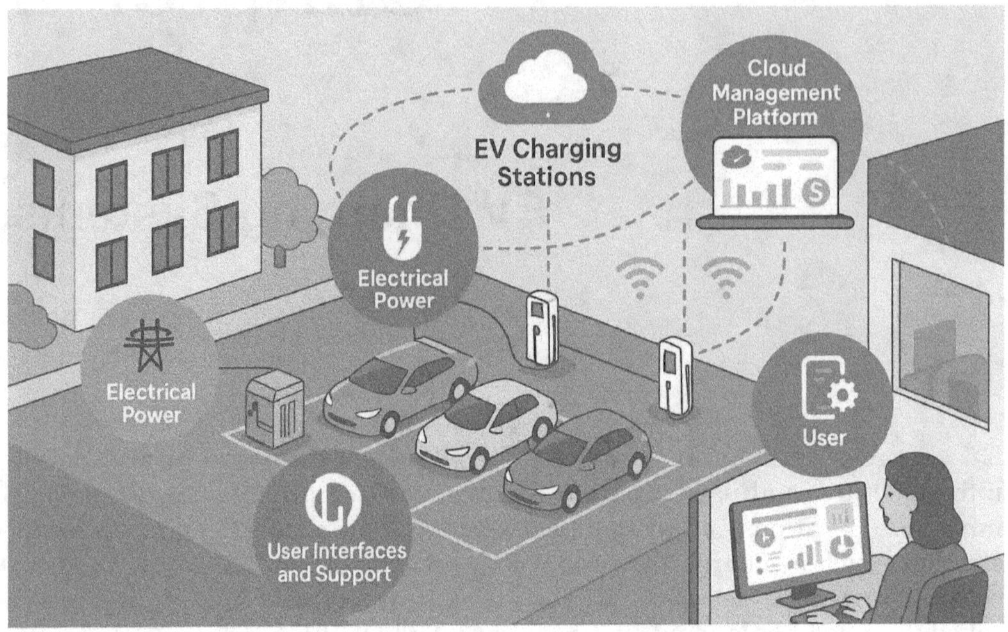

EV Charging System at an Apartment Complex

Charging or Level 3 (high-power for rapid energy delivery). Apartment EV charging stations typically range from Level 1 chargers, which provide basic charging via standard outlets, to Level 2 chargers and DC fast chargers that offer faster, more efficient power delivery. Modern chargers often include smart features, such as scheduling, load balancing, and real-time monitoring, which help optimize energy usage. It's also important to select chargers that are open charge point protocol (OCPP) ready, ensuring they are compatible with multiple management platforms and can be upgraded or integrated with future systems without replacing the hardware.

Electrical Power

The electrical infrastructure at an apartment complex converts and distributes power from utility transformers to EV Chargers. Utility service, building panels, and overall load capacity must be carefully evaluated to avoid costly upgrades. Effective load management systems can dynamically allocate power among multiple chargers, allowing the property to maximize usage while staying within existing electrical limits. Proper planning ensures that the property can support current demand and scale efficiently as more residents adopt EVs.

Data Network

EV chargers are connected to a management system through a data network. Data connections can be hardwired via Ethernet, use Wi-Fi, or cellular networks depending on site conditions and coverage reliability. Choosing a dependable data link ensures uptime, supports remote diagnostics, and allows the system to provide accurate usage data for reporting and future planning.

Cloud Management Platform

An EV charging system management platform is the central hub for operating an apartment's EV chargers. It controls access permissions, pricing, billing, and reporting, enabling property managers to monitor usage, enforce policies, and streamline revenue collection. A well-chosen platform also supports future expansion, integrates with utility demand management programs, and allows for flexible configurations to meet the unique needs of residential communities. This includes administrative access for the apartment complex staff and contractors.

User Interfaces and Support

EV charging user interfaces include mobile apps, web portals, and onsite support features that allow tenants and guests to locate chargers, schedule sessions, make payments, receive notifications, and resolve issues efficiently. Effective user interfaces make EV charging convenient for residents while reducing administrative overhead for property staff. Mobile apps and web portals allow tenants to locate chargers, schedule sessions, make payments, and receive notifications. Support tools, including remote diagnostics, spare parts management, and clear signage, further enhance the user experience and ensure that issues can be resolved quickly. Strong user support ensures residents feel confident using the chargers, leading to higher satisfaction and adoption rates.

***Surprising Fact** - While Public EV Chargers in the United States have a 20% vandalism rate, adding well lit EV Chargers in apartment complexes and MDUs with video surveillance typically results in a significant reduction of vandalism, theft and crime. These monitored safety zones can also reduce insurance premiums.*

EV Charging System Features and Services

Apartment EV charging systems have a mix of features and services that go beyond simply providing electricity. Key capabilities include secure access, automated billing, user-friendly mobile apps, reservation options, property branding, and potential advertising revenue streams. Together, these features enhance the resident experience, streamline property management, and create opportunities for added value or income for apartment owners.

Charger Access Control

Secure access is a critical component of apartment EV charging systems. Residents can authenticate their sessions using RFID cards, mobile apps, or even license plate recognition systems. Effective access control ensures that only authorized users can operate the chargers, protecting both the property's investment and the safety of residents while simplifying user management for property staff.

Automated Billing

Automated billing capabilities allow properties to seamlessly collect payment for EV charging sessions. These systems can integrate with accounting software or property management platforms to reconcile usage and revenue efficiently. By leveraging automated billing, apartment owners can recover costs, generate revenue, and reduce administrative effort associated with manual tracking or invoicing.

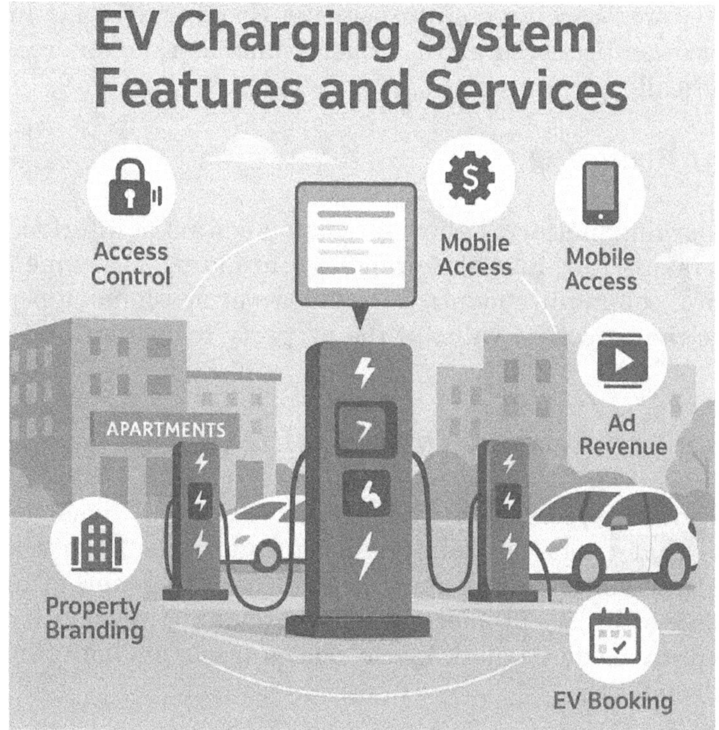

EV Charging System Features and Services

Charging Mobile App

EV charging system mobile applications provide residents with a convenient interface to manage their EV charging experience. Through the app, users can check charger availability, initiate and monitor charging sessions, make payments, and receive real-time status updates. A well-designed user mobile app enhances the tenant experience while reducing the need for property staff to manage daily operations manually.

EV Charging Booking

Reservation and booking capabilities allow residents to schedule charging sessions in advance, ensuring fair access to limited chargers. This feature is particularly important in shared parking environments where multiple tenants may require charging simultaneously. Booking systems improve efficiency, reduce conflicts, and allow property managers to enforce usage policies automatically.

Apartment Branding

Many EV charging platforms allow for customization of interfaces or mobile app graphic skins to reflect the property's branding. Apartment branding helps reinforce community identity, provides a professional appearance, and can enhance the perceived value of the property to current and prospective tenants.

Advertising and Revenue Opportunities

Some EV charging systems offer ad-supported screens, dashboards, or app integrations that create an additional revenue stream for the property. Advertising capabilities allow apartment owners to generate income from digital signage or in-app promotions while providing information or promotions relevant to residents, making the charging system both functional and financially beneficial.

Types of EV Chargers

The types of EV chargers installed at apartment complexes vary in level, connector type, usage model, and smart integration, allowing properties to meet diverse resident needs while optimizing energy use. Effective charger selection combines hardware, software, and power management features to deliver a seamless, efficient, and scalable EV charging experience.

EV Charger Levels

EV chargers at apartments are available in multiple levels to suit different charging needs. Level 1 chargers use standard household outlets and provide slow charging, typically adding 2–5 miles of range per hour. Level 2 chargers are the most common for residential properties, offering standard charging with 10–25 miles of range per hour. DC Fast Chargers deliver

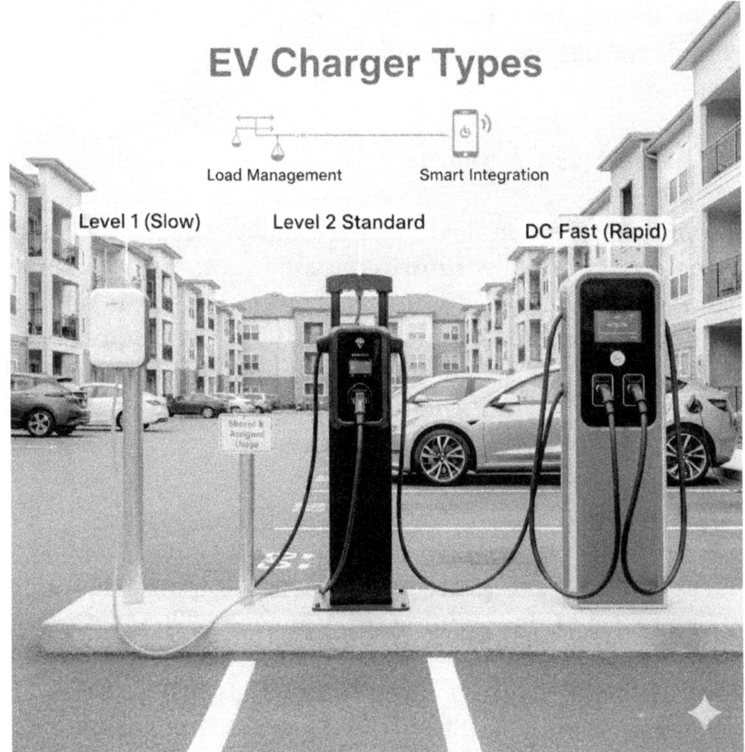

EV Charger Types

rapid charging and are ideal for high-turnover or short-duration sessions, although they require higher power and infrastructure investments. Selecting the right charger levels helps balance resident convenience with installation and operational costs.

Connector Types

Connector compatibility is essential to support a range of EV models. Most electric vehicles use J1772 connectors, while Tesla vehicles require their proprietary connectors, although adapters are available. Some newer installations also include Combined Charging System (CCS) or North American Charging Standard (NACS) ports to accommodate a broader variety of EVs, ensuring future-proofing as vehicle technology evolves. Apartment EV chargers may use a NEMA 14-50 or Type 2 socket which are standard electrical plugs for high-power appliances—making it a simple, cost-effective, and code-compliant option for Level 2 EV charging without requiring a hard-wired station.

Shared vs. Assigned Chargers

Apartment complexes can deploy chargers under shared or assigned usage models. Shared chargers allow multiple residents to use the same unit on a first-come, first-served basis or via a reservation system, maximizing efficiency when demand is moderate. Assigned chargers dedicate a unit to a specific tenant or parking space, offering guaranteed access but requiring more infrastructure. Choosing the right model depends on resident needs, parking layouts, and expected EV adoption rates.

Smart Integration

Modern chargers often integrate with software platforms that manage billing, access, reservations, and energy usage. This smart integration allows property managers to automate payments, enforce access controls, and monitor usage remotely. By combining hardware and software, apartments can create a seamless, user-friendly experience for residents while reducing administrative effort.

Electrical Load Management

Efficient power distribution is critical to prevent electrical overloads and manage costs. Load management systems use smart meters and algorithms to allocate available power dynamically among multiple chargers based on demand and priority. This ensures that the building's existing electrical infrastructure is not exceeded and allows the property to support more EVs without expensive utility upgrades.

Surprising Fact: *Many apartment complexes can add EV chargers without upgrading electrical panels or transformers. Smart EV charger load management dramatically caps daytime charging speeds while prioritizing off-peak nighttime charging—when most residents plug in and rates are lowest. Since the average EV requires only about 7 kWh per day, dynamic load management ensures total charging demand stays within the property's existing electrical capacity, avoiding costly infrastructure upgrades.*

EV Charger Access Types

EV charger access control at apartment complexes defines how residents, guests, and service staff initiate charging sessions, track usage, and process payments. Selecting the right access methods ensures secure, efficient, and scalable operations while providing transparency and convenience for all users.

User Identification Options

Residents and authorized users can access chargers through a variety of identification methods. Common options include RFID cards or fobs, mobile app logins, user ID and password systems, and plug-and-charge technologies that authenticate the vehicle automatically. These methods allow users to track their own charging sessions, while enabling property managers to monitor usage, enforce access policies, and generate accurate billing records.

Public Access Control

Some apartment properties choose to provide public or visitor access to chargers for guests, delivery drivers, or external EV drivers. Proper public access control ensures that these users can charge securely and that usage can be tracked for billing or revenue sharing purposes. Policies for guest access and time-based controls help prevent misuse while generating additional income for the property.

Payment Integration

Each access type is closely linked to payment processing. Payment systems can be integrated with resident accounts, public access apps, or plug-and-charge systems to handle per-use fees, subscriptions, or electricity-based billing. This integration simplifies revenue collection, ensures accurate billing, and reduces administrative workload for property staff.

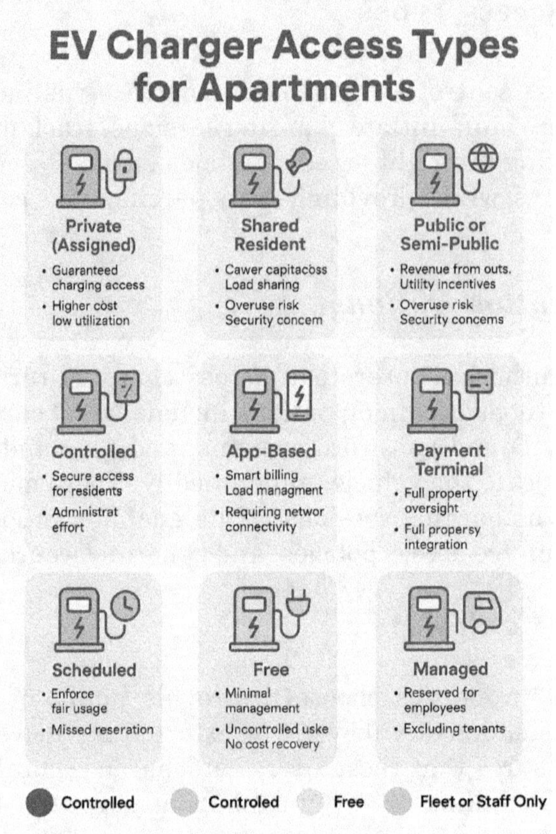

EV Charger Access Types

Network Connectivity Requirements

Access methods rely on robust network connectivity and backend systems to operate effectively. Mobile apps, RFID systems, and plug-and-charge solutions require real-time data communication for authentication, session monitoring, and billing. Ensuring reliable connectivity—through Wi-Fi, Ethernet, or cellular networks—is essential for uninterrupted operation.

Data Collection and Privacy

Different access methods impact the type and amount of data collected, including user identity, session duration, energy consumption, and billing information. Managing this data responsibly is critical to protect user privacy while allowing property managers to analyze usage patterns, optimize operations, and comply with relevant regulations.

EV Charging Reservation and Booking

EV charging reservation and booking systems are essential for ensuring fair, efficient, and convenient access to chargers at apartment complexes. These systems combine mobile app-based booking, automated scheduling, integrated billing, and data reporting to optimize usage, improve tenant satisfaction, and simplify management for property staff.

User Access Management

Reservation systems help ensure fair access to limited charging stations among multiple residents. By implementing rules for session length, priority access, or first-come-first-served scheduling, property managers can prevent conflicts and ensure that all tenants have equitable opportunities to charge their vehicles.

Mobile App Booking Features

Mobile apps and web portals provide a user-friendly interface for residents to locate available chargers, reserve time slots, start sessions, and make payments. Intuitive app features reduce confusion, minimize staff involvement, and enhance the overall tenant experience by offering convenience and transparency.

Booking Management

Advanced reservation systems include scheduling tools, time limits, and automated notifications to manage charger availability. Tenants can be

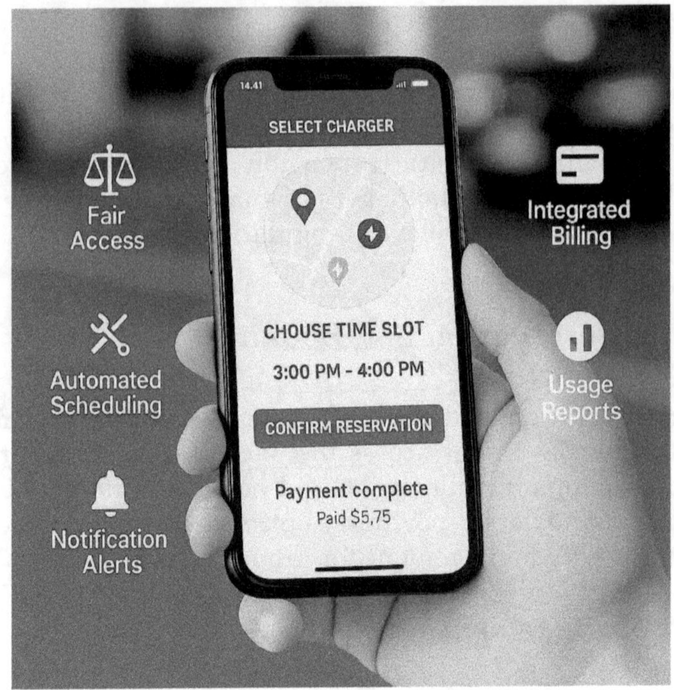

EV Charger Reservation and Bookings

reminded of upcoming sessions, and idle chargers can be released for others to use, ensuring maximum utilization of the charging infrastructure.

Suprising Fact - *Most apartment-based EV drivers plug in after work and let their vehicles charge overnight, when electricity demand — and pricing — is at its lowest. Data from the U.S. Department of Energy shows that roughly 80% of EV charging takes place at home and primarily during nighttime hours, rather than during the day. For multifamily property owners, this means on-site charging can satisfy the majority of resident demand while taking advantage of lower off-peak rates, improving load balance, and reducing exposure to higher daytime peak pricing.*

Billing and Payment Integration

Reservation platforms often integrate with payment gateways to handle per-use fees, subscription plans, or electricity-based billing. This seamless integration simplifies revenue collection, reduces administrative work, and provides tenants with transparent, accurate billing for their charging sessions.

Data Analysis and Reporting

Reservation and booking systems also collect usage data, including session duration, frequency, and energy consumed. Property managers can use this data to optimize policies, plan for future expansion, and ensure that the EV charging infrastructure meets current and projected tenant demand.

EV Charging System Electrical Power

EV charging systems at apartment complexes require careful electrical distribution system planning to ensure safety, reliability, and scalability. Properly designing energy capacity, disconnects, grounding, conduits, load centers, switchgear, and utility connections allows properties to support current EV demand while accommodating future growth efficiently and safely.

Electric Energy Requirements

Determining energy requirements is critical to sizing the electrical system for an apartment EV installation. Energy demand depends on tenants' driving habits, charger types, and charging schedules. Most EV owners drive 20–30 miles daily, which equates to roughly 7 kWh, often charged overnight. Understanding these patterns helps managers avoid overestimating load while ensuring sufficient capacity for peak periods.

EV Charger Electric Disconnects

Each charger circuit requires a manual electric disconnect for safety and maintenance, as mandated by NEC Article 625. Disconnects allow technicians or emergency personnel to safely isolate power to a specific charger without affecting the entire system, improving both safety and operational flexibility.

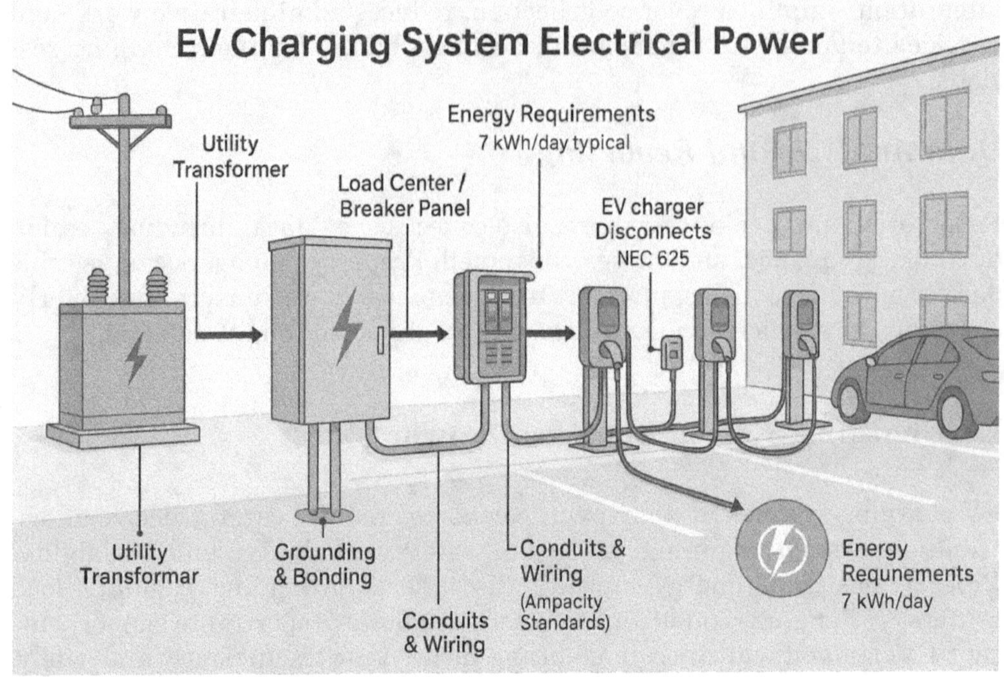

EV Charging System Electrical Power Disribution at Apartment Complexes

Grounding & Bonding Systems

Proper grounding and bonding are essential to prevent shock hazards, stabilize voltage, and ensure reliable operation. Ground rods, bonding jumpers, and connections to the main grounding system protect residents, staff, and equipment from electrical faults while maintaining code compliance.

Conduits and Wiring

Conduits and wiring carry electrical current from panels to chargers and must meet NEC standards for ampacity, environmental protection, and mechanical safety. Proper sizing, insulation, and routing reduce the risk of overheating, short circuits, and system failure while supporting long-term reliability.

Electrical Panels (Load Centers)

Load centers house breakers that feed individual charger circuits. Each breaker must be appropriately rated, clearly labeled, and capable of handling the expected load. Sufficient panel capacity ensures that additional chargers can be added without overloading the system.

Main Switchgear

The main switchgear serves as the central control point for distributing and isolating power throughout the EV charging system. It should include spare breaker capacity for future charger installations, allowing expansion without major retrofits while ensuring safety and operational control.

Utility Transformer

The utility transformer connects the apartment property to the electrical grid and steps down high-voltage electricity to site-level voltage. It must be properly sized to handle the aggregate EV load without overheating or reducing service reliability, supporting both current charging demand and potential future expansion.

EV Charging System Data Network

EV charging systems depend on reliable data communication networks to support billing, monitoring, energy management, maintenance, and cybersecurity. Apartment owners or managers should understand how these networks operate, who manages them, and what risks and opportunities they present to ensure reliable, secure, and efficient EV charging operations.

Charger Data Network System

EV chargers connect to cloud systems, management platforms, and property networks using wired, Wi-Fi, or cellular connections. The choice of network affects reliability, latency, and integration capabilities, making it

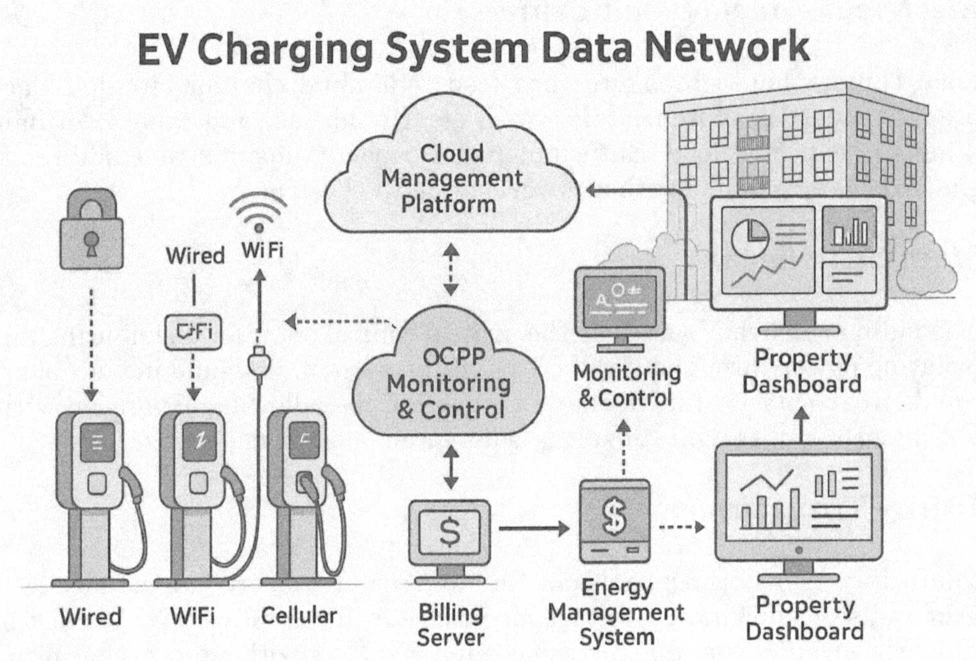

EV Charging System Data Network

essential to select systems that maintain consistent uptime and support the property's operational needs.

Data Flow and Access Control

Data flows between chargers, networks, and management platforms to enable session authentication, usage tracking, and billing. Access control determines who can view, manage, or modify this information, ensuring that sensitive data is protected and that property managers retain operational oversight. Protocols such as Open Charge Point Protocol (OCPP) enable standard monitoring and control across compatible devices.

Cybersecurity and Privacy

Protecting resident data and preventing unauthorized system access is critical and may be legally required. Cybersecurity measures include encrypted communications, secure authentication, and network monitoring to prevent tampering, data breaches, or service disruptions, while privacy policies govern how resident and usage data is stored and used.

Building System Network Integration

Networked EV chargers can integrate with other building technologies, such as smart energy management systems, renewable energy sources, or load balancing controls. Integration allows properties to optimize energy usage, reduce costs, and coordinate charging operations with broader building systems.

Network Maintenance, Monitoring, and Vendor Responsibilities

Effective operation requires ongoing maintenance and monitoring of the communication network, often managed by vendors or service providers. Understanding who is responsible for updates, troubleshooting, and uptime ensures reliability, prevents downtime, and protects the property's investment in the charging infrastructure.

EV Charging Management System (CMS)

The EV Charging Management System (CMS) is the central hub that controls access, billing, load balancing, fault detection, and performance analytics for an apartment's EV chargers. Apartment owners rely on the CMS to ensure smooth system operation, provide a positive tenant experience, and manage revenue, maintenance, and future scalability.
Account Management and Access Control

The CMS manages how residents, guests, and staff access and use the EV chargers. Through account creation, authentication, and permissions, the system ensures that only authorized users can operate the chargers. This functionality also supports user-level tracking of sessions, enabling property managers to monitor usage patterns and enforce policies.

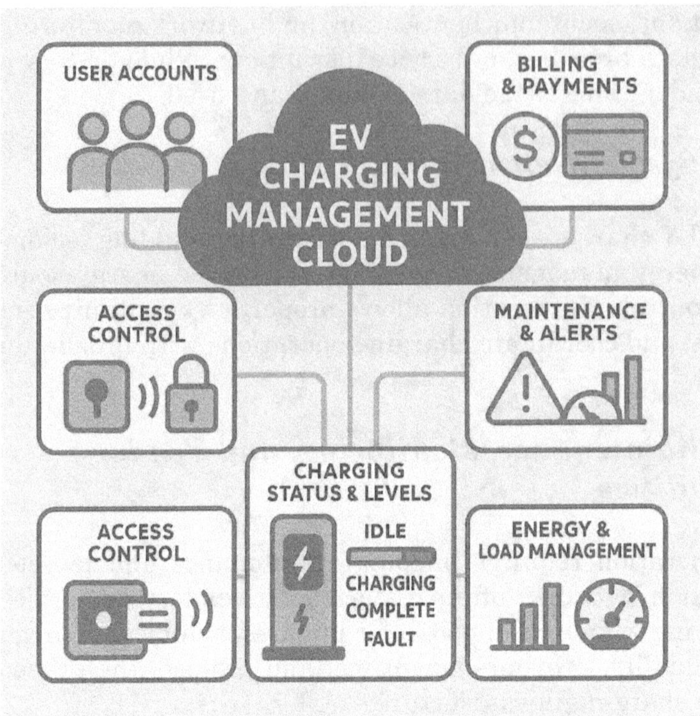

EV Charging System Management

Charger Power Management

A CMS helps manage electrical load across multiple chargers to balance energy use and avoid overloading building systems. By dynamically allocating power based on demand and priority, the system maximizes charger utilization while preventing electrical faults or costly utility upgrades. Effective power management is critical for both operational safety and long-term scalability.

Monitoring and Maintenance

The CMS enables real-time monitoring of charger performance and fault detection, allowing property owners or service partners to respond quickly to issues. Automated alerts and reporting help reduce downtime, streamline maintenance, and ensure a reliable charging experience for tenants.

Billing and Payments

Billing and payment functions within the CMS allow seamless financial transactions for per-use fees, subscriptions, or energy-based billing. Integrated reporting tools generate performance and compliance reports, simplifying revenue collection and providing insights into usage trends, system efficiency, and return on investment.

Value-Added Services

Some CMS platforms offer opportunities for advertising, sponsorships, or other revenue-generating services. These features can enhance the property's income potential while providing additional engagement or information to residents, creating a more versatile and financially beneficial system.

Systems Integration and Scalability

A modern CMS is designed to grow and adapt with the property's needs. OCPP compliance (versions 1.6 or 2.0.1) ensures interoperability with multiple charger brands, allowing easy integration of new hardware and software updates. This scalability makes the system future-proof and capable of supporting evolving EV adoption rates and technology upgrades.

Public EV Charging Network Connection

Connecting apartment EV chargers to public EV charging networks allows residents, guests, and the public to access charging infrastructure while creating potential new revenue streams for property owners. Effective network integration requires careful planning around charger selection, billing, technical compatibility, maintenance responsibilities, and user support to ensure reliable, secure, and profitable operations.

Public Charging Options

Apartment properties can choose between dedicated chargers for private resident use and shared chargers that are connected to public EV charging

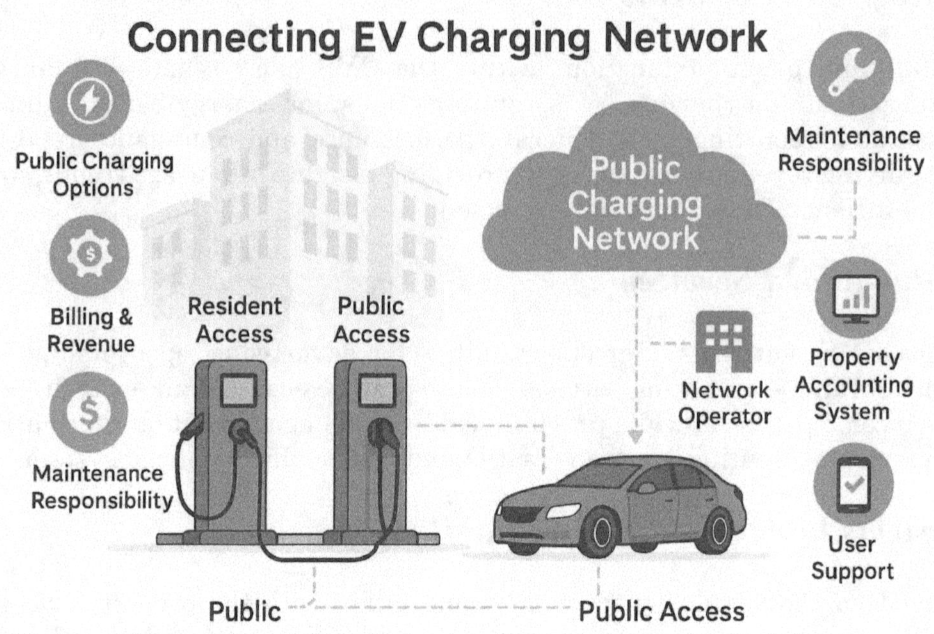

Public EV Charging System Connections

networks. Shared chargers allow public access, increasing utilization and providing additional revenue, while dedicated chargers prioritize resident access and convenience. Choosing the right model depends on property goals, parking layouts, and expected EV demand.

Billing & Revenue Management

Connecting to public networks requires reliable billing and revenue management systems. Methods may include per-use fees, subscription plans, or revenue sharing with network operators. Integration with property accounting systems ensures accurate financial reporting and allows apartment owners to capture value from public usage without adding administrative complexity.

Network Compatibility & Standards

To operate seamlessly, chargers must support the protocols and standards of public networks. OCPP compliance, along with CCS and NACS connector compatibility, ensures interoperability with multiple network operators and future-proofs the property for evolving EV technologies. Proper standardization simplifies system integration and avoids costly replacements or upgrades.

Liability, Maintenance & Service Agreements

Defining maintenance responsibilities and liability coverage is critical when chargers are publicly accessible. Agreements should specify who maintains equipment, guarantees uptime, and covers insurance or liability for users, protecting both the property and residents while ensuring safe and reliable service.

Services & Support

A clear plan for services and support ensures that user questions, technical issues, or charger malfunctions are addressed promptly. Designating responsible personnel or vendors improves system reliability, minimizes downtime, and enhances the overall experience for residents and public users alike.

EV Charging System Operation

EV charging system operation encompasses the full range of functions that keep chargers running efficiently, secure access for residents, and property management informed. Key operational areas include automated management, user access, monitoring and maintenance, billing, and tenant communication, all of which work together to ensure a reliable and convenient charging experience.

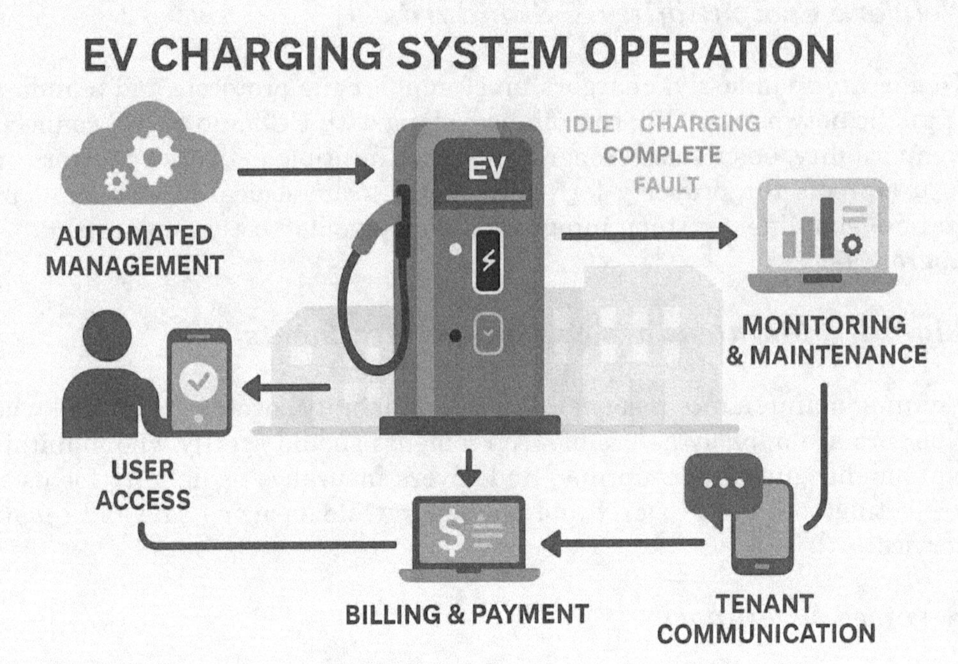

EV Charging System at Apartments Operation

Automated Management

Smart EV charging systems can self-manage once configured, automatically controlling start and stop times, load distribution, and session scheduling. Automation reduces the need for manual intervention, ensures consistent performance, and allows property managers to focus on strategic oversight rather than daily operational tasks.

User Access

Effective user access management ensures that residents can authenticate and use chargers securely while enforcing any restrictions or priority rules. Methods may include RFID cards, mobile app credentials, or vehicle-based plug-and-charge authentication, providing convenience for tenants and control for property management.

Monitoring and Maintenance

Routine maintenance schedules, real-time system monitoring, and available service support ensure chargers remain operational and safe. Monitoring and maintenance programs allow property managers and service partners to quickly detect faults, schedule repairs, and prevent extended downtime, maintaining tenant satisfaction and system reliability.

Billing and Payment Processing

EV charging systems track usage and process payments accurately for tenants or external users. Billing and payment processing can integrate with property accounting or third-party payment platforms to simplify revenue collection, reconcile energy costs, and provide transparency for both residents and property managers.

Tenant Communication

Clear tenant communication is essential for smooth operations, including notifications about charger availability, maintenance schedules, or system issues. Timely alerts and responsive support ensure residents have a positive charging experience while reducing administrative burden on property staff.

EV Charging System User Support

EV charging user support is a critical component of apartment charging systems, ensuring residents can access chargers efficiently, resolve issues quickly, and have a positive experience. Key support elements include mobile app and account assistance, notifications, onboarding and training, and helpdesk services for troubleshooting technical problems.

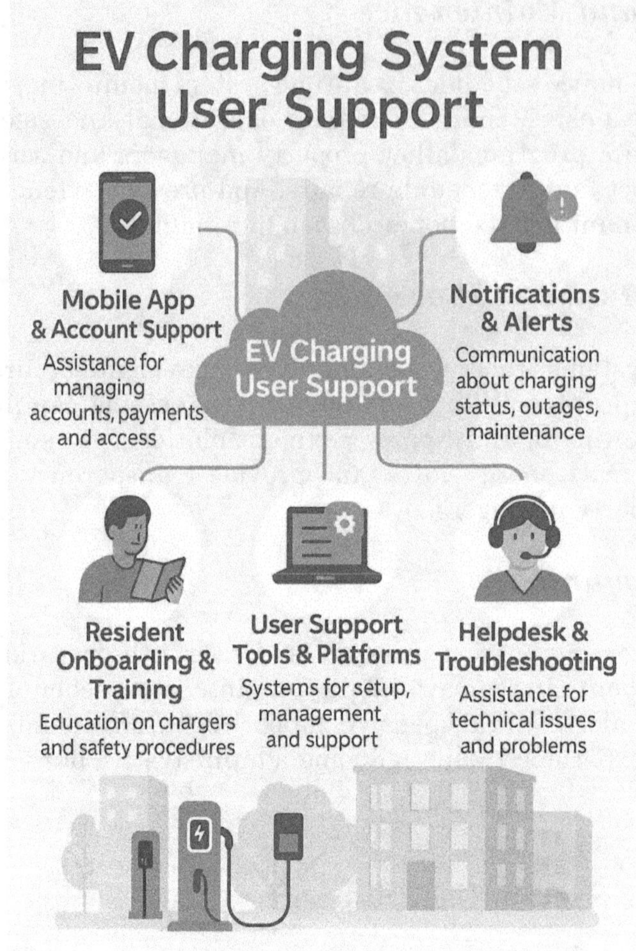

EV Charging System User Support

Mobile App & Account Assistance

Residents require support for managing accounts, payments, access permissions, and booking through mobile apps or web portals. Providing clear instructions and responsive assistance ensures that tenants can use the charging system independently and reduces the administrative burden on property staff.

Notifications & Alerts

Effective user support includes proactive notifications and alerts to communicate charging status, outages, maintenance schedules, or software updates. Timely messages keep residents informed and prevent confusion or frustration when chargers are unavailable or undergoing service.

User Support Tools and Platforms

Support systems and platforms must be carefully selected and managed to ensure smooth operations. Property managers need to understand which tools are used, who has access, and how to configure them for account management, communication, and troubleshooting, creating a structured and reliable support environment.

Resident Onboarding & Training

Proper onboarding and training educates tenants on using EV chargers, mobile apps, reservation systems, and safety procedures. Training programs improve user confidence, reduce errors, and encourage higher adoption of the charging system.

Helpdesk & Troubleshooting

A responsive helpdesk provides technical support for charger malfunctions, network issues, or user difficulties. Clear escalation procedures, defined response times, and access to technical experts ensure that problems are resolved quickly, maintaining resident satisfaction and system reliability.

Chapter 3

EV Charging System Feasibility

Feasibility analysis determines whether adding EV chargers to an apartment complex is technically, financially, and operationally practical — and how to plan for successful implementation. It provides the foundation for making informed investment decisions, ensuring that property owners, managers, and technical partners understand both opportunities and constraints before moving forward with installation.

Feasibility Purpose – Plan Before Install

The primary purpose of feasibility planning is to assess readiness before committing funds or resources. This process identifies key technical, financial, and operational factors—such as electrical capacity, parking availability, and management support—that influence the success of an EV charging project. Early planning reduces costly mistakes and ensures the project aligns with property goals and tenant needs.

Demand & Capacity

A thorough feasibility study evaluates current and projected tenant EV demand, parking configurations, and available electrical infrastructure. Understanding these factors helps determine the appropriate number and type of chargers, optimal placement, and whether existing systems can support future growth. Demand forecasting also ensures scalability as EV adoption among tenants increases over time.

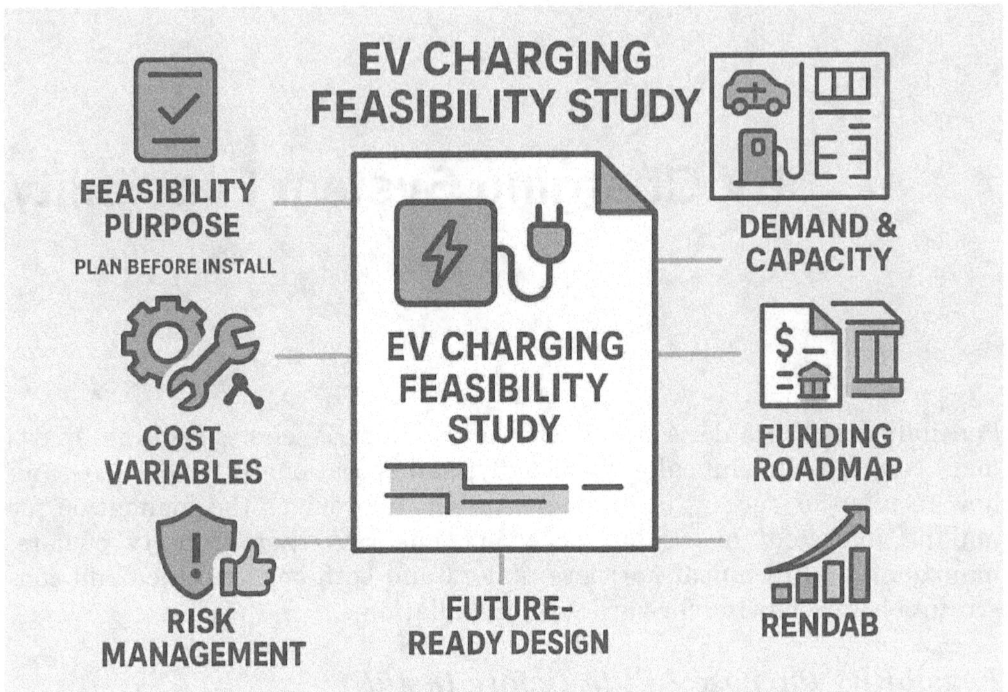

EV Charging Systems at Apartments Feasibility Study

Cost Variables

Feasibility analysis defines the major cost categories that affect project budgeting, including hardware, installation, software, electrical upgrades, permitting, and ongoing maintenance. Evaluating these variables provides a clear picture of total project cost and identifies opportunities to reduce expenses through design optimization, load management, or phased implementation.

Risk Management

Identifying and mitigating risks early is critical to a successful EV charging project. The feasibility process highlights potential challenges—such as utility coordination, equipment delays, or regulatory hurdles—and establishes strategies to address them. Collaboration among property owners, utilities, and system integrators during the planning phase minimizes disruptions and enhances project reliability.

Funding Roadmap

A well-documented feasibility study supports funding and incentive applications by providing evidence of project viability. Lenders, investors, and grant programs often require this level of due diligence before committing financial support. A clear roadmap also increases confidence in long-term returns by outlining expected costs, benefits, and performance outcomes.

Future-Ready Design

Feasibility analysis enables long-term, scalable planning for EV charging infrastructure. By anticipating future technological advances, increased EV adoption, and evolving standards, property owners can design systems that expand cost-effectively over time. This forward-thinking approach protects the investment and ensures continued relevance in a rapidly evolving mobility landscape.

EV Charging Systems Integration Companies

EV charging system integration companies provide end-to-end expertise—combining engineering, construction, and financial analysis—to design, assess, and implement cost-effective, compatible EV charging solutions for apartment properties. Their role bridges the gap between technical requirements and business objectives, ensuring that each system is not only compliant and reliable but also financially and operationally viable for property owners.

What EV Charging Systems Integrators Do

EV charging systems integrators combine multiple areas of specialized knowledge to deliver complete solutions. Their electrical engineering expertise includes load analysis, service panel evaluation, and coordination with

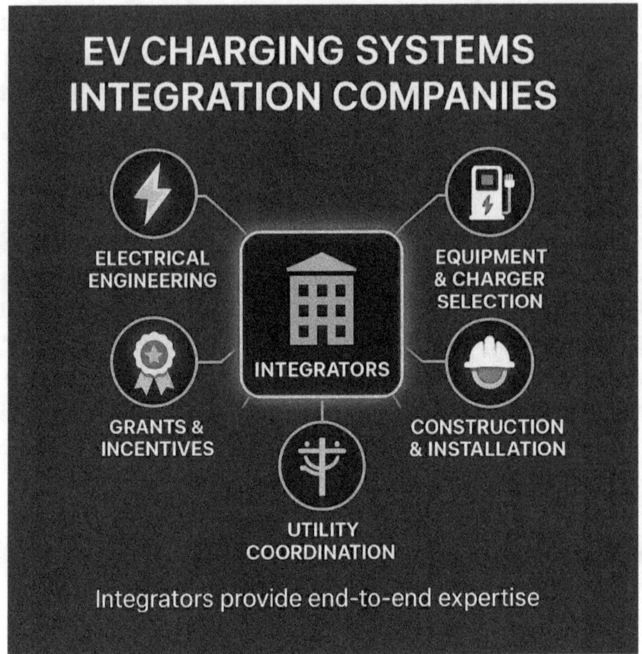

EV Charging Systems Integration Companies

utilities. They also bring deep product and network knowledge—understanding charger specifications, communication protocols, and system interoperability. On the construction side, integrators manage site layout planning, permitting, and installation logistics. Additionally, they incorporate financial modeling such as ROI projections, incentive applications, and phased rollout strategies to align technical decisions with investment goals.

Suprising Fact - *Few apartment property owners realize that EV charging systems integrators who help with feasibility and design often receive 10–35% vendor discounts or bundled pricing from multiple charger, software, and electrical-equipment manufacturers. These discounts aren't publicly advertised and aren't available to most buyers. In exchange, integrators help with system setup, configuration, network onboarding, and long-term support, meaning one skilled integration company can dramatically reduce project costs simply by bringing their vendor relationships to the table.*

System Integrator Activities

A systems integrator typically begins with a detailed site inspection and data collection to assess existing infrastructure. This includes evaluating electrical capacity, reviewing parking layouts, and developing preliminary cost estimates. They also manage utility coordination, explore available grants and incentives, and prepare feasibility summaries that help property owners make informed decisions. Their findings often culminate in a report that outlines technical options, cost ranges, and a recommended implementation strategy.

Benefits of Working with a Systems Integrator

Engaging a qualified EV charging systems integrator provides significant advantages. Acting as a single point of contact, integrators streamline communications and ensure accountability across all project phases. Because they remain vendor-neutral, they can present unbiased equipment and software options, helping property owners select the best-fit technologies. Their established relationships with vendors often result in equipment discounts, while their experience reduces compatibility risks and overall project costs.

Feasibility Study Costs and Deliverables

The cost of a feasibility study conducted by an EV charging systems integrator typically ranges from $1,500 to $7,500 for multifamily properties, depending on the size and complexity of the site. The process generally takes 2–4 weeks and concludes with a comprehensive report that includes an executive summary, cost and design recommendations, and a feasibility rating. This assessment provides property owners with the technical clarity and financial confidence needed to proceed with EV charging installations strategically.

Resident EV Charging Needs and Adoption Forecasting

Understanding resident EV needs and adoption forecasting helps property owners anticipate future charging demand, plan infrastructure investments wisely, and design scalable, equitable EV charging programs that attract and retain tenants. By combining data analysis with resident engagement, owners can align charging capacity with real-world usage trends and evolving tenant expectations.

Tenant EV User Growth Forecast

Forecasting resident EV ownership is the foundation of effective charging infrastructure planning. Property owners should measure current EV adoption rates and estimate future growth based on market trends, regional EV sales data, and demographic profiles. This helps determine how many chargers are needed now and when additional units should be phased in, avoiding both underinvestment and costly overbuilding.

Surprising Fact - *Some apartment complexes run EV charging launch parties or setup community groups to involve tenants in the design and setup of charging systems at their apartments. In addition to gathering key information on tenant EV charging needs, it also motivates tenants to share the news with their friends creating a new tenant marketing campaign.*

EV Charger Usage Patterns

Analyzing resident charging behaviors—such as frequency, session duration, and preferred charging times—provides insight into how and when tenants use EV chargers. Understanding these patterns helps property managers optimize power capacity, select the right charger mix (Level 1, Level 2, or DC Fast), and design scheduling systems that reduce congestion during peak charging hours.

EV Charger Parking Access

Parking design plays a key role in determining how residents interact with EV charging infrastructure. Matching charger placement to tenant parking assignments, guest spaces, or shared lots ensures convenience and fairness. Integrating EV chargers into accessible, well-lit, and clearly marked areas also improves safety and usability, while supporting compliance with local codes and ADA requirements.

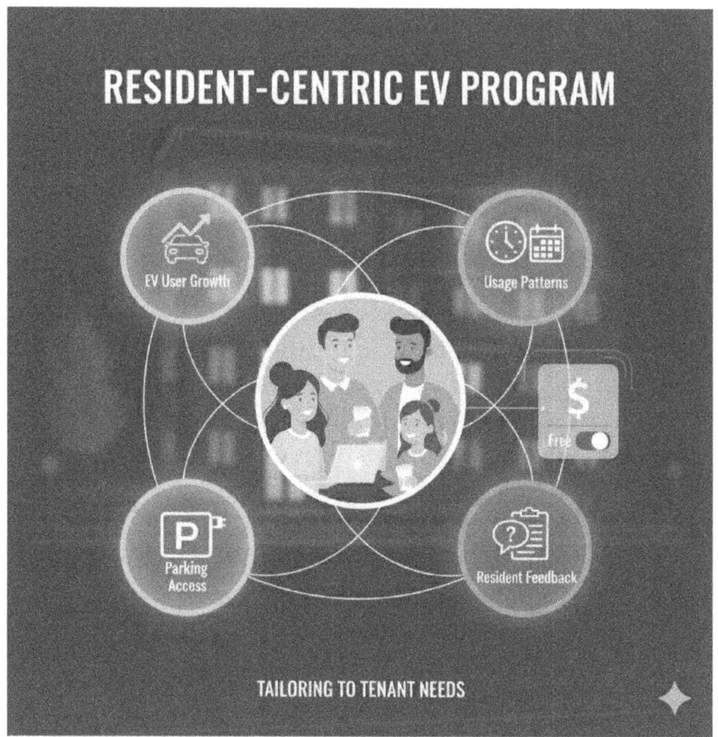

Apartment Resident EV Charging Needs and Adoption Forecasting

Resident Feedback

Ongoing resident engagement is critical to understanding evolving EV charging needs. Conducting surveys and open communications helps track adoption trends, identify satisfaction levels, and collect suggestions for improvement. Resident input also supports data-driven decision-making, allowing property owners to adjust charger numbers, pricing, or access models as adoption grows.

EV Charging Fees and Demand Impact

Pricing models have a direct influence on charging demand and resident behavior. Understanding how external factors—such as free workplace charging or public charging availability—affect on-site usage can guide fee structures that balance convenience and cost recovery. Setting appropriate EV charging rates ensures that the system remains both financially sustainable and attractive to tenants.

Assessing Property Needs & Parking Configurations

EV charger placement strategy balances installation cost, resident convenience, accessibility, and efficient utilization. By carefully planning charger locations, assignments, and supporting infrastructure, property owners can create a charging environment that meets tenant needs, complies with regulations, and maximizes return on investment.

EV Charger Placement Strategy

The placement of EV chargers directly impacts installation cost, convenience for residents, and overall system utilization. Well-located chargers reduce wiring and trenching costs while ensuring that residents can easily access charging stations without disrupting parking flow. A thoughtful layout should consider proximity to electrical rooms, traffic patterns, lighting, and visibility to promote both safety and ease of use.

Assigned vs. Shared EV Chargers

Property owners must decide whether chargers will be assigned to specific tenants or shared among residents. Assigned chargers are ideal for high-demand tenants or those willing to pay premium rates for guaranteed access. Shared chargers, on the other hand, help reduce the total number of chargers required, lowering upfront costs. However, they require clear scheduling systems, usage monitoring, and fair enforcement policies to ensure equitable access.

Accessibility Design (ADA)

Accessibility design, such as compliance with the Americans with Disabilities Act (ADA), is an essential component of EV charger placement. Typically, 5–10% of total EV charging spaces must be accessible, including

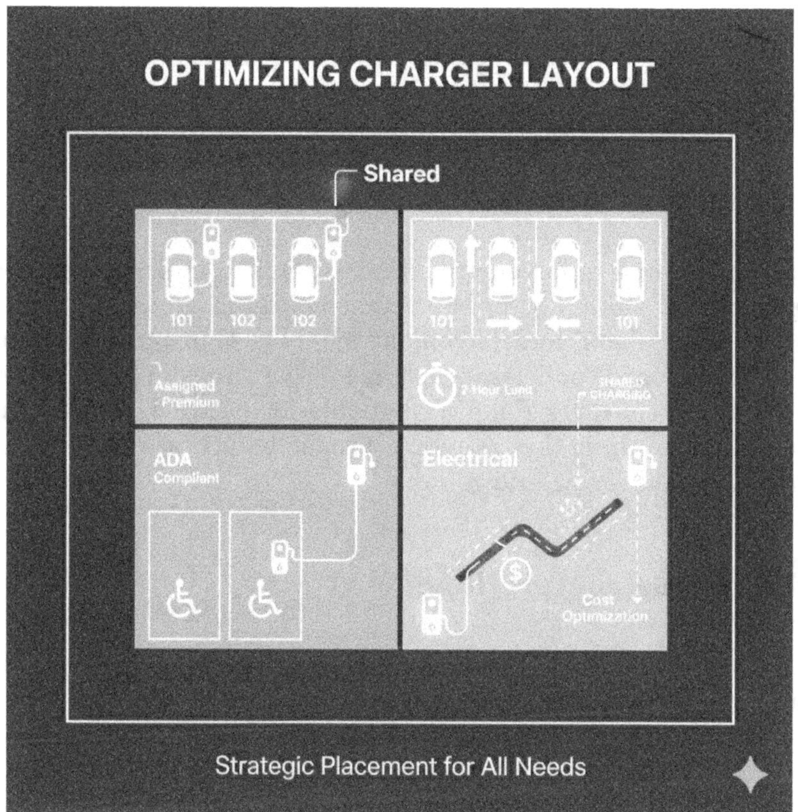

EV Charger Layout at Apartment Complexes

both standard and van-accessible designs. Key considerations include appropriate reach ranges for plugs, adequate space for mobility devices, and unobstructed pathways between parking areas and building entrances. Ensuring accessibility not only meets legal requirements but also enhances inclusivity for all residents and visitors.

Electrical Distance and Cost Optimization

Electrical distance—the length between the charger location and the main electrical service—has a significant impact on installation cost. Longer distances require more trenching, conduit, and wiring, which can quickly increase expenses. To optimize costs, chargers should be placed as close as possible to existing electrical infrastructure. In some cases, pre-installing conduits during repaving or renovation projects can provide major savings for future EV charger expansions.

Signage and Enforcement

Effective signage and enforcement are essential to maintaining a positive user experience in shared or public-access charging areas. Clearly marked spaces, time-limit signs, and pavement symbols help prevent misuse and confusion. Enforcement policies—such as tow warnings or digital access control—ensure that chargers remain available for active EV use. Consistent visibility and communication reinforce proper behavior and help residents feel that the system is fair and reliable.

Electrical Infrastructure Review

Electrical load planning for apartment EV charging systems involves assessing available power, managing energy through smart controls, coordinating with utilities for upgrades and rebates, and ensuring all installations meet NEC safety and compliance standards. A well-executed infrastructure review provides the foundation for reliable, efficient, and scalable EV charging deployment.

Electrical Load Analysis

The first step in designing an apartment EV charging system is to evaluate how much electrical capacity is currently available. This includes reviewing service panels, transformers, feeder circuits, and spare breaker space to determine how many chargers can be supported without upgrades. Accurate load analysis helps prevent overloading and identifies where additional capacity or redistribution may be required for future expansion.

EV Charger Energy Management

Smart energy management systems play a crucial role in optimizing power use and avoiding costly infrastructure upgrades. Strategies such as dynam-

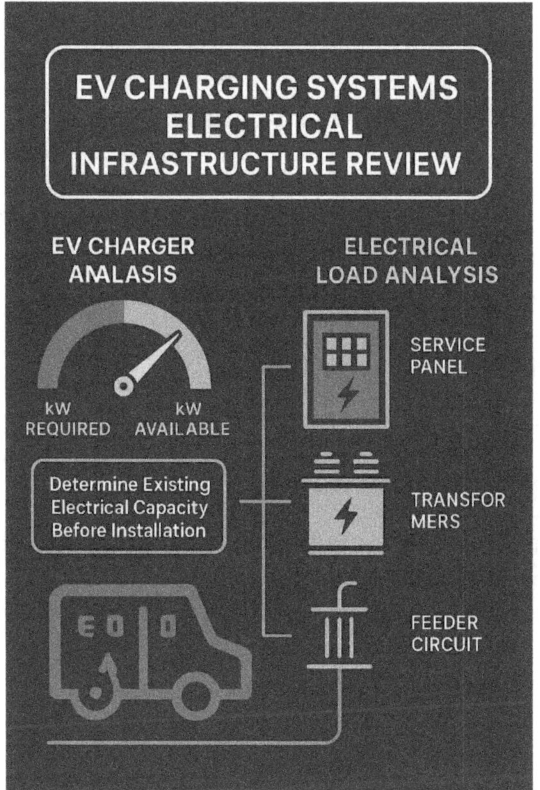

EV Charging Systems Electrical Infrastructure Review

ic load balancing, time-of-use optimization, and demand response programs allow the system to distribute available power efficiently across chargers. Software-based controls can adjust charging rates in real time, lowering peak demand and reducing utility costs while maintaining user satisfaction.

Electrical Upgrade Requirements

In cases where existing infrastructure cannot support the planned number of EV chargers, upgrades may be necessary. This can include enhancing main electrical panels, upgrading transformers, installing new conduits, or expanding feeder capacity. Integrating these improvements into broader building renovation or maintenance schedules can minimize disruption and leverage cost efficiencies.

Suprising Fact - Some apartment complexes are doing building efficiency upgrades to unlock enough electrical capacity for EV charging—without expensive transformer replacements. In fact, switching to LED lighting and high-efficiency HVAC systems can cut building energy use by 20–40%, freeing up thousands of watts of load that can be redirected to Level-2 or even DC fast chargers. This means a property that thought it needed a costly electrical service upgrade may actually be able to install EV chargers just by modernizing lighting and climate systems—turning an energy efficiency project into an EV-infrastructure accelerator.

Utility Coordination

Coordinating with the local utility company is essential to ensure proper interconnection, grid reliability, and access to available incentives. Utilities can provide guidance on transformer capacity, grid impact assessments, and rebate programs that offset equipment or installation costs. Because transformer and service upgrades often have long lead times, early engagement with utility providers helps prevent delays in project execution.

Permission to Operate (PTO) Grid Interconnection

Permission to Operate (PTO) is a formal approval from the utility company that allows a distributed energy resource (such as solar panels or EV charging infrastructure) to connect and operate in parallel with the electric grid. The PTO process typically involves inspection, verification of safety and compliance, and confirmation that the system will not adversely affect grid stability.

For EV charging infrastructure, obtaining PTO is crucial before activating chargers that may export power (such as bi-directional or V2G systems). The utility may require documentation, testing, and sometimes coordination with local authorities before granting PTO.

Electrical Safety and Compliance

Safety and compliance are fundamental to EV charging infrastructure design. All installations must adhere to National Electrical Code (NEC) Article 625 and related local standards, covering grounding, conduit sealing,

GFCI protection, and proper circuit labeling. Detailed documentation and inspection ensure long-term reliability, prevent hazards, and protect both residents and property assets from electrical risks.

Number & Types of Chargers Needed

Determining the number and types of EV chargers for an apartment complex involves assessing tenant demand, sele3cting the most appropriate charger technologies, balancing installation costs with utilization rates, and planning for future growth. A well-structured approach ensures that property owners invest efficiently while providing convenient, reliable charging access for residents.

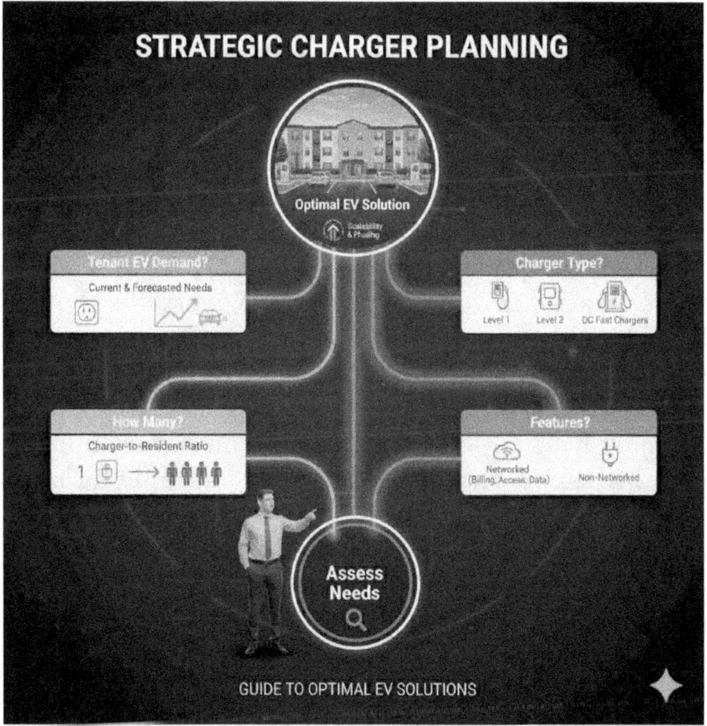

Determining Number & Types of EV Chargers Needed at Apartment Complexes

Tenant EV Demand

The first step in planning an EV charging system is to assess both current and projected tenant EV ownership. Surveys, parking usage data, and regional EV registration trends can help estimate near-term demand. Forecasting future growth—based on increasing EV adoption rates—ensures that the infrastructure remains relevant and scalable for years to come, preventing costly retrofits or capacity shortfalls.

Charger Types

Selecting the right charger type is essential to match tenant needs and property capabilities. Level 1 chargers offer low-cost, slow charging suitable for long-term parking areas. Level 2 chargers are the most common choice for apartments, providing a balance of speed and cost-efficiency. DC Fast Chargers deliver rapid charging but require substantial electrical capacity and higher installation costs, making them better suited for shared or public-access areas. The mix should reflect both resident habits and available electrical infrastructure.

In many apartment installations, lower-cost electrical outlet options can also play a role in the charging strategy. For example, NEMA 14-50 outlets are often used as a simple and inexpensive way to provide higher-power charging where residents supply their own portable Level 2 charger. Similarly, NEMA 5-20R 20-amp outlets can be an economical solution for overnight charging in long-term parking spaces, delivering enough energy during extended parking periods without requiring the cost of installing full charging stations. These outlet-based options can reduce upfront infrastructure costs while still supporting practical daily charging for many residents.

Charger Quantity and Use

Determining the ideal number of chargers requires balancing accessibility with cost control. A realistic charger-to-resident ratio—often between 1:5 and 1:10 depending on EV ownership levels—ensures sufficient access without overbuilding infrastructure. Usage modeling and scheduling software can further optimize charger utilization, allowing a smaller number of chargers to effectively serve a larger resident base.

Charger Features

Modern EV chargers offer varying levels of functionality that affect both operations and resident satisfaction. Networked chargers enable features such as user authentication, billing, energy management, and remote monitoring. Non-networked chargers are simpler and less expensive but lack data insights and access control. The choice should align with property management goals—whether focused on convenience, revenue generation, or operational oversight.

Scalability and Future-Proof Planning

Future-proofing the EV charging infrastructure is critical to long-term success. Planning for phased installation, with pre-installed conduits and electrical capacity for additional chargers, allows expansion as demand grows. Selecting chargers and software that comply with open standards such as OCPP ensures flexibility for future integrations. A scalable strategy protects the property's investment and supports smooth transitions as EV adoption accelerates.

Disabilities Access Compliance

Planning EV charging spaces that meet disabilities access requirements (such as ADA) ensures that all residents and visitors—regardless of mobility—can safely and conveniently access charging infrastructure. Compliance with federal and local accessibility standards not only fulfills legal obligations but also demonstrates a property's commitment to inclusivity and equitable access.

Disabilities Access Requirements

The Americans with Disabilities Act (ADA) establishes the framework for making EV charging stations accessible to individuals with disabilities.

EV Charging ADA Accessibility Compliance.

Typically, 4–10% of total EV charging spaces must be designated as accessible, depending on the property size and whether chargers are for residents, visitors, or public use. Both standard accessible and van-accessible stalls are required, with van-accessible spaces offering wider access aisles and additional clearance. These guidelines ensure that users with wheelchairs, mobility aids, or specialized vehicles can charge safely and comfortably.

Layout Planning

Proper layout design is essential to accommodate accessible EV charging spaces. Accessible stalls must be positioned to provide unobstructed access to chargers, allow sufficient maneuvering space, and maintain a clear path to building entrances or sidewalks. Locating accessible EV chargers close to elevators, ramps, and accessible routes enhances safety and convenience. Designers should also account for weather protection, lighting, and surface conditions to ensure usability in all environments.

Accessible Signage

Clear and consistent signage is a critical component of ADA-compliant EV charger design. Each accessible charging stall should feature pavement markings and vertical signs displaying the International Symbol of Accessibility and the label "EV Charging Only." Proper signage helps prevent misuse by non-EV or non-disabled drivers and ensures that accessible spaces remain available for those who need them. Adding wayfinding or directional signs within larger parking areas can further improve visibility and ease of navigation.

EV-Only Parking Enforcement

Designated EV charging spaces should be reserved for vehicles that are actively charging to ensure the chargers remain available for residents who need them. Without clear enforcement policies, non-EV vehicles—or EVs that remain parked after charging is complete—can block access and reduce the effectiveness of the charging infrastructure. Apartment managers should establish clear rules for EV-only parking, including time limits where appropriate, and communicate these policies to residents. Enforcement measures may include warning notices, parking citations, or towing policies consistent with local regulations.

Signage, Visibility, and Accessibility of Chargers

EV charging stations should be clearly identified and easy for residents and visitors to locate. This includes both physical visibility within the property and digital visibility through charging apps and mapping platforms. Best practices include installing clear signage indicating EV-only parking, painting pavement markings such as "EV Charging Only," and ensuring adequate lighting around the charging area. Effective wayfinding—such as directional signs at property entrances or within parking structures—can help drivers quickly locate charging stations. Clear markings and signage not only improve user experience but also support enforcement by making the intended use of the spaces unmistakable.

Code Regulation Variations

While ADA provides federal-level guidance, state and local regulations often include additional accessibility amendments or stricter requirements. These may specify differences in stall dimensions, slope tolerances, signage placement, or surface treatments. Property owners and integrators should consult local building departments or accessibility experts early in the design phase to confirm compliance. Staying current with evolving regulations ensures that EV charging installations remain both legally compliant and functionally accessible for years to come.

Public vs. Resident-Only Access

Choosing between resident-only and public EV charger access models requires balancing financial, operational, and community considerations. Property owners must evaluate how access policies affect revenue opportunities, liability exposure, and tenant satisfaction while ensuring proper coordination with utilities and network systems. The right approach depends on property goals—whether focused on resident amenities, community engagement, or revenue generation.

User Charger Access Options

EV charger access models typically fall into three categories: resident-only, guest, and public.

- Resident-only access limits charger use to tenants, providing exclusivity and convenience while simplifying management.
- Guest access extends availability to visitors, often through limited-time or code-based authorization.
- Public access allows anyone to use the chargers, typically through a networked payment platform.

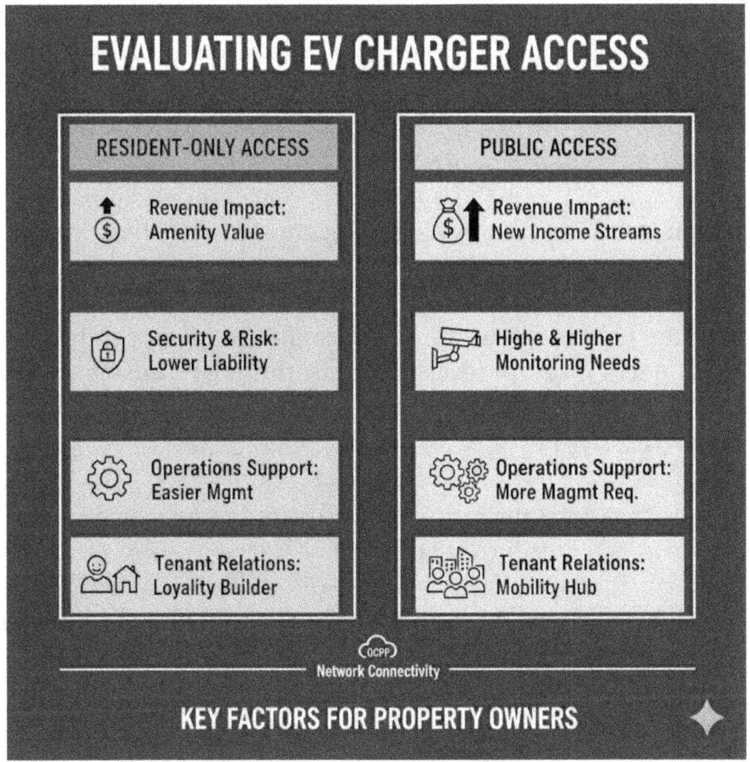

EV Charging at Apartments Private and Public Access Options

Resident-only chargers are typically reserved for tenants, often with assigned spots or subscription-based access. These systems may use billing models tailored for long-term use and can be a valuable amenity, increasing property value and rental rates.

Each model requires distinct pricing, maintenance, and operational policies, and the choice should align with property goals and available resources.
Revenue Impact

Public-access chargers create new income opportunities through per-kWh billing, session fees, or parking premiums, potentially offsetting installation and maintenance costs. However, resident-only systems often deliver stronger long-term tenant retention and marketing value by positioning charging as a premium amenity. A hybrid model—reserving some chargers for residents and others for public use—can provide both steady revenue and tenant satisfaction.

Security & Risk

Expanding charger access increases exposure to liability, vandalism, and unauthorized use. Property owners must implement clear operational policies, access controls, and safety measures such as surveillance cameras and lighting. Limiting charger availability to registered users or tenants reduces misuse and supports more predictable maintenance and insurance costs.

Insurance and Safety

Adequate lighting, video surveillance, and signage are critical for both user safety and insurance compliance. Insurance carriers may require documentation of safety features and usage policies for public-access sites. Incorporating physical protections—such as bollards and barriers—also reduces risk of damage to chargers and vehicles.

Operations Support

Whether public or private, effective operations management ensures chargers remain reliable and user-friendly. Designating responsibility for uptime monitoring, maintenance dispatch, payment processing, and dispute resolution is key. Many property owners partner with EV network operators or integrators to manage these functions, reducing administrative burden and ensuring professional oversight.

Utility Coordination

Public chargers often require separate metering and permitting to comply with commercial use regulations. Coordination with the local utility ensures that proper interconnection, load balancing, and billing structures are in place. Utility programs may also offer incentives or rate options specifically for public-access chargers, which can improve ROI when managed correctly.

Network Connectivity

Using OCPP-compliant (Open Charge Point Protocol) systems provides flexibility to manage various access levels and integrate with multiple software platforms. Networked systems allow property managers to set user permissions, monitor activity, and track revenue across both public and private chargers on multiple properties. Open standards also future-proof the investment by maintaining compatibility with evolving technologies.

OCPP Version 2.0

OCPP version 2.0 is a major version of the open standard protocol used for communication between EV charging stations and central management systems (CPMS). OCPP 2.0 introduces advanced features for smart charging, security, device management, and support for new use cases such as bidirectional charging and energy management. It enables interoperability between different charger brands and network operators, allowing for seamless integration and data exchange. Key improvements include enhanced transaction handling, better diagnostics, support for firmware updates, and improved user authentication. OCPP 2.0 is designed to support future innovations in EV charging, including integration with energy management systems and grid services.

Tenant Relations and Community Impact

Access decisions can shape tenant perceptions and community engagement. Resident-only charging systems foster a sense of exclusivity and loyalty among tenants, enhancing property value and satisfaction. In contrast, public-access systems can position the property as a community mobility hub, improving sustainability visibility and attracting eco-conscious residents or visitors. Balancing these dynamics ensures the EV charging program supports both resident needs and the property's broader brand identity.

Billing & Payment Models

EV charging billing and payment systems for apartments provide property owners and residents with flexible and transparent ways to manage charging costs. By combining appropriate pricing models, regulatory compliance, and accessible payment technologies, apartment communities can ensure fair cost recovery while enhancing the resident experience and encouraging EV adoption.

Billing Options

Apartment charging programs can use several billing models depending on the property's goals and infrastructure. Flat-rate billing offers simplicity, charging residents a fixed monthly fee for unlimited or limited charging access. Per-kWh billing is the most precise method, charging based on actual energy consumed, though it may require compliance with local utility regulations. Session-based or time-based fees charge for the duration or number of charging sessions, often used in shared or public-access systems. Each option can be applied differently for resident-only versus public chargers to balance fairness, revenue, and convenience.

Utility Regulations

Because EV charging involves the resale of electricity, many jurisdictions impose utility and metering regulations on how energy costs can be passed to users. Not all apartment properties are permitted to directly resell electricity to residents. In such cases, operators may charge for access, parking, or time instead of energy use. It's important to consult local utility guidelines or partner with a certified EV charging network that ensures billing compliance and handles regulatory reporting.

Payment Methods

Smart EV charging systems support multiple payment methods to accommodate diverse user preferences. Residents can pay via credit card, mobile app, RFID key, or integrated billing through rent statements. Networked chargers often allow automated user authentication and payment process-

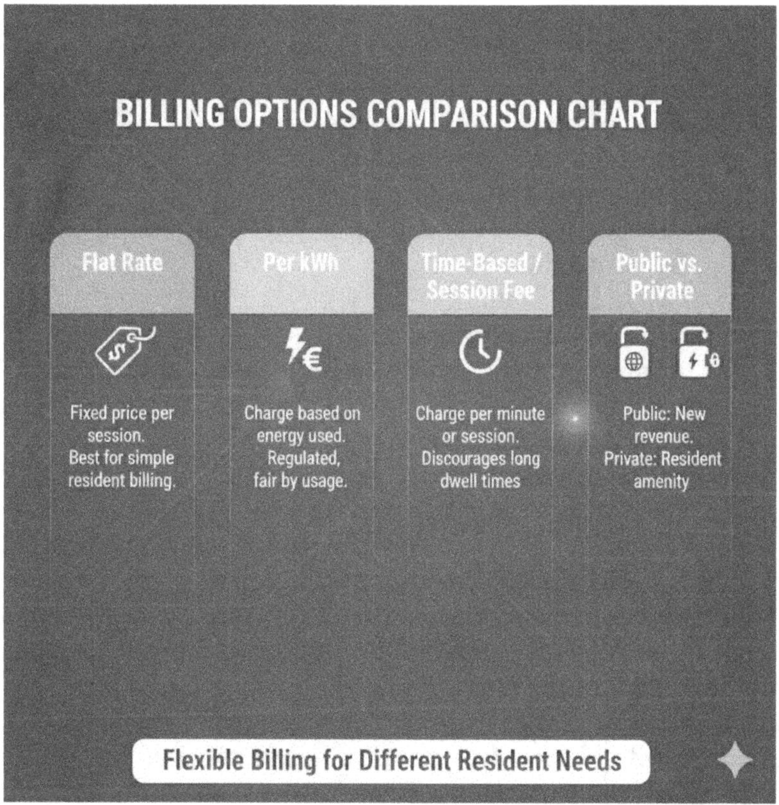

EV Charging Billing Options

ing, simplifying administration for property managers. Flexible payment options increase convenience and encourage more consistent charger use.

Data Reports

Accurate and transparent data reporting is mission critical for both residents and property management. Networked systems can generate detailed usage summaries that show energy consumption, costs, and reimbursement breakdowns by user or apartment unit. These reports help maintain accountability, support cost allocation across tenants, and provide valuable insights into energy use patterns that inform future expansion or pricing adjustments.

Data reporting is vital to EV charging because it provides the visibility needed to manage energy use, track utilization, ensure reliability, and support accurate billing. Reporting also prepares properties for compliance with CEC 2026 charging requirements, which increase the number of required EV-ready spaces and mandate load management capabilities. Without detailed reporting, it is not possible to verify compliance, optimize energy loads, plan for infrastructure upgrades, or participate in utility programs that depend on accurate data.

The 2026 California Energy Code establishes new electric vehicle charging infrastructure requirements for multifamily residential buildings. The code requires a defined percentage of parking spaces to be EV Ready, EV Capable, or fully equipped with charging hardware. EV Ready spaces must include a dedicated branch circuit, an installed receptacle or charging device, and the necessary electrical capacity to deliver Level 2 charging. EV Capable spaces must include electrical raceways, panel capacity allocation, and termination points that allow future installation of charging equipment without significant construction. Load management systems are permitted and are encouraged because they allow multiple circuits to share power while remaining compliant with required charging availability. For multifamily dwellings, central load management is often required to maintain panel capacity limits, distribute charging power efficiently, and reduce the need for costly service upgrades. Transformers, distribution panels, and branch circuits must be sized to meet the combined requirements of EV Ready and EV Capable spaces while ensuring compliance with allowable diversity factors. These provisions ensure that new residential buildings are constructed with infrastructure capable of supporting long duration overnight charging, grid interaction, and increased EV adoption over time.

Billing Policies

Clear billing policies promote fairness, transparency, and resident engagement. Communicating how rates are set, when charges occur, and how usage is tracked builds trust and reduces disputes. Providing residents with real-time access to charging data or monthly summaries fosters awareness and encourages energy-efficient behaviors. Transparent billing also strengthens resident confidence in the property's commitment to sustainability and equitable cost management.

Building Systems Integration

Integrating EV charging with existing building systems allows property owners to create a coordinated and efficient energy ecosystem. By connecting chargers to smart meters, energy management systems (EMS), building management systems (BMS), and renewable energy sources, apartment complexes can optimize energy use, prevent overloads, enhance reliability, and ensure secure communication across the property's infrastructure.

EV Charging Systems at Apartments Smart Energy Integration with Building Systems

Energy Dashboard

Building systems integration refers to the coordinated design of electrical, mechanical, and digital subsystems so they operate as a unified architecture. An Energy Dashboard functions as the centralized interface that aggregates real-time data from these subsystems, including energy consumption profiles, demand response signals, load management behavior, EV charging activity, solar or storage output, and utility rate structures. By integrating these components through standardized communication protocols and centralized controls, the building can optimize power distribution, improve operational efficiency, and support advanced functions such as load shifting, energy monitoring, and participation in grid interaction programs.

Smart Metering Integration

Smart metering integration provides precise tracking of EV charging energy use, enabling accurate billing, tenant cost recovery, and utility data reporting. By linking EV chargers to individual or shared smart meters, property managers gain insight into real-time consumption patterns and can allocate costs fairly among residents. Smart metering also matters for time of use (TOU) billing in certain energy Markets. This data-driven approach supports both financial transparency and compliance with utility or local reporting requirements.

Energy Management Control

Because EV chargers can significantly increase a building's electrical load, active energy management is critical to prevent service overloads and reduce peak demand costs. Intelligent load balancing systems dynamically distribute available power among chargers based on total building consumption, ensuring optimal performance without exceeding capacity limits. This proactive control not only enhances electrical safety but also lowers operating expenses by minimizing demand charges from utilities.

Energy Management Systems (EMS) Integration

Integrating EV chargers with Energy Management Systems (EMS) or Building Management Systems (BMS) allows for centralized control and monitoring of energy resources. Compatibility with common communication protocols—such as BACnet, Modbus, and OCPP—enables real-time data exchange between chargers, meters, and building systems. This integration supports automated load optimization, fault detection, and maintenance alerts, ensuring consistent operation and long-term system reliability.

Charge Point Management System (CPMS)

A Charge Point Management System (CPMS) can integrate with a Building Management System or an Energy Management System to provide coordinated control of EV charging loads within a multifamily property. A CPMS collects real time data from EV charging equipment, including current, voltage, power consumption, and session status, and provides this information to the BMS or EMS

Renewable and Energy Storage Options

Combining EV charging infrastructure with renewable energy and storage systems enhances sustainability and energy resilience. Solar power and battery energy storage can offset grid demand during peak hours, while advanced technologies such as vehicle-to-grid (V2G) and vehicle-to-building (V2B) allow EVs to return stored energy to the property when needed. These integrations reduce carbon footprint, improve grid stability, and demonstrate the property's commitment to environmental stewardship.

V2B allows electric vehicles to discharge stored energy back into a building, enabling the building to function as a hybrid energy system rather than relying solely on grid supply. When paired with an energy management system, V2B can shift a large portion of a building's electrical load to the battery capacity of resident vehicles. This reduces peak demand charges, which are often the most expensive part of a commercial or multifamily electric bill.

By supplying building loads during peak pricing periods, V2B can reduce the effective energy cost by as much as half, depending on load profiles and available stored energy. During a storm or grid outage, the building can disconnect from the utility supply and draw power from connected vehicles. A typical EV can store enough energy to power critical building loads such as lighting, elevators, emergency circuits, and communication systems for many hours. In cases with multiple participating vehicles, a building can maintain essential services for an extended period. The BMS uses real time data to regulate the discharge rate, prioritize critical loads, and ensure the vehicles retain enough energy for resident mobility. This creates a resilient energy architecture that combines grid power, distributed storage, and intelligent load control.

Security Coordination

With greater system interconnectivity comes the need for strong data security and maintenance coordination. EV chargers and building systems exchange sensitive operational and user data, making cybersecurity measures—such as encryption, access authentication, and continuous monitoring—essential. Coordinating maintenance schedules and security protocols across all integrated systems ensures reliability, protects resident information, and safeguards the property's energy infrastructure from potential digital or physical threats.

Cybersecurity Considerations in EV Charging System Design

As EV charging systems become increasingly connected, they also become potential targets for cyber threats. Protecting these systems requires a comprehensive approach that secures hardware and networks, safeguards user data, enforces authentication protocols, and ensures continuous monitoring. A strong cybersecurity framework not only protects residents and property owners but also maintains trust in the reliability of the charging infrastructure.

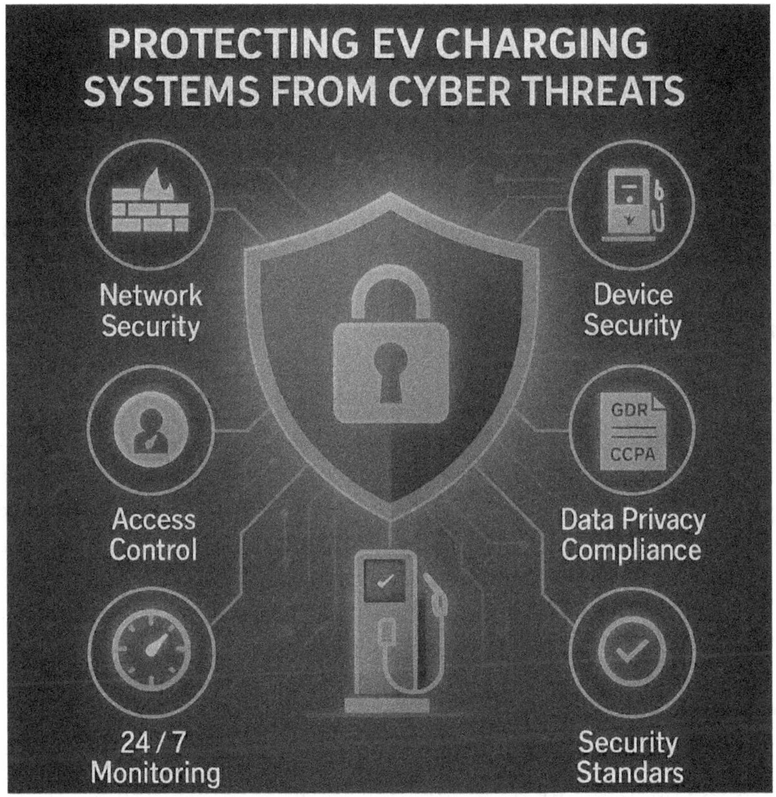

Cybersecurity Considerations in EV Charging System Design

Network and Device Security

Network and device security form the first line of defense against cyberattacks. Each charger, router, and data gateway must be properly configured with firewalls, secure communication protocols, and regular firmware updates to prevent unauthorized access. Segregating EV charging networks from other building systems, such as security cameras or Wi-Fi, helps reduce vulnerabilities and limits the spread of potential breaches across the property's infrastructure.

Data Privacy

EV charging systems collect and transmit sensitive information, including user identities, billing data, and usage patterns. Ensuring data privacy means protecting this information under relevant laws such as GDPR, CCPA, and state-level consumer protection acts. Encryption of all transmitted data, anonymization of user records, and clear privacy policies help maintain compliance while building resident confidence in the system's integrity.

Platform Security Standards

Partnering with vendors that meet recognized cybersecurity certification standards—such as ISO 27001 for information security management or SOC 2 for service organization controls—ensures a higher level of protection across the charging ecosystem. Certified vendors follow strict security protocols, including regular audits, data handling procedures, and incident response plans. Using these certified platforms reduces the likelihood of vulnerabilities and provides assurance that systems meet global cybersecurity benchmarks.

Access Control and User Authentication

Effective access control and user authentication mechanisms prevent misuse by unauthorized users—both digitally and physically. Networked chargers should require secure logins, token-based credentials, or RFID authorization before initiating a charge session. Administrative access should be limited to authorized personnel, with multi-factor authentication (MFA) and role-based permissions enforced. Physical safeguards, such as lockable enclosures and tamper detection, further enhance system integrity.

Continuous Security Monitoring

Cybersecurity is not a one-time setup—it requires continuous monitoring, maintenance, and incident response. Regular system audits, vulnerability scans, and firmware updates help identify and address emerging threats. Establishing an incident response plan ensures that any breach or anomaly is quickly contained and mitigated. Ongoing staff training and periodic reviews of cybersecurity policies also help maintain readiness and resilience as technology and threat landscapes evolve.

EV Charging System Communication Design

EV charging systems rely on robust communication networks to ensure smooth operation, secure data exchange, and seamless integration with management and maintenance platforms. These systems use a combination of wired, wireless, and cellular connections to support data transfer between chargers, software platforms, users, and utilities—enabling efficient control, billing, and diagnostics across the property. Charging Networks require this for Public Charging real time reporting.

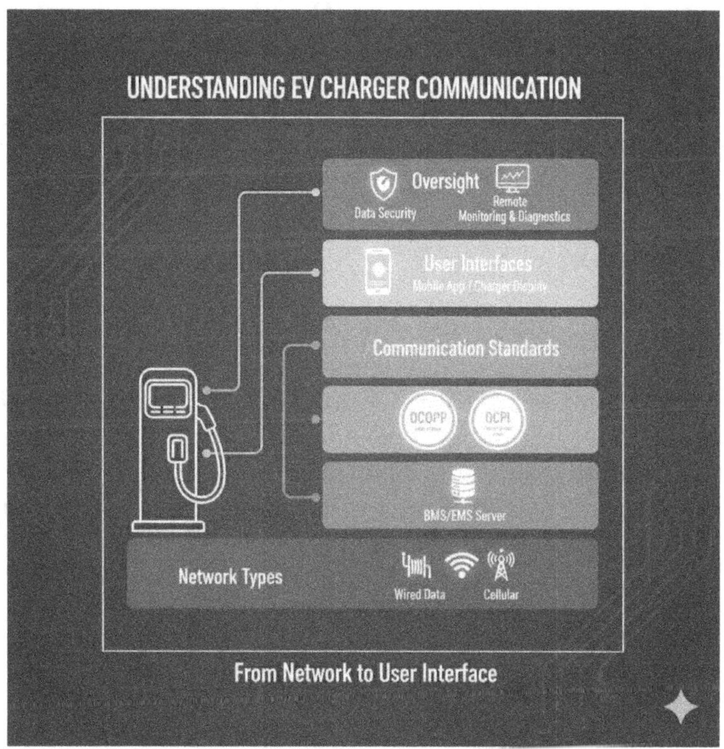

EV Charger Communication Design

Network Types

EV chargers use various network types to connect and exchange information. Wired Ethernet connections provide the most stable and secure communication for fixed installations. Wi-Fi offers flexibility in areas with good local coverage, while cellular networks (such as 4G/5G) are ideal for remote or outdoor sites where wired access is limited. Selecting the right network depends on property layout, signal strength, data requirements, and cost considerations, ensuring reliable connectivity for both real-time operations and long-term monitoring.

Communication Standards

To ensure compatibility between different equipment and software systems, EV chargers follow established communication standards and data protocols. The Open Charge Point Protocol (OCPP) governs charger-to-network communication, handling system control, authentication, and power management. The Open Charge Point Interface (OCPI) enables roaming between different charging networks, allowing users to access chargers across multiple platforms. Adhering to these open standards prevents vendor lock-in and supports future scalability as technology evolves.

System Integration

Seamless system integration allows EV chargers to connect with property management systems, energy management systems (EMS), and billing platforms. This connection enables automated reporting, user authentication, energy optimization, and unified operational control. Integrating EV infrastructure with building systems also improves efficiency by coordinating charging activity with overall energy consumption, supporting sustainability and load management goals.

User Interfaces and Communication Displays

The user interface is the primary point of interaction between residents and the charging system. On-screen menus, LED indicators, or mobile apps guide users through authentication, payment, and session monitoring. In some cases, chargers may include media and content displays—such as digital signage or advertisements—that communicate real-time information or generate additional revenue. Clear, user-friendly interfaces reduce confusion and enhance the overall resident experience.

Data Security

Strong data security practices protect both system integrity and user privacy. All communication between chargers, networks, and management systems should be encrypted to prevent unauthorized access. Compliance with privacy regulations (such as GDPR or CCPA) ensures that personal and billing information remains protected. Regular software updates, secure authentication, and firewall protections are essential to maintain cybersecurity resilience.

Maintenance and Remote Monitoring

Smart EV charging systems rely on remote monitoring and diagnostics to maintain reliability and reduce downtime. Networked chargers can automatically report faults, performance data, and usage metrics to a central dashboard, allowing technicians to address issues proactively. Ai Predictive Maintenance can predict when a charger needs maintenance. Companies like WattsApp use AI-driven analytics to monitor EV charging systems, detect potential failures, and optimize maintenance before issues disrupt charging operations. Remote access also supports firmware updates, configuration changes, and load management without requiring on-site intervention—minimizing maintenance costs and maximizing system uptime.

EV Charging System Energy Efficiency and Sustainability Design

Integrating energy efficiency and sustainability into EV charging system design helps apartment properties lower operating costs, reduce environmental impact, and enhance long-term value. Smart energy management, renewable integration, and adherence to sustainability frameworks such as LEED and ESG not only optimize performance but also position the property as a forward-thinking, eco-conscious community that appeals to residents and investors alike.

Smart Energy Management

Smart energy management focuses on optimizing how and when EV chargers draw electricity to prevent overloading and reduce costs. Tools like Dynamic Load Management (DLM) automatically distribute available power among chargers based on real-time demand, while time-of-use optimization shifts charging to off-peak hours when energy is cheaper and cleaner. Incorporating power factor correction ensures more efficient use of electricity, lowering overall utility expenses and minimizing strain on the grid.

Renewable Energy Integration

Pairing EV charging with renewable energy sources such as solar panels, battery storage, or microgrids enhances sustainability and energy resilience. Solar power can directly offset the electricity used for charging, while battery storage systems help balance loads and provide backup power during outages or peak demand. Microgrid integration enables properties to operate partially independent from the main grid, improving reliability and supporting local sustainability goals.

EV Charging System Efficiency and Sustainability Design

Advanced Energy Management and Bidirectional Charging

Emerging energy technologies are expanding the role of EV charging systems beyond simple electricity consumption. Demand response programs allow charging systems to automatically adjust charging loads in response to utility signals or electricity price changes, helping properties reduce peak demand charges and support grid stability. Bidirectional charging technologies enable electric vehicles to both receive and deliver energy, turning parked EVs into distributed energy resources. Through Vehicle-to-Building (V2B) and Vehicle-to-Home (V2H) systems, stored energy in EV batteries can be used to power buildings or homes during peak pricing periods or power outages, improving energy resilience and potentially lowering electricity costs. As these technologies mature, EV charging infrastructure can become an important part of broader building energy management strategies, integrating vehicles, renewable energy, and the electric grid into a flexible energy ecosystem.

Sustainable Design Certification

Aligning EV charging projects with recognized sustainable design certifications, such as LEED (Leadership in Energy and Environmental Design) or ESG (Environmental, Social, and Governance) frameworks, adds both environmental and market value. Certification-ready infrastructure demonstrates compliance with green building standards, supports property value appreciation, and provides a strong marketing advantage to attract eco-conscious tenants and investors. It also ensures that the project aligns with evolving sustainability regulations and reporting expectations.

Energy Monitoring and Optimization

Continuous energy monitoring allows property owners to track EV charging performance, identify inefficiencies, and measure sustainability outcomes. Advanced monitoring systems provide data on consumption trends, peak usage times, and carbon offset performance. This information supports predictive maintenance, cost optimization, and transparent reporting to stakeholders, making it easier to demonstrate measurable progress toward sustainability goals.

Carbon Reduction Strategies

Implementing carbon reduction strategies helps protect long-term asset value and maintain regulatory compliance. Reducing energy waste, sourcing renewable power, and enabling carbon-neutral charging options all contribute to a smaller environmental footprint. Many investors and government programs now favor or even require low-carbon operations, making proactive carbon management a strategic financial decision as well as an environmental one.

EV Charging System Cost Estimation

Accurately estimating EV charging system costs is essential for developing a financially sustainable project plan. This process involves evaluating key cost categories, understanding site-specific variables, identifying cost-saving opportunities, leveraging available incentives, and modeling long-term lifecycle expenses and returns. A detailed cost estimation provides property owners with the clarity needed to make informed investment decisions and secure funding with confidence.

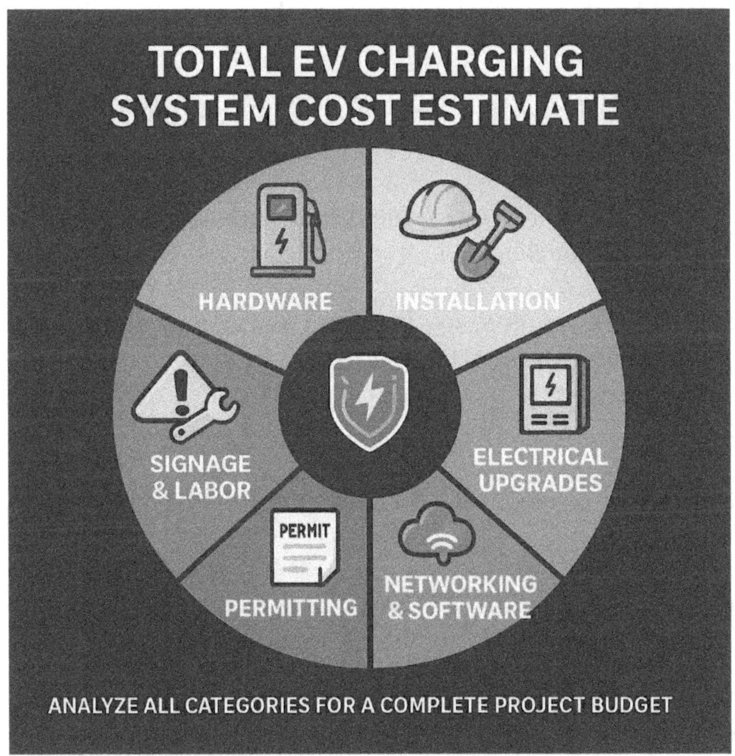

EV Charging System Design Cost Estimation

Cost Categories

The total cost of an EV charging system is composed of several core categories:

Hardware – chargers, mounting equipment, and protective enclosures. Also includes spare parts such as couplers (the plug at the end of the charging cable) that get run over a lot.

Installation – labor for trenching, conduit installation, and electrical connections.

Electrical upgrades – new panels, transformers, or capacity enhancements.

Networking and software – communications systems, user access, and billing platforms.

Permitting and inspection – local government and utility fees for approvals and safety checks.

Legal and contractual costs – legal review of installation agreements, utility interconnection contracts, charging service provider agreements, property lease considerations, liability protections, and compliance with local regulations.

Signage and labor overheads – markings, instructional signs, and project management costs.

Understanding how each category contributes to the total budget helps owners identify where to prioritize spending or reduce costs.

Site Condition Variables

Each property's site conditions significantly influence installation costs. Key factors include the distance from electrical service, which affects the amount of trenching and conduit needed; surface type (asphalt, concrete, or gravel), which impacts labor and equipment requirements; and panel access and spare capacity, which determine whether upgrades are necessary. Additionally, ADA and code compliance can affect layout and construction expenses, while local labor rates and permitting fees may vary by region, further shaping overall project costs.

Cost Optimization Strategies

Cost optimization focuses on reducing upfront expenses without compromising quality or functionality. Phased installation allows property owners to start with a few chargers and expand as demand grows. Implementing load management software can delay or reduce the need for costly electrical upgrades. Pre-installing conduits during parking lot resurfacing or renovation projects lowers future installation costs, while bulk purchasing equipment through partnerships or networks can yield volume discounts. These strategies help balance affordability with scalability.

Grants, Incentives, and Tax Credits

Federal, state, and local governments often offer grants, rebates, and tax credits to offset EV infrastructure costs. These incentives can cover a portion of hardware, installation, or design expenses, making projects more financially viable. Understanding application timing and eligibility requirements is crucial, as many programs operate on a first-come, first-served basis or have annual funding cycles. Partnering with experienced consultants or integrators can help identify and secure the most relevant funding opportunities.

Lifecycle Cost Modeling

Beyond initial installation, it's important to evaluate lifecycle costs—including maintenance, insurance, software subscriptions, and energy use—

against projected revenue streams. Common revenue models include tenant subscriptions, per-kWh billing, and amenity premiums added to rent. A comprehensive ROI analysis, typically spanning 3–7 years, helps determine payback periods under different scenarios. Scenario modeling further allows property owners to compare financial outcomes based on varying adoption rates, energy prices, and incentive structures, ensuring that the investment remains profitable and sustainable over time.

Chapter 4

EV Charging System Design & Planning

EV charging system design for apartment complexes involves balancing technical, operational, and user considerations. A well-designed system ensures reliable charging access for residents while optimizing installation costs and future scalability. Core design areas include charger placement, electrical infrastructure, networking and communication systems, management platforms, and compliance with all safety and code requirements.

EV Charger Placement

Proper charger placement is one of the most important design decisions. Chargers should be positioned close to electrical power sources to minimize trenching, conduit runs, and installation costs. Designers must balance the mix between shared-use and assigned chargers to meet both resident needs and budget goals. ADA-compliant routes, lighting, and clear signage enhance safety, accessibility, and ease of use. A thoughtfully planned layout not only improves utilization but also supports efficient maintenance and long-term property aesthetics.

Some states such as California now require all new apartment buildings to include electric vehicle charging infrastructure. The goal is to make sure residents have access to convenient overnight charging without costly retrofits later. Here is what property owners need to know:

1. A certain number of parking spaces must be EV Ready

These spaces must already have a working outlet or charger installed, along with the electrical wiring needed for a resident to plug in immediately. This allows new tenants with EVs to move in without waiting for upgrades.

2. Additional spaces must be EV Capable

These do not need chargers installed yet, but they must include conduit, wiring paths, and electrical panel capacity so chargers can be added later without major construction. This protects owners from expensive retrofits.

3. The building must support smart load management

California allows buildings to use load management systems to control how much power each charger uses. This reduces the need to upgrade transformers or electrical service.

4. The rules apply to all new multifamily residential construction

Any new apartment complex must include EV Ready and EV Capable parking spaces according to state code.

Electrical Infrastructure Design

A reliable electrical infrastructure provides the foundation for safe and efficient EV charging. This includes evaluating existing electrical panels, transformers, and feeder lines to determine available capacity and future requirements. Engineers should anticipate long-term EV adoption by designing for scalability—installing oversized conduits, reserving breaker spaces, and planning for future transformer upgrades. By incorporating flexibility during the design phase, properties can expand charging capacity later without major construction or downtime.

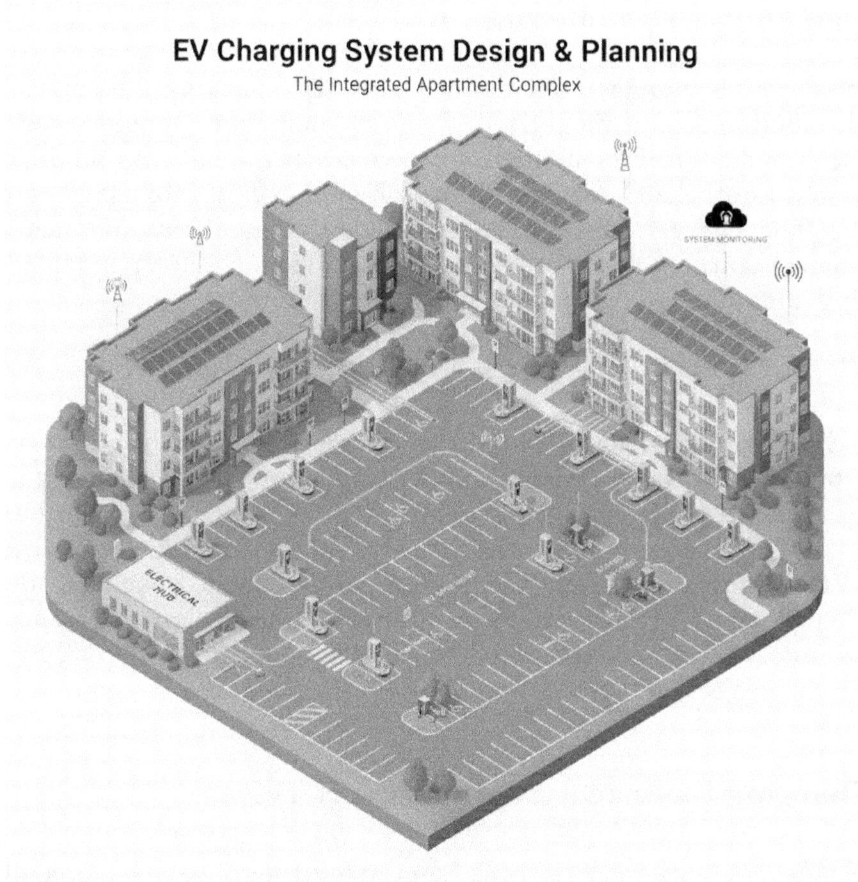

EV Charging System Design and Planning

Networking & Communication

Networking and communication systems enable smart charging operations. Each charger should have dependable data connectivity through wired Ethernet, Wi-Fi, or cellular networks to support monitoring, access control, and billing. Adopting open communication standards such as OCPP and ISO 15118 ensures interoperability among different hardware and software providers. Integration with centralized management platforms allows for real-time data tracking, diagnostics, and remote control, helping operators improve efficiency and resident satisfaction.

EV Charging System Management

Effective system management defines how the charging network is controlled, monitored, and monetized. Property managers should select platforms that handle user authentication, access control, billing, and payments seamlessly. Centralized dashboards can provide insight into usage patterns, revenue, and charger health. Integrating automated maintenance alerts and support features ensures uptime and convenience for residents while reducing administrative workload for property staff.

Safety and Code Compliance

Every EV charging system must adhere to strict safety and regulatory standards to protect users, property, and equipment. Electrical design must comply with the National Electrical Code (NEC) Article 625, local building codes, and fire safety regulations. Critical measures include proper grounding, GFCI protection, labeled circuits, and adherence to spacing and clearance requirements. Prioritizing compliance in the design phase not only ensures safety but also streamlines inspections and prevents costly rework later in the project.

EV Charging Electrical Engineering Services

Electrical engineering services are essential for designing safe, efficient, and scalable EV charging systems at apartment complexes. These services encompass detailed electrical analysis, system integration, and compliance with utility and code requirements. Engineers assess existing power infrastructure, plan for capacity expansion, and develop complete construction-ready documents. Typical engineering design projects cost between $3,000 and $15,000 and take about 3 to 6 weeks to complete, depending on the number of chargers, site complexity, and utility coordination needs. Some companies offer turnkey solutions: Engineering, installation, and training.

EV Charging Electrical Engineering Companies

Electrical Engineering Companies

Electrical engineering firms with EV charging system design experience play a vital role in EV charging infrastructure development. Their expertise includes performing power load analyses, designing distribution systems, coordinating with utilities for transformer and service upgrades, and creating efficient panel and conduit layouts. These professionals ensure that all designs comply with the National Elcctrical Code (NEC), local building regulations, and fire safety standards. Their detailed engineering ensures systems are safe, properly sized, and future-ready.

Benefits of Electrical Engineering Companies

Hiring an experienced electrical engineering firm offers significant advantages for apartment property owners. These companies provide precise load calculations and fully compliant designs that reduce installation risks and improve efficiency. Their coordination with utilities and contractors helps prevent design errors, delays, and costly rework. By delivering accurate budgets and permit-ready documentation, engineering firms help streamline project approval, optimize energy performance, and ensure long-term reliability and scalability as EV adoption increases.

Designs and Drawings

Electrical engineering firms develop detailed engineered drawings and one-line diagrams that serve as blueprints for construction and permitting. These plans define equipment locations, conduit routes, grounding systems, and breaker configurations. Engineers also optimize designs for power efficiency and safety, ensuring all systems operate within electrical and fire code standards. Their involvement continues through construction oversight and commissioning, verifying that installed systems meet performance expectations and regulatory compliance.

Electrical Design and Code Compliance

Compliance with electrical and safety codes is a cornerstone of professional EV charging design. Engineers must design circuits, conduit pathways, grounding systems, and protective devices in accordance with NEC Article 625, ADA accessibility standards, and applicable fire codes. Adhering to these regulations ensures system safety, prevents electrical faults, and protects both property and residents. Proper documentation and labeling are essential to meet inspection requirements and maintain long-term operational integrity.

Electrical Engineering Design Study Cost and Timeline

The cost and duration of electrical engineering design depend on the complexity of the property and system scope. Most projects for apartment complexes range from $3,000 to $15,000 and require approximately 3 to 6 weeks to complete. Smaller properties with minimal upgrades fall on the lower end of this range, while larger or older sites with limited electrical capacity may require additional utility coordination and design time. Investing in a thorough engineering design study ensures a smooth installation, accurate budgeting, and a system that is both code-compliant and expansion-ready.

Layout Design

Layout design for apartment EV charging systems focuses on strategic positioning, accessibility, and long-term scalability. A well-planned layout ensures chargers are easy to use, visually integrated into the property, and cost-effective to install. Proper layout design connects aesthetic, electrical,

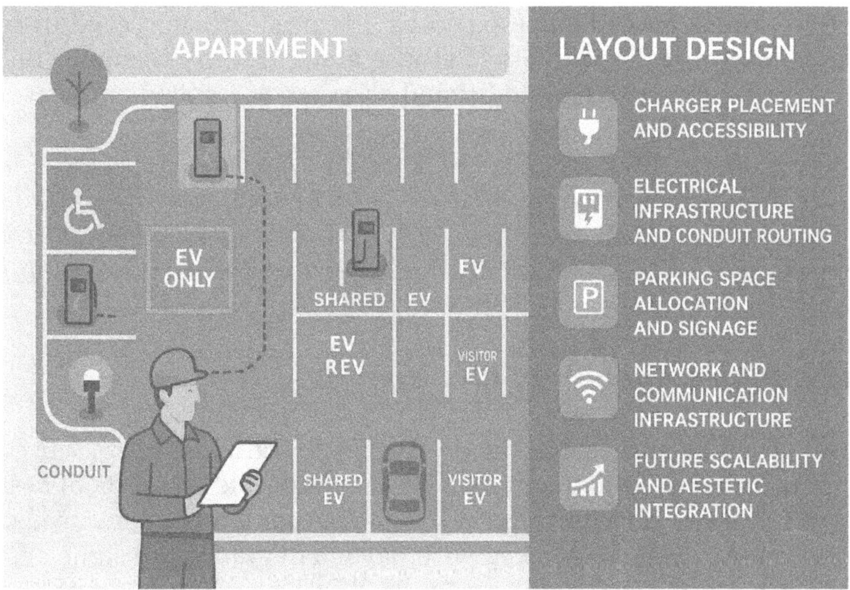

EV Charging Systems Charger Layout Design

and operational factors—balancing user convenience, compliance, and infrastructure efficiency.

Charger Placement and Accessibility

Determining where chargers are positioned within parking areas is a crucial part of layout planning. Chargers should be located close to existing power sources to minimize installation costs while ensuring fair and convenient access for all residents. Designers must also consider ADA accessibility, clear approach paths, adequate lighting, and charger visibility for safety and ease of use. A thoughtful placement plan improves overall utilization and enhances the resident charging experience.

Electrical Infrastructure and Conduit Routing

Charger layout and electrical design are closely linked. The distance between chargers and electrical panels affects voltage drop, conduit runs, trenching requirements, and overall installation costs. Strategically placing chargers along logical conduit paths minimizes disruption to paved areas and reduces material and labor expenses. Planning efficient conduit routing not only lowers installation costs but also simplifies maintenance and supports future expansion when additional chargers are added.

Surprising Fact - *Wall- or pole-mounted EV chargers can reduce installation costs by up to ~70% compared to pedestal-style units. By eliminating trenching, concrete pads, and long conduit runs — often the most expensive part of an install — these mounts typically require less wiring, install faster, and carry lower long-term maintenance risk.*

Parking Space Allocation and Signage

Allocating parking spaces specifically for EV charging helps organize usage and enforce policies. Apartment owners should decide on a mix of assigned, shared-use, and visitor charging spaces to best match resident needs. Each EV space must be clearly marked with pavement stencils or signs designating “EV Charging Only,” along with ADA-compliant symbols where required. Proper signage and markings reduce misuse, ensure accessibility, maintain regulatory compliance. To enforce only EVs in charging spots, tow cars that are not an EV which are in an EV space.

Network and Communication Infrastructure

Reliable data connectivity is essential for networked EV chargers. Each charging location must have access to Wi-Fi, cellular, or Ethernet connections to support real-time monitoring, billing, and load management. Early planning of communication pathways—both wired and wireless—prevents connectivity issues after installation. Coordinating with network providers and IT teams ensures seamless charger operation and integration with property management systems.

Load Management System Data

EV charging systems can use load management to share electrical loads. Guides and regulations such as CEC 2026 allows and encourages load management so multiple chargers can share circuits. To do this safely and stay within electrical limits, the system must continuously monitor:

- current
- voltage
- available panel capacity
- charging load on each circuit

This is essentially real time reporting, even though the code does not use that exact phrase. Compliance verification requires accurate data tracking. CEC 2026 requires proof that:

- EV Ready spaces are powered
- circuits stay within limits
- load management rules are being enforced

This does not explicitly say "real time reporting," but the only practical way to verify compliance is to use systems that gather and track operational data.

Future Scalability and Aesthetic Integration

A forward-thinking design approach prepares apartment complexes for future EV adoption growth. Oversizing conduits, reserving electrical panel capacity, and leaving space for additional chargers make expansion straightforward and affordable. Designers should also consider aesthetics—integrating chargers, bollards, and cable management systems in ways that complement the property's architectural style. A scalable, visually cohesive layout enhances property value while ensuring long-term functionality and sustainability.

Electrical Design

Electrical design for apartment EV charging systems focuses on assessing electrical capacity, configuring panels and circuits for safe operation, incorporating load management technologies, and ensuring compliance with all applicable electrical and safety codes. A well-engineered design not only supports current charging needs but also provides scalability for future expansion as EV adoption increases across the property.

Electric Vehicles Charging Infrastructure

The EV charging infrastructure comes with varying types such as: AC Slow Charging and DC Fast Charging. AC slow chargers that are powered via an outlet at homes is the most cost effective and simplistic solution. There are higher power output AC slow chargers that are capable of improving the charging session times. DC fast chargers are capable of reducing the charging session times significantly from hours to minutes. From an electric grid loading standpoint, AC slow charging sessions add a more stabilized demand over an elongated period of four to eight hours. Whereas, DC fast chargers add a significantly higher demand in shorter durations of 10-60 minutes. Suitability of the type of charger (AC slow vs DC fast) for apartments goes in the hands of the electrical designer. Usually, DC fast charging at rated voltage of 480V is less feasible due to designated 240V systems specified for apartments. However, current technological advancements have resulted in development of DC fast chargers at lower operating voltages such as 208 or 240V.

EV Charging System at Apartment Complex Electrical Design

Electrical Load Capacity and Utility Service

The first step in EV charging electrical design is evaluating the property's existing electrical service. This includes assessing transformer size, available spare capacity, and service entrance ratings. Many apartment complexes have limited excess capacity, so engineers must determine whether upgrades, new subpanels, or load-sharing technologies are required. Coordination with the local utility company helps verify available supply, identify upgrade timelines, and align the design with future energy requirements. Proper capacity analysis prevents overloads and ensures long-term system stability.

Surprising Fact - By integrating a battery-energy storage system (BESS) alongside EV chargers, properties can reduce the required grid (service) capacity by roughly 50 %–80 % compared with a charger setup that draws directly from the grid. This may be expensive to setup, but it can be worth it.

Power Purchase Agreement (PPA)

A power purchase agreement (PPA) is a contract between a utility or energy provider and a customer, usually a building owner, business, or large energy user. It defines how electricity will be supplied, priced, and delivered. For an apartment complex, a PPA typically covers:

- How much power the utility provides. This can include base load, peak load, or a fixed amount of electricity.
- The cost of electricity. Often structured as a long term fixed or semi fixed rate to protect against price increases.
- The length of the agreement. Usually between 10 and 25 years.
- Who maintains the equipment. If solar or backup systems are included, the provider often handles maintenance.

A Power Purchase Agreement can significantly reduce the cost and complexity of adding EV charging to a multifamily property. Instead of the property paying upfront for electrical upgrades, solar, or battery storage, a PPA allows a third party to build and maintain the energy system while the property pays only for the electricity the system produces.

Apartments are billed not only for energy use but also for peak demand. EV charging can raise those peaks. Solar paired with storage under a PPA can supply energy during high demand periods, helping to keep demand charges low and a PPA typically provides fixed or stable energy pricing. This makes EV charging cost planning easier and protects the property from utility rate increases.

Panel Configuration and Circuit Distribution

Panel and circuit design define how charging stations are connected to the building's electrical system. Engineers must calculate load distribution across circuits, specify breaker sizes, and design efficient conduit routing to minimize voltage drop and installation costs. Clear labeling and logical panel layouts simplify troubleshooting and maintenance. A well-organized configuration also supports system scalability—allowing new chargers or panels to be added later without disrupting existing infrastructure.

Load Management and Energy Optimization

Smart load management is a key feature in smart EV charging designs. These systems dynamically balance available power among active chargers to prevent exceeding building demand limits or triggering costly demand charges. Software-based load control enables multiple vehicles to charge simultaneously using limited capacity, optimizing both performance and energy efficiency. Integrating load management systems ensures reliable operation without requiring major electrical upgrades, making it a cost-effective solution for multifamily properties.

Safety, Compliance, and Code Requirements

Safety and regulatory compliance form the backbone of every electrical design. EV charging systems must adhere to NEC Article 625, local electrical codes, and relevant fire and building standards. Proper grounding, GFCI protection, conduit sizing, and circuit protection are essential to prevent hazards. Engineers also ensure all equipment is UL- or ETL-listed and installed according to manufacturer specifications. Adhering to these standards guarantees resident safety, code approval, and system reliability throughout the charger's lifespan.

Scalability and Future-Ready Infrastructure

A future-ready design anticipates increasing EV adoption and evolving technology. Engineers plan for expansion by oversizing conduits, reserving breaker space in panels, and designing circuits that can handle additional capacity. Including spare conduit paths and upgrade-ready service panels allows for easy addition of new chargers without major rework. Scalable electrical infrastructure ensures the apartment complex remains adaptable to growing resident demand while protecting the owner's long-term investment.

EV Charger Hardware Options

Selecting the right charger hardware is a critical component of designing EV charging systems for apartment complexes. Hardware decisions affect charging speed, user experience, maintenance costs, and future scalability. Choosing appropriate charger types, ensuring compatibility, and verifying quality and integration features help property owners create reliable, efficient, and future-ready charging solutions for residents and visitors.

Charger Types and Power Levels

EV chargers are generally categorized into three levels—Level 1, Level 2, and DC Fast Chargers—each suited for different property needs and budgets. Level 1 chargers use standard 120-volt outlets and provide slow charging, ideal for overnight use or low-demand sites. Level 2 chargers, operating at 208–240 volts, are the most common for apartments, offering a practical balance between cost and charging speed, typically adding 20–30 miles of range per hour. DC Fast Chargers deliver rapid charging but require significant electrical infrastructure and higher installation costs, making them best suited for high-traffic or public-access areas rather than resident-only use.

Smart vs. Basic Chargers

When selecting chargers, owners must decide between smart (networked) and basic (non-networked) models. Smart chargers connect via Wi-Fi, cellular, or Ethernet and support advanced features such as user authentication, payment processing, energy load management, and real-time monitoring—ideal for multi-tenant environments. Basic chargers, by contrast, are simpler and lower-cost but lack remote control, billing, and data reporting capabilities. For most apartment properties, smart chargers provide better long-term value by simplifying management and enabling revenue generation.

Connector Types

Charger connector compatibility ensures that residents with different EV models can use the system without restrictions. The most common standard

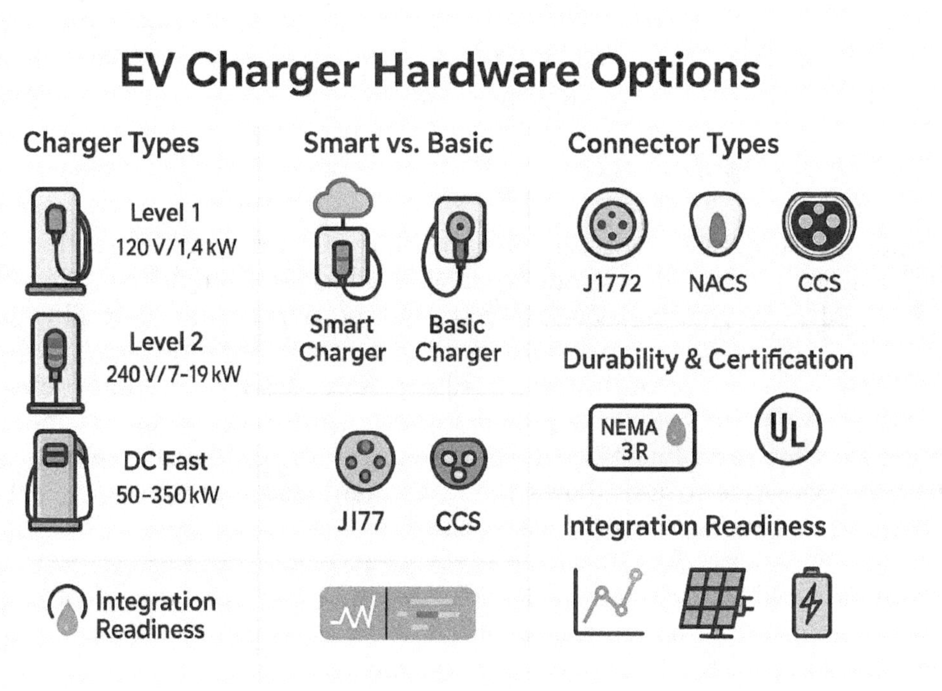

EV Charger Type and Feature Options

in North America is the J1772 connector, used by nearly all non-Tesla vehicles. NACS (North American Charging Standard), originally developed by Tesla, is rapidly becoming an industry-wide standard as many automakers adopt it. CCS (Combined Charging System) connectors are used for DC Fast Charging. Apartment owners should prioritize chargers with dual or adaptable connector support to maximize usability and future-proof the investment against evolving vehicle standards.

Durability and Warranty

Hardware durability directly affects reliability and maintenance costs. Chargers installed outdoors must meet NEMA enclosure ratings for weather and dust resistance and should carry UL or ETL safety certifications to verify electrical safety. Investing in commercial-grade equipment designed for continuous operation helps prevent downtime and warranty claims. Property owners should also compare warranty terms—typically 3 to 5 years—and evaluate the manufacturer's reputation for support and parts availability to ensure consistent performance.

Integration Readiness

Future-proofing the charging infrastructure requires hardware that supports system integration and expansion. Chargers should be compatible with load management systems, payment platforms, and emerging technologies such as solar generation, battery storage, or vehicle-to-grid (V2G) systems. Selecting open-protocol hardware (e.g., OCPP-compliant) ensures flexibility to switch software providers or integrate with property management systems as technology evolves. Integration-ready hardware helps protect the investment and allows the apartment complex to adapt easily as charging demand and energy strategies grow.

Surprising Factoid - *Many EV chargers used in commercial properties include displays that can display advertising messages. Some ad networks can integrate with EV charger displays meaning ads can be selected, sold and served automatically — no manual scheduling or local sales needed. If you select EV chargers with displays that are advertising enabled, they can become revenue machines providing hundreds or thousands of dollars per year for each EV charger.*

Vendor Selection

Vendor selection for apartment EV charging systems is a critical step that determines the success, reliability, and long-term manageability of the project. Property owners should seek experienced providers who understand the unique requirements of multifamily environments, offer interoperable hardware and software solutions, and provide dependable post-installation support. The right vendor can also help navigate financing, incentive programs, and permitting, ensuring a smooth and cost-effective deployment.

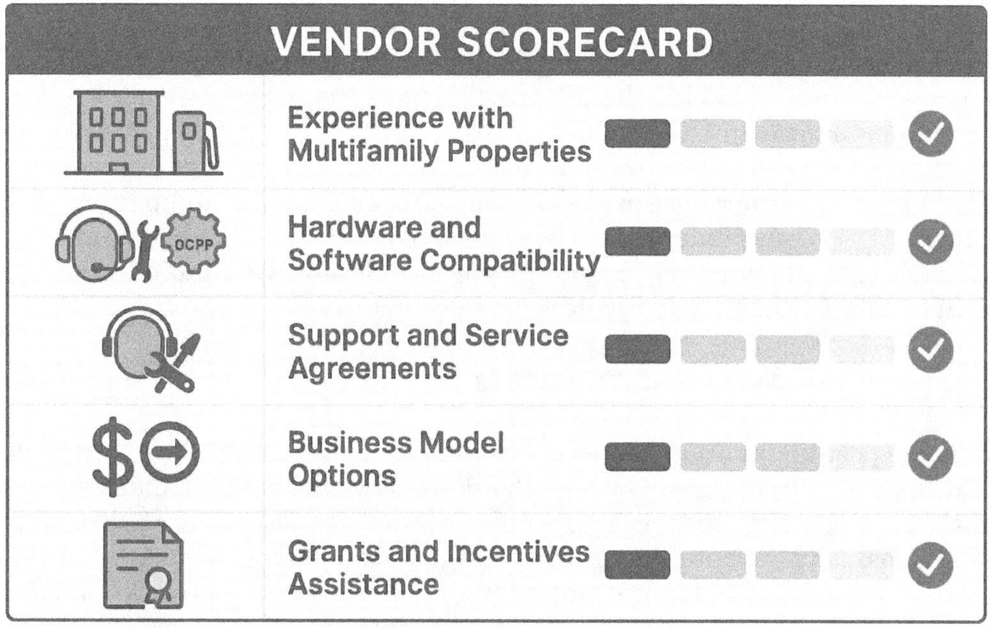

EV Charger System Vendor Selection

Experience in Multifamily Properties

Choosing a vendor with demonstrated experience in multifamily or mixed-use properties is essential. These vendors understand the complexities of shared infrastructure, tenant billing, and parking space allocation common to apartment environments. They can recommend practical configurations—such as assigned versus shared chargers—and integrate systems with existing property management or access control platforms. A vendor familiar with multifamily operations can anticipate resident needs, streamline implementation, and ensure a positive charging experience for both tenants and management.

Hardware and Software Compatibility

Interoperability is key to ensuring flexibility and longevity in an EV charging installation. Vendors should provide open-standard systems, such as those compliant with OCPP (Open Charge Point Protocol), which allow integration with various hardware brands, utilities, and payment processors. This prevents vendor lock-in and enables property owners to upgrade components or software independently as technology evolves. Compatibility also ensures that systems can communicate seamlessly with building energy management systems and future smart grid programs.

Support and Service Agreements

Reliable post-installation support is critical for maintaining charger uptime and resident satisfaction. Owners should review the vendor's maintenance offerings, including response times for service requests, software update schedules, and remote monitoring capabilities. Comprehensive service agreements often include preventive maintenance visits, network management, and extended warranty options. Partnering with a vendor that provides consistent support helps reduce downtime, ensure safety compliance, and protect the investment over time.

Business Model Options

EV charging vendors offer a range of business models to fit different property budgets and goals. Traditional outright purchase models provide full ownership but require higher upfront costs. Alternatively, subscription, lease, or revenue-sharing models—often referred to as "charging-as-a-service"—can minimize initial expenses while outsourcing management and maintenance responsibilities. Each model affects long-term costs, cash flow, and control, so owners should carefully evaluate which approach aligns best with their financial and operational objectives.

Grants and Incentives Assistance

An experienced vendor can also be a valuable partner in securing grants, rebates, and tax incentives. Many utilities and government agencies offer funding for EV infrastructure, but the application and compliance processes can be complex. Vendors familiar with these programs can guide property owners through eligibility checks, documentation, and permitting, often accelerating project timelines and lowering total installation costs. Choosing a vendor that provides incentive navigation support can significantly improve project affordability and return on investment.

Smart Charging & Load Balancing

Smart charging and load balancing technologies form the backbone of smart EV charging system design for apartment complexes. These systems intelligently manage energy distribution to prevent overloading electrical infrastructure, reduce energy costs, and enhance user convenience. By integrat-

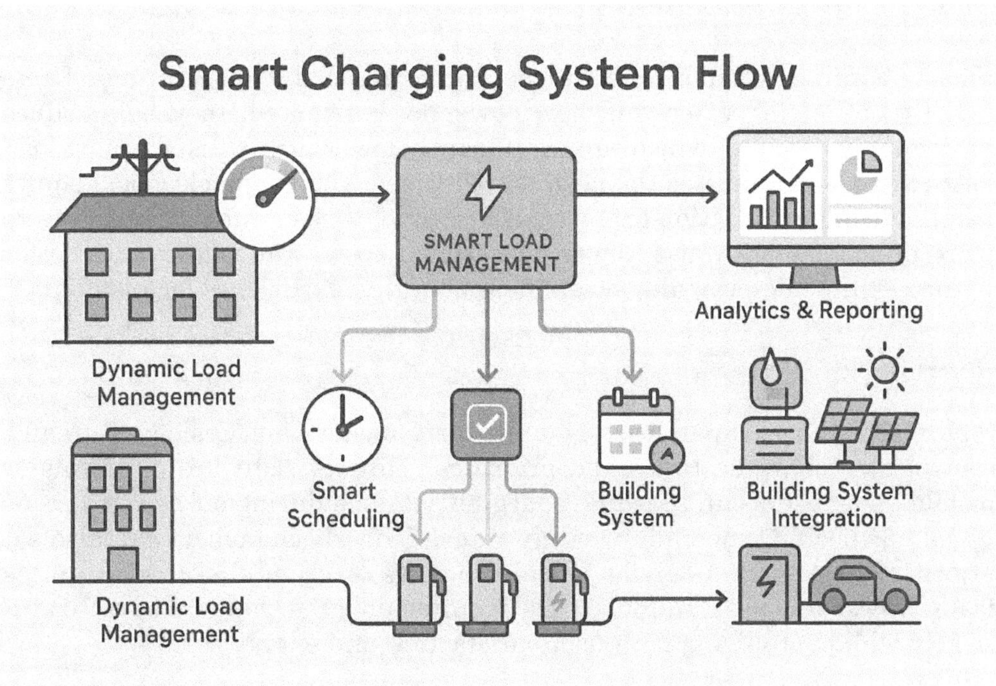

Smart EV Charging & Load Balancing

ing with building systems and renewable energy sources, they improve operational efficiency, support sustainability goals, and allow for scalable expansion as EV adoption increases.

Dynamic Load Management (Smart Charging)

Dynamic load management is the core feature of smart charging. It continuously monitors the electrical demand across all active chargers and automatically adjusts power distribution to stay within the building's available capacity. This ensures that charging remains balanced, even when multiple vehicles are plugged in simultaneously. By preventing overloading of circuits or transformers, dynamic load management allows more chargers to operate on existing infrastructure—avoiding expensive utility upgrades or additional service connections.

Smart Charging Benefits

Smart charging systems deliver measurable financial and operational benefits. By optimizing when and how power is distributed, they help reduce peak energy demand, which can significantly lower utility costs. Smart load balancing also minimizes the need for oversized wiring and electrical equipment, cutting installation expenses. Over time, these systems contribute to more efficient energy use, lower operational costs, and improved charger uptime—all while providing a seamless charging experience for residents.

Smart Scheduling

Smart scheduling capabilities give property owners and residents greater control over charging times and priorities. Through software platforms or mobile apps, users can schedule charging sessions during off-peak hours or based on specific time-of-day energy rates. Property managers can also set priority rules—such as giving certain tenants or premium parking spaces faster access to power. Automated scheduling ensures chargers operate efficiently while optimizing both user satisfaction and energy costs.

Building System Integration

Integrating EV charging systems with broader building management systems (BMS) creates new opportunities for energy optimization. When connected to solar arrays, battery storage, or demand response programs, smart chargers can use renewable or stored energy when available and adjust consumption during grid peaks. This integration enhances energy resilience, reduces carbon footprint, and aligns with sustainability goals. Coordinated operation across systems allows apartment complexes to maximize efficiency and participate in utility incentive programs.

Analytics, Reporting, and Future Scalability

Advanced smart charging platforms provide real-time analytics and reporting tools that help owners and operators make informed decisions. These systems track metrics such as energy consumption, usage patterns, and revenue generation, offering insights for future infrastructure planning. Data reporting simplifies billing and compliance with incentive programs, while scalability features—such as modular software and open communication protocols—allow easy expansion as EV demand grows. Together, analytics and scalability ensure that apartment charging systems remain adaptable, efficient, and profitable over the long term.

Utility Company Coordination

Utility company coordination is a vital component of planning and operating EV charging systems at apartment complexes. Early collaboration with the local utility helps ensure that the property's electrical infrastructure can support additional charging demand, while also unlocking opportunities for cost savings and efficiency through rate optimization, rebates, and participation in demand management programs. Effective coordination not only reduces project risk and costs but also ensures long-term grid reliability and compliance with utility communication standards.

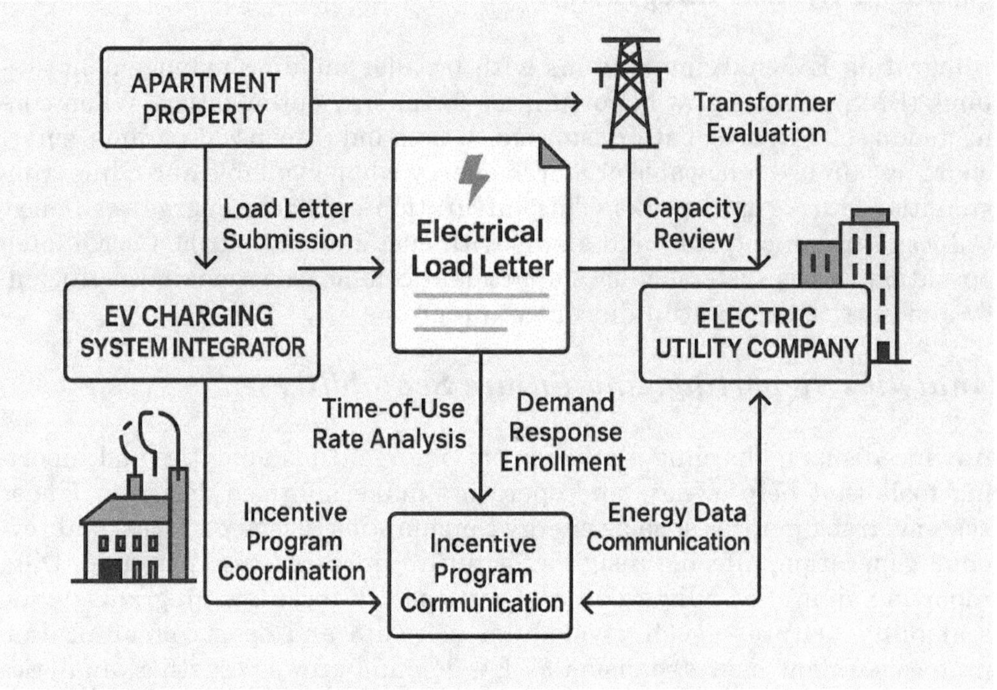

EV Charging System and Utility Company Coordination

Grid Capacity Requirements

Assessing grid and service capacity is the first step in coordinating with the utility. Engineers must evaluate the property's electrical load, transformer capacity, and service connection options to determine whether upgrades are needed. This typically involves submitting a load letter to the utility, outlining the anticipated charging demand and infrastructure requirements. Early engagement allows utilities to plan transformer upgrades or new service connections in time for the project, preventing costly delays. Understanding grid limits helps owners design right-sized systems that balance capacity, performance, and expansion potential.

Time-of-Use (TOU) Rate Optimization

Many utilities offer time-of-use (TOU) electricity rates, which vary based on the time of day and overall grid demand. Coordinating EV charger operations with TOU pricing can significantly reduce energy costs for apartment complexes. By scheduling charging during off-peak hours—typically at night or midday—property owners and residents can take advantage of lower rates. Smart charging platforms can automate this process, ensuring chargers draw power only when electricity prices are most favorable, further improving cost efficiency and grid balance.

Utility Incentives and Rebates

Utilities across the U.S. are increasingly offering rebates, incentives, and make-ready funding to encourage EV charging adoption. These programs can cover portions of hardware, installation, or even electrical infrastructure upgrades. Coordinating with the utility early allows property owners to identify which programs are available and ensure that their design meets eligibility requirements. In some cases, utilities may even assist with engineering support, equipment selection, or permitting. Leveraging these incentives can reduce upfront costs and improve project ROI.

Grid Load Management Participation

Participation in demand response or grid load management programs provides another opportunity to reduce operational costs while supporting grid stability. In these programs, utilities temporarily adjust or limit charging power during peak grid demand periods in exchange for financial credits or rate reductions. For apartment complexes, enrolling in such programs can help offset operating expenses, demonstrate environmental responsibility, and integrate the property into broader energy resilience initiatives.

Energy Use Communication

Smart EV charging systems often need to meet specific utility communication and data-sharing standards to qualify for incentives or grid integration. Protocols such as OpenADR (Open Automated Demand Response) and

OCPP (Open Charge Point Protocol) enable two-way communication between the utility, the charging network, and the property's energy management system. These standards allow for remote monitoring, load control, and real-time energy reporting. Ensuring compliance with utility data protocols enhances transparency, simplifies coordination, and enables long-term participation in future grid-interactive programs.

EV Charging Systems Design

An EV Charging Systems Design provides a complete blueprint for deploying EV charging infrastructure at an apartment property, covering the electrical, technical, construction, and compliance elements required to create a safe, scalable, and cost-effective system. A well-developed design plan ensures the installation meets tenant needs, aligns with property constraints, and supports long-term adaptability as EV adoption grows. By addressing electrical capacity, charger selection, networking, construction logistics, regulatory requirements, and essential installation documents, apartment owners and integrators can confidently plan and implement a charging system that delivers reliable performance and long-term value.

Electrical Upgrades

A key part of the design process involves evaluating the property's existing electrical infrastructure to determine whether upgrades are needed to support EV charging. Service panels, transformers, feeder circuits, and load capacity are assessed to define available power and identify constraints. When upgrades are required, strategic solutions such as dynamic load management (DLM) can significantly reduce costs by distributing charging power intelligently and minimizing the need for heavy infrastructure expansion. Properly planning electrical capacity ensures the system can safely support today's charging needs while allowing room for future growth.

EV Charger Types, Quantities & Placement Strategy

Choosing the appropriate mix of Level 1, Level 2, and DC fast chargers is essential to aligning the design with resident demand, parking layout, and

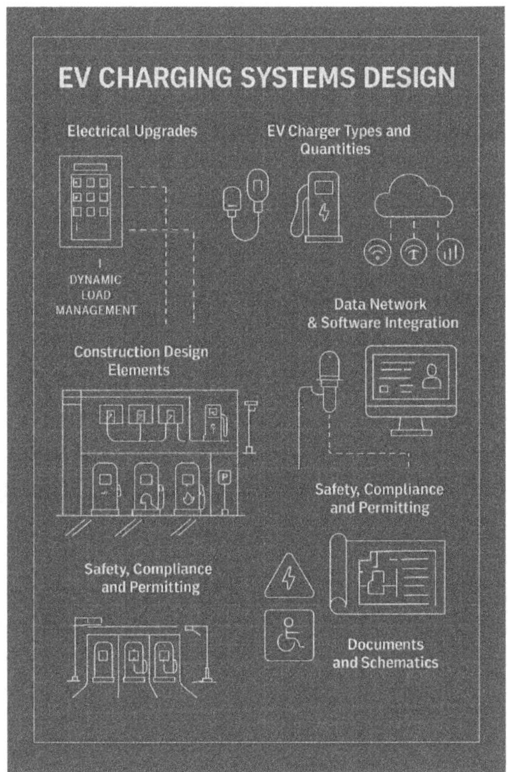

EV Charging Systems Design

budget. The placement strategy considers accessibility, convenience, and efficiency—ensuring ADA-compliant spaces, minimizing trenching distances, and optimizing charger locations for both cost control and user experience. Determining the right number of chargers helps avoid overbuilding while keeping the system scalable for increasing EV adoption. A thoughtful approach ensures the charging infrastructure is both practical and future-ready.

Data Network & Software Integration

A robust communication and control layer is central to smart EV charging systems. The design must define how chargers will connect—using wired Ethernet, Wi-Fi, or cellular networks—and identify which management platform will handle billing, access control, performance monitoring, and remote diagnostics. Integration with building systems such as Energy Management Systems (EMS) and Building Management Systems (BMS) ensures coordinated energy use and consistent reporting. Strong networking and software design ensures reliable charger operation and supports long-term operational efficiency.

Construction Design Elements

The construction component of the design plan outlines the physical installation requirements, including site layout, trenching needs, conduit routing, and mounting methods such as wall-mounted or pedestal-mounted chargers. It also addresses parking lot modifications, signage placement, and lighting improvements to create a safe and accessible charging environment. These construction considerations directly impact installation costs and long-term maintenance, making it essential to design pathways and components that are durable, efficient, and compliant with site conditions.

Safety, Compliance & Permitting

Ensuring compliance with all applicable regulations is a foundational element of EV charging system design. This includes adherence to electrical codes such as NEC Article 625, ADA accessibility requirements, local fire and building codes, and all utility interconnection rules. The design must specify the documentation needed for permitting and inspection, ensuring that the installation is legally compliant and eligible for activation. Addressing safety and compliance early prevents costly redesigns and delays later in the project.

Documents and Schematics

A complete EV charging system design package includes all drawings, schematics, equipment lists, and construction documentation required for installation. This typically includes site plans, single-line electrical diagrams, conduit routing maps, panel schedules, networking diagrams, and product specification sheets. Providing accurate and comprehensive documentation ensures installers, inspectors, contractors, and utility partners can coordinate effectively and execute the project without uncertainty. Clear documentation is essential to achieving a smooth, code-compliant installation that aligns with the property's long-term operational strategy.

Installation Plan

Installation planning for apartment EV charging systems requires careful coordination among utilities, contractors, and property management to ensure a smooth and cost-effective process. Proper planning addresses

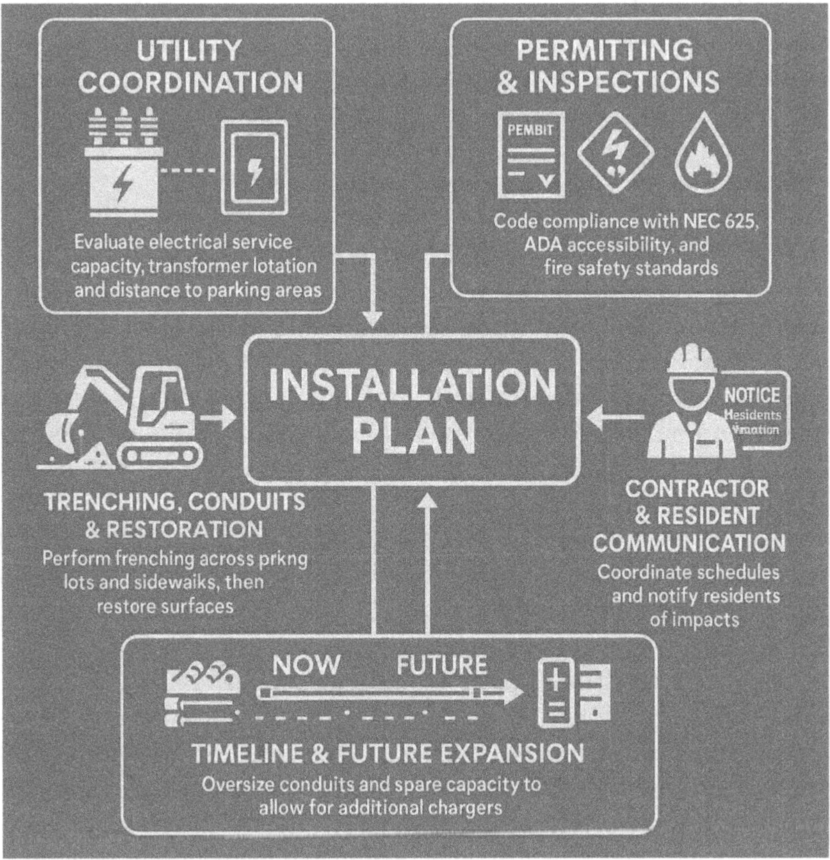

EV Charging System for Apartments Installation Plan

everything from trenching and electrical service preparation to permitting, code compliance, and resident communication. By anticipating site challenges and integrating scalability into the design, apartment owners can minimize disruptions, control costs, and prepare for future charging expansion.

Utility Coordination

Successful installation begins with early and proactive utility coordination. Engineers and property managers must evaluate existing electrical service capacity, transformer locations, and available grid connections. Working with the local utility helps determine whether service upgrades are required and identifies optimal connection points for new chargers. This step also includes submitting load letters, confirming transformer access, and aligning with any utility incentive or interconnection requirements. Early engagement with the utility helps avoid delays and ensures the system's design aligns with available electrical infrastructure.

Trenching, Conduits, and Restoration

Trenching and conduit installation represent one of the most labor-intensive and costly aspects of an EV charging project. Planning efficient conduit routes—across parking lots, sidewalks, or landscaped areas—reduces excavation costs and surface disruption. In some cases, directional boring may be used to minimize pavement removal. The plan should also specify how surfaces will be restored after installation, ensuring minimal visual impact and compliance with property standards. Combining conduit installation with other planned maintenance projects (such as resurfacing or lighting upgrades) can yield additional savings.

Permitting, Inspections, and Code Compliance

Every installation must comply with local permitting, inspection, and electrical code requirements. This includes adherence to NEC Article 625, ADA accessibility standards, and applicable fire and building safety codes. The permitting process typically involves submitting detailed electrical drawings, obtaining municipal approvals, and scheduling inspections throughout construction. Ensuring code compliance at every step prevents rework, accelerates approval timelines, and guarantees a safe, legally compliant charging system for both residents and property managers.

Installation Timeline and Future Expansion

A well-planned installation should balance immediate needs with long-term scalability. During initial construction, installing oversized conduits, reserving breaker capacity, and pre-wiring additional panels can greatly reduce costs for future charger additions. This "build once, expand later" approach avoids costly retrenching and ensures the system can adapt as more residents adopt EVs. Planning for phased expansion allows the property to meet current demand efficiently while maintaining flexibility for future growth.

Contractor Scheduling and Resident Communication

Coordinating multiple contractors—electrical, paving, signage, and network technicians—requires a structured timeline and clear communication. Property managers should develop a resident communication plan to inform tenants of temporary parking changes, power interruptions, and construction schedules. Regular updates through email, notices, or community portals help maintain resident satisfaction and reduce complaints. Effective scheduling and transparent communication ensure that installation proceeds smoothly, minimizing disruption to daily property operations.

Chapter 5

EV Charging System Installation

EV charging system installation requires the integration of project management, permitting, utility coordination, equipment procurement, and contractor scheduling to ensure a smooth and timely deployment. Each phase must be carefully planned—from selecting hardware with long lead times to sequencing electrical, civil, and data work—to avoid delays and minimize disruption for residents. A structured approach using work orders, milestone tracking, and commissioning procedures ensures that every component is installed correctly, tested, and handed over to property management with confidence.

Project Management

Effective project management establishes a clear installation plan that aligns timelines, personnel, and resources needed to deploy EV charging systems efficiently. Using structured tools and defined workflows helps track progress, document inspections, verify quality, and ensure compliance with design and safety standards such as NEC 625 and local codes. Contractor payments should be tied to milestone achievements—such as trenching completion, panel upgrades, or passed inspections—to maintain accountability and prevent cost overruns. A well-managed project framework keeps the installation on schedule and reduces risks throughout the build process.

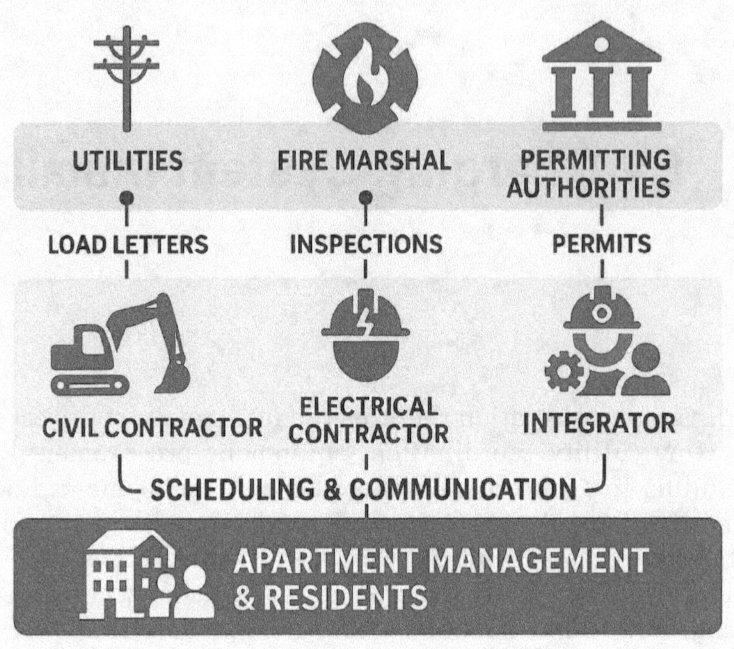

EV Charging System Installation at Apartments

Permitting and Utility Coordination

Permitting, inspections, and utility coordination form the backbone of the installation timeline and often determine the project's critical path. Local authorities, fire marshals, and utilities each require documentation, site plans, and scheduled reviews before work can begin or be energized. Delays in interconnection approvals or meter upgrades can extend schedules by weeks or even months, making it essential to start these steps early in the process. Maintaining open communication with permitting departments and utility representatives ensures faster issue resolution and smoother transitions between phases.

Equipment Selection and Lead Times

Choosing the right chargers—Level 2 or DC fast—along with supporting hardware such as network controllers, mounting systems, and communication modules significantly affects project timing. Many EVSE products have long procurement cycles, with lead times ranging from 8 to 20 weeks. Early equipment selection and purchase orders are critical to preventing installation slowdowns or prolonged site inactivity. Understanding firmware compatibility, network requirements, and manufacturer support also ensures the installation team has everything needed once construction begins.

Contractor Selection & Scheduling

Coordinated contractor scheduling ensures that electrical, civil, and data work happens in the correct order, reducing inefficiencies and disruptions for property residents. Trenching, conduit installation, panel upgrades, and network wiring must be sequenced to align with property operations, minimize downtime, and prevent unnecessary re-work. Selecting experienced EV charging contractors improves reliability, while well-defined construction phasing prevents idle labor, missed inspections, and budget creep. Clear communication between contractors and property managers ensures that the installation progresses smoothly and safely.

Work Orders

Work orders define the individual tasks, timeline, labor, and material requirements needed to complete each phase of the installation. Detailed work orders help contractors understand the scope of work, prioritize activities, and ensure that all necessary materials and approvals are in place before tasks begin. Using work orders as part of the project workflow increases accountability, enhances documentation, and supports efficient scheduling across multiple crews and trades.

Testing & Project Handover

The installation process concludes with a structured commissioning phase that verifies proper operation of all charging equipment and network systems. This includes software setup, charger activation, load-management configuration, safety testing, and full network validation. After final inspections and approvals, installers conduct staff training and provide documentation packages—such as as-built drawings, warranty details, and user guides—to ensure the property team can manage the system effectively. A structured handover process ensures the charging system is fully operational and ready for long-term use.

Selecting Certified Installers and Contractors

Choosing the right contractors and integrators is one of the most critical decisions apartment owners make when installing EV charging systems. Effective selection requires careful evaluation of certifications, licenses, insurance, technical experience, safety practices, and the ability to manage all elements of EVSE deployment—from electrical and civil work to data networking and software configuration. Firms with proven multifamily experience, transparent proposals, and clear communication processes ensure higher quality, fewer delays, and greater long-term system reliability. Certified, well-equipped installers reduce risk, ensure code compliance, support better resident experiences, and provide owners with confidence that the charging system will operate safely and efficiently for years.

Certifications, Licenses, and EV-Specific Credentials

Qualified contractors must hold the proper licenses and certifications required for safe and compliant EV charging system installation. Core requirements include a state electrical contractor license, proof of completed Electric Vehicle Infrastructure Training Program (EVITP) certification, and manufacturer-specific training from companies such as ChargePoint, Wallbox, Blink, or Enel X. Contractors with experience installing OCPP-compliant systems demonstrate an understanding of modern communication protocols and long-term system interoperability. Verifying these cre-

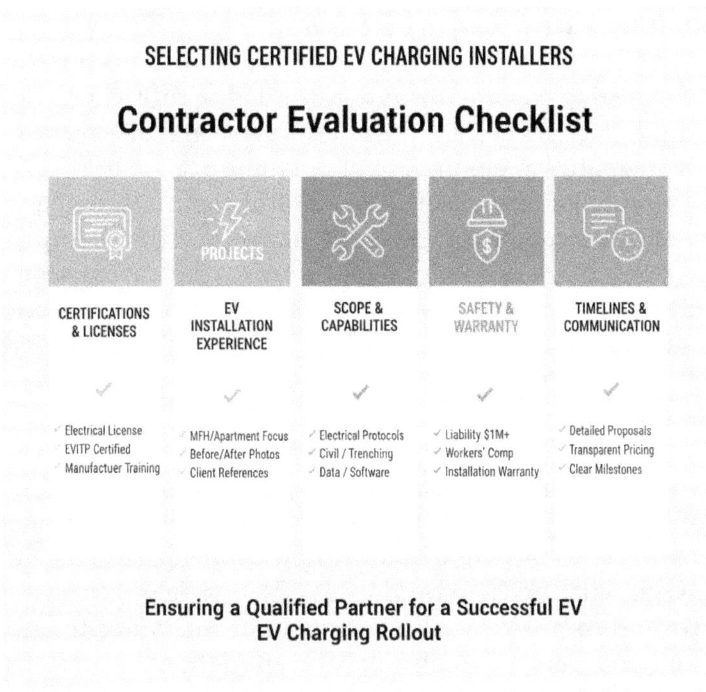

EV Charging System Installation at Apartments Contractor Selection

dentials protects apartment owners from code violations, unsafe installations, and warranty issues.

EV Charging Installation Experience

Installing EV charging stations requires specialized skills that go well beyond traditional electrical work. Apartment owners should look for contractors with documented experience in multifamily charging installations, including examples of trenching, panel upgrades, load management setup, and resident-facing charger configurations. Before-and-after photos, case studies, client references, and testimonials help validate real-world experience. Contractors familiar with the operational needs of apartment communities—such as minimizing resident disruption and coordinating with property maintenance teams—deliver more efficient and reliable outcomes.

Scope Awareness and Capabilities

A top-tier EV charging contractor understands the full scope of EVSE installation, including electrical, civil, data, and software integration work. This comprehensive capability ensures that a single contractor—or coordinated integrator—can manage trenching and conduit installation, panel upgrades, networking, charger configuration, and backend CMS setup. Contractors who manage the entire scope reduce delays, prevent miscommunication between trades, and provide a more seamless installation process for property owners and residents.

Safety and Quality Practices

Safety is a core requirement for EV charging installation, especially in active residential environments. Contractors must demonstrate strong safety protocols for electrical work, excavation, and operations near resident areas, complying with OSHA standards, NEC Article 625, and local codes. Quality control procedures—such as inspection-ready documentation, proper labeling, and adherence to manufacturer guidelines—are essential to prevent hazards and ensure system reliability. Contractors with strong safety records reduce liability risks and ensure long-term performance.

Insurance and Warranty Coverage

Apartment owners should only work with contractors who carry appropriate insurance coverage, including general liability insurance (commonly $1M–$2M or more) and workers' compensation for all employees. These protections limit owner risk in case of damage, injury, or unforeseen issues during the project. Additionally, reputable contractors provide clear warranty terms for both workmanship and installed materials, along with documentation suitable for inspections, rebates, and future maintenance. Strong insurance and warranty coverage are indicators of professionalism and accountability.

Timelines and Communication Methods

The most reliable contractors provide detailed written proposals outlining scope, drawings, equipment lists, labor costs, and all expected materials—from trenching and conduit to panels and communication hardware. Transparent pricing prevents budget surprises, while well-defined timelines with milestone checkpoints help owners track progress. Effective communication—through scheduled updates, project management tools, and clear points of contact—keeps all parties aligned. Contractors who communicate well reduce confusion, support on-time delivery, and enable a smooth installation process.

Managing Permits & Inspections

Managing permits and inspections is essential to ensuring apartment EV charging projects are built safely, legally, and without costly delays. Successful installation depends on securing the correct permits, coordinating closely with local authorities and utilities, preparing detailed engineering documents, and meeting all code and inspection requirements. Proper planning not only reduces project risk but also keeps timelines on track, minimizes resident disruption, and ensures the system is fully approved for operation once construction is complete.

Permit Types and Coordination

EV charging installations typically require a range of permits—electrical, building, zoning, and in some cases fire safety approvals—depending on the property's location and project scope. These permits are overseen by different Authorities Having Jurisdiction (AHJs), such as electrical inspectors, planning departments, and fire marshals. Early coordination with these agencies helps apartment owners understand requirements, submission timelines, fees, and any site-specific rules. Proactive communication with permitting offices ensures the project moves efficiently through each approval stage, avoiding unnecessary delays.

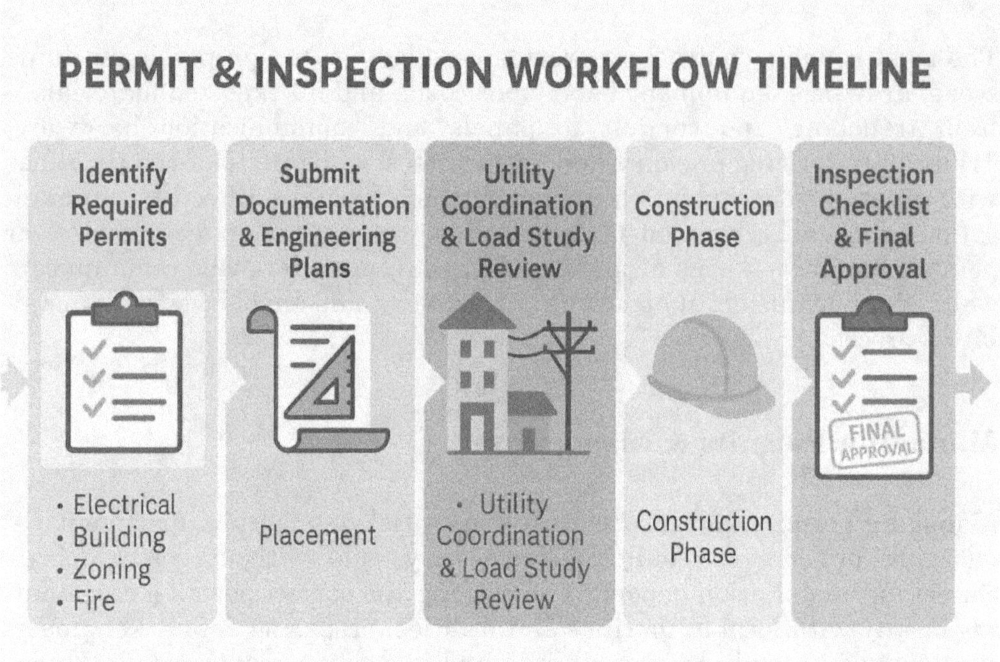

Managing Permits and Inspections for EV Charging Systems

Utility Coordination

Utility coordination is often one of the most time-sensitive components of the permitting and inspection process. Utilities may need to review load studies, approve service upgrades, or verify transformer capacity before construction can begin. Lead times for transformer replacements or new service drops can span weeks or months, making early submission critical to maintaining the project schedule. Apartment owners should work closely with the utility's engineering and metering departments to track approvals, understand any required infrastructure changes, and stay aligned with utility planning timelines.

Documentation, Drawings & Engineering Plans

Most permits require detailed, code-compliant documentation, including site plans, single-line electrical diagrams, conduit layouts, load calculations, ADA parking diagrams, and manufacturer specifications. Clear and accurate engineering drawings help reviewers quickly assess compliance with NEC Article 625, accessibility requirements, and safety standards. Apartment owners should ensure their contractors provide complete, well-organized documentation that matches field conditions to avoid resubmissions or correction notices that can slow down the approval process.

Inspection Readiness

Preparing thoroughly for inspections is essential to passing on the first attempt and avoiding costly rework. Inspectors commonly check for correct grounding and bonding, GFCI protection, proper conduit depth and support, accurate labeling, bollard placement, and ADA-compliant charging spaces. A walkthrough by the contractor prior to calling for inspection helps identify issues early. Passing inspections the first time protects the project timeline, reduces labor costs, and ensures the installation meets all safety and code requirements.

Inspection Schedule Impacts

Permits and inspections have a direct impact on construction sequencing, resident access, and overall project timing. Scheduling inspections too late can idle contractors, while scheduling too early risks incomplete work. Coordinating inspection times with trenching, concrete restoration, electrical tie-ins, and charger activation helps minimize disruption to residents and maintain predictable project flow. Clear communication with property management ensures parking areas, access routes, and common spaces remain safely managed during inspection activities.

Construction Planning (Trenching, Conduit, Mounting)

Effective construction planning is essential for deploying EV charging systems in apartment communities with minimal disruption, safe installation practices, and long-term scalability. Understanding the physical requirements—such as trenching paths, conduit selection, mounting methods, and electrical panel access—helps owners anticipate costs, coordinate work across multiple trades, and ensure compliance with NEC 625, ADA rules, and other local codes. Thoughtful construction planning creates a smoother installation process, reduces rework, and ensures the charging infrastructure meets both current needs and future expansion goals.

Trenching and Surface Restoration

Trenching is one of the biggest cost drivers in EV charging construction, especially when chargers are located far from electrical panels or utility service points. Planning the trenching route—including its distance, depth, and path across asphalt, concrete, landscaping, or curbs—directly affects labor, materials, and resident disruption. Surface restoration must also be considered, as parking lots, sidewalks, and landscaped areas will require patching, paving, or replanting after conduits are installed. Understanding these factors early helps owners make informed decisions about charger placement, routing efficiency, and construction timing.

Conduit Routing and Capacity Planning

Proper conduit selection and routing ensure a safe, durable, and scalable installation. Contractors typically choose from PVC, EMT, or rigid metal conduit depending on local code requirements, environmental exposure, and the depth of trenching. Conduit sizing must account not only for current charger needs but also future expansion, allowing additional circuits to be pulled later without reopening trenches. Good capacity planning includes clear routing diagrams, appropriate bends and junction points, and compliance with conduit-fill limits to ensure long-term usability and simplified maintenance.

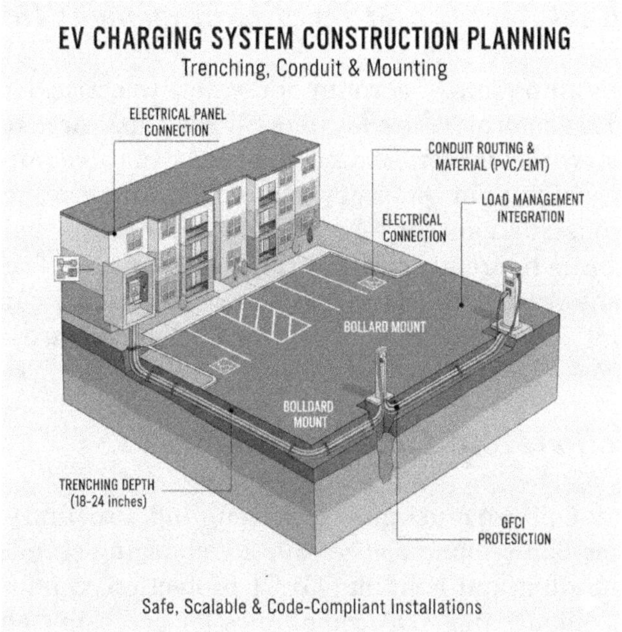

EV Charging System Construction Planning

Surprising Fact - By creating a predefined Backup Weather EV charger installation plans — with alternate task sequencing, indoor or covered work tasks, material staging, and weather-triggered rescheduling — installers can avoid many of the 45% of projects that get hit by weather, and avoid the 23–26% cost/time inflation that typically follows. The result: lower risk, fewer delays, and reduced labor and overhead cost.

Charger Mounting Options

Charge point mounting must align with parking layouts, property aesthetics, and structural requirements. Options include wall-mounted chargers for garages or building façades, pedestal-mounted units for open parking lots, and dual-port pedestals for maximizing charging density in limited spaces. Mounting methods must also consider bollard protection, cable management, and ADA accessibility requirements to create a safe and user-friendly charging experience. Selecting the right mounting method early in planning prevents costly redesigns and ensures consistent appearance across the property.

Electrical Panel Access and Load Management Integration

Construction planning must account for where electrical panels, service equipment, and transformers are located. Shorter distances to panels reduce trenching costs, while larger service upgrades may require coordination with the utility or installation of new subpanels. Integrating load management into the construction plan—such as dynamic power balancing, breaker sharing, or branch-circuit load control—can reduce infrastructure costs and avoid expensive service upgrades. Discussing panel capacity, breaker availability, and load-management options early ensures the electrical design is both cost-efficient and future-ready.

Safety Inspections and Code Compliance

Every construction phase must meet local building, fire, and electrical codes, with NEC Article 625 serving as the core EV charging standard. Inspectors will review grounding and bonding, GFCI protection, conduit depth, labeling, bollard placement, and ADA compliance for accessible charging spaces. Proper planning includes preparing inspection-ready documentation, coordinating with inspectors for timely site visits, and ensuring all work areas are safe for residents. Prioritizing code compliance early reduces rework, accelerates approvals, and ensures a safe and reliable installation.

Equipment Procurement and Delivery Coordination

Successful EV charging installation projects depend on securing the right equipment, verifying specifications, managing long lead times, and coordinating deliveries with construction phases. Apartment owners must ensure chargers, network components, switchgear, and mounting hardware are compatible with site conditions and electrical capacity while also mitigating supply chain risks. Proper equipment staging, pre-installation testing, and delivery scheduling help avoid downtime, prevent installation errors, and keep the project on track from procurement to commissioning.

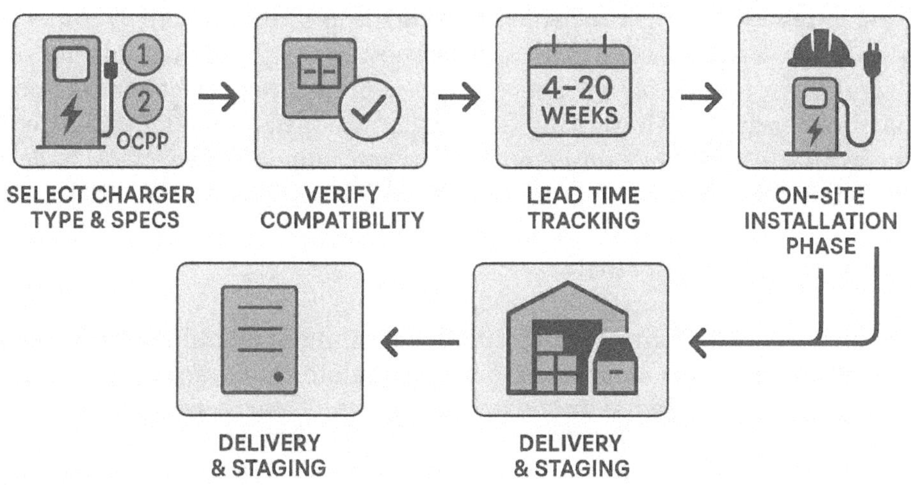

EV Charging Equipment Procurement and Delivery Coordination

Charger Types, Specifications & Compatibility

Selecting the right charger equipment begins with evaluating the property's electrical capacity, resident charging demand, and long-term operational goals. Apartment owners must choose between Level 1 and Level 2 chargers, balancing convenience, speed, and cost. Equipment specifications—including durability, weatherproofing ratings, cable length, connector type (such as J1772), and compatibility with network management systems—determine how well the chargers perform in daily use. OCPP compatibility is especially important for future flexibility, allowing properties to switch software providers without replacing hardware. Proper specification review ensures that equipment aligns with both current needs and future expansion plans.

Lead Times and Supply Chain Risks

Lead times for EV charging equipment vary widely and can impact the overall project schedule if not managed proactively. Chargers may take 4–20 weeks to arrive depending on the manufacturer and model. Network controllers, gateways, or SIM-based communication units typically require 2–8 weeks, while critical electrical infrastructure such as transformers or switchgear can take 8–52 weeks—often becoming the project's longest critical-path dependency. Monitoring supply chain status, placing orders early, and coordinating delivery dates with contractors help prevent costly delays and construction gaps.

Pre-Installation Testing

Before installation begins, all delivered equipment should be thoroughly inspected and tested to ensure that it is complete, undamaged, and matches the specifications listed in purchase orders. Contractors should verify that chargers have the correct power ratings, connector types, mounting hardware, and configuration options. Early identification of missing parts, shipping damage, or incorrect models prevents installation stalls and allows time for replacements to be ordered. Pre-installation testing ensures that installation teams have exactly what they need when construction begins.

Storage & Site Staging

Because equipment often arrives ahead of installation, proper storage and staging are essential to protecting the investment. Chargers, electrical components, pedestals, and network equipment should be stored in secure indoor areas or locked job-site containers protected from weather exposure, theft, and vandalism. Staging materials in an organized way near the installation area also helps contractors work efficiently and minimizes handling time. Good storage and staging practices ensure equipment remains in optimal condition and ready for deployment.

Construction Scheduling and Equipment Delivery

Coordinating equipment arrival with construction phases is critical to maintaining workflow efficiency and avoiding project delays. Key items—such as conduits, panels, chargers, and network hardware—must be on-site when contractors need them, but not so early that they require excessive storage. Aligning delivery with trenching, wiring, mounting, and commissioning phases ensures that each trade has the materials required for its scheduled work. Effective delivery planning keeps the installation on track, reduces idle time, and supports a smooth transition from construction to system activation.

Surprising Fact: *Pre-commissioning EV chargers can reduce final activation time by 30–50%. By completing software setup, network linking, user-access control, and diagnostics before the chargers are powered onsite, installers eliminate most of the configuration bottleneck. The result is a fast, near plug-and-play activation process that dramatically cuts labor time on installation day.*

Site Preparation

Site preparation is a critical phase of EV charging system installation, involving upgrades to electrical infrastructure, verification of utility-service capacity, conduit routing, trenching, protective measures, and charger foundation work. By planning these steps carefully, apartment owners can reduce disruption, minimize construction risk, and ensure the site is physically ready for safe, efficient, and code-compliant EV charger deployment. Thorough preparation sets the stage for smoother installation, better long-term performance, and scalable infrastructure that meets the evolving needs of residents.

Electrical Infrastructure Upgrades

Preparing the site begins with evaluating the existing electrical infrastructure to determine whether current panels, breakers, and service equipment can support additional EV charging load. Some installations may use spare

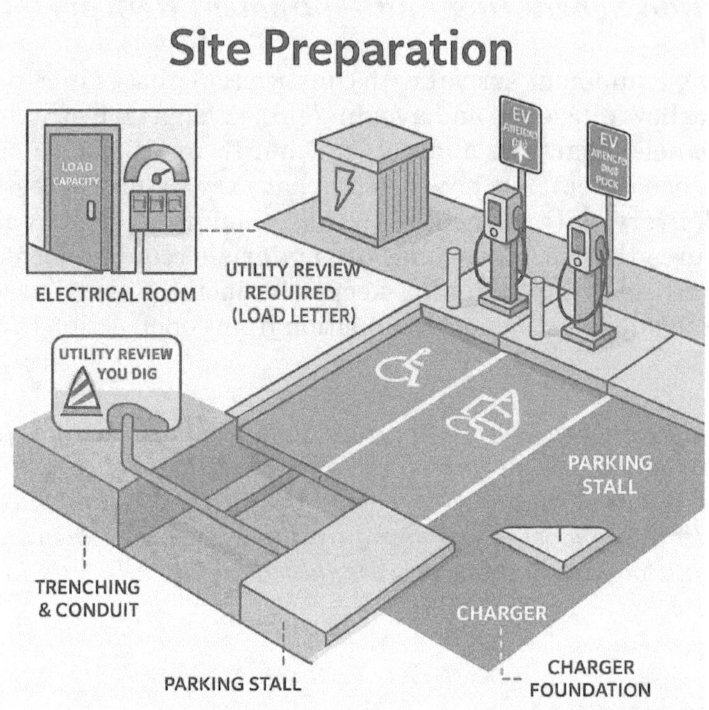

EV Charging System at Apartments Site Preparation

breaker capacity in an existing panel, while others require panel upgrades, new subpanels, or dedicated EV charging distribution sections to support future expansion. Load calculations help determine whether load management can be used to avoid costly upgrades. Ensuring the electrical system is properly sized and configured is essential for safe, reliable EV charging operations.

Utility-Service Readiness

Utility-service readiness focuses on assessing whether the property's existing transformer can safely handle the additional load introduced by EV chargers. Utilities often require a load letter or engineering documentation before approving service upgrades or energizing the chargers. If the transformer is undersized, the utility may need to replace it or install additional infrastructure, which can introduce long lead times. Early utility coordination ensures the project remains on schedule and that new chargers operate within safe electrical limits.

Trenching and Conduit Installation

Trenching and conduit installation establish the physical pathways required to deliver power to each charging location. Planning should prioritize the shortest, most cost-efficient routes while avoiding landscaped areas, pavement cuts, or disruptions to lighting, drainage, or existing utilities. Underground utility locating is essential to prevent safety hazards and ensure compliance with local clearance requirements. Properly sized and routed conduits also support future expansion and facilitate smoother installation when additional chargers are needed.

Surprising Factoid - *EV charging system installers that use ground-penetrating radar (GPR) before digging can identify underground utilities — water, gas, electrical, telecom lines — with extremely high accuracy, dramatically reducing the risk of utility line strikes. Using GPR can easily save tens of thousands of dollars per project — including avoided repair costs, downtime, rework, and legal or safety expenses.*

Parking Stall Protection and Signage

Preparing the site includes adding protective and user-access elements within each parking stall. Bollards, wheel stops, or curbing protect charging equipment from vehicle impact, while clearly marked signage ensures residents understand charging rules, time limits, and ADA-accessible stall locations. ADA pathways and required dimensions must be integrated into the site layout to support equitable access. These protective and informational elements enhance user safety, charger longevity, and operational clarity.

Charger Foundation Preparation

Foundation preparation ensures chargers are securely mounted and aligned with site specifications. For pedestal-mounted chargers, this typically includes pouring concrete pads or installing robust mounting bases designed to support the charger's weight and withstand outdoor conditions. Proper alignment with conduit stubs, spacing standards, and accessibility requirements prevents rework during installation. A well-prepared foundation ensures the chargers remain stable, safe, and visually consistent across the property.

Network and Management System

Network and communication setup is a core component of apartment EV charging installations, enabling remote monitoring, access control, billing, user authentication, and integration with property management systems. Whether using cellular, Wi-Fi, or wired Ethernet connections, proper configuration of the Charging Management System (CMS) ensures reliable operation, secure user access, and accurate revenue tracking. Clear access control methods, robust user account management, and seamless payment processing provide a smooth charging experience for residents while giving property owners the tools to manage utilization, recover costs, and support long-term system scalability.

Data Networks

Each EV charging system requires a stable communication connection, and selecting the right network type depends on site conditions and equipment capabilities. Cellular networks offer the highest reliability and simplest installation because they do not rely on the building's Wi-Fi; however, they may require subscription fees. Wi-Fi can be cost-effective but depends on signal strength, distance, and network security within the property. Wired Ethernet provides the most stable and secure connection but requires additional trenching or conduit for data cabling. Choosing the correct data network ensures chargers remain online, report accurate data, and support advanced features like load management and real-time monitoring.

Charging Management System (CMS)

The Charging Management System is the digital backbone of an EV charging installation, enabling property owners to control how chargers operate.

EV Charging at Apartment Network System

The CMS handles access permissions, monitors system health, allocates power to avoid overloading electrical panels, and generates usage reports for billing and operational planning. Proper setup involves connecting chargers to the CMS, configuring pricing models, defining load-balancing rules, enabling alerts, and validating communication between the chargers and the cloud platform. A well-configured CMS improves uptime, supports energy efficiency, and enhances the overall user experience.

Charger Access Control

Access control ensures that only authorized users can operate and pay for EV charging at the property. Apartment charging systems commonly support several methods: RFID cards or fobs for secure physical access; mobile apps for flexible digital access; QR codes for quick guest use; and credit card readers for direct payment. The chosen method should align with the property's management style—whether prioritizing resident-only access, guest charging, or public availability. Proper access control setup prevents misuse, ensures accurate billing, and simplifies account assignments for residents.

User Account Management

User account management defines how residents register, authenticate, and interact with the charging system. Through the CMS or mobile app, residents create accounts, add payment methods, reserve chargers (if supported), and view charging history. Clear onboarding instructions—often including QR codes, welcome emails, or property-issued RFID cards—help reduce support requests. User account management also enables property staff to assign accounts to units, deactivate access when residents move out, and set charging policies such as time limits or pricing tiers.

Billing and Payment Processing

Accurate billing and payment processing are essential for cost recovery and revenue generation. Smart EV charging systems integrate with payment processors such as Stripe, PayPal, or built-in vendor billing systems, enabling automated per-kWh, per-hour, or session-based charges. Advanced systems can also connect to property management platforms or tenant portals for consolidated billing. Revenue-sharing configurations allow property owners and operators to divide income, while utility incentive integration helps automatically track credits or rebates. A well-structured billing system ensures transparency, reduces administrative burden, and supports long-term financial sustainability.

Energy Management and Load Optimization

Effective energy management is essential for installing EV charging systems in apartment communities without overwhelming electrical infrastructure or increasing utility costs. By using dynamic load control, implementing peak-demand strategies, participating in utility demand-response

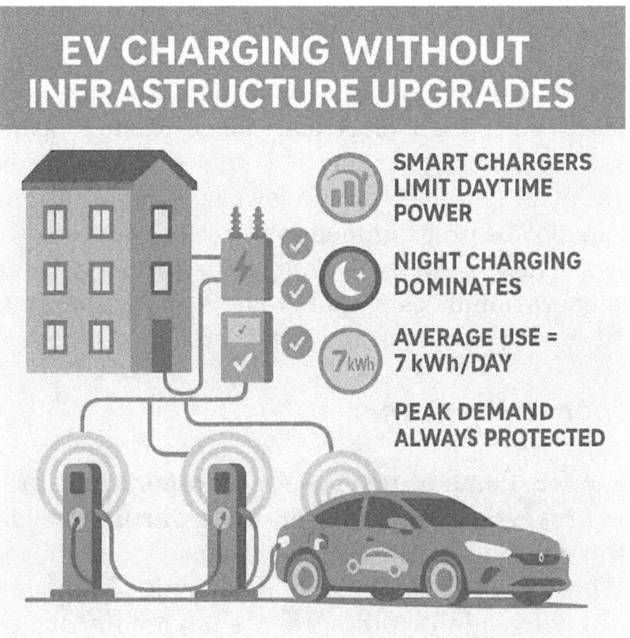

Energy Management and Load Optimization

programs, integrating with the building's management systems, and planning for scalable electrical capacity, apartment owners can maximize charging availability while minimizing upgrades and long-term energy expenses. These strategies ensure a cost-efficient, flexible, and reliable charging system that evolves with resident demand and future EV adoption.

Dynamic Load Management (DLM)

Dynamic Load Management allows multiple chargers to operate on limited electrical capacity by intelligently allocating power based on real-time demand. Instead of requiring expensive panel, feeder, or transformer upgrades, DLM systems automatically reduce charging speeds during periods of high usage, ensuring total demand stays within available limits. This approach enables properties to install more chargers with lower upfront costs while maintaining a consistent and reliable user experience. DLM is one of the most powerful tools for deploying EV charging at scale in apartment communities.

Peak-Demand Reduction Strategies

Peak-demand strategies help apartment owners manage and reduce utility charges associated with high electrical usage during peak hours. Using time-of-use (TOU) policies, charging systems can encourage residents to charge during off-peak periods through lower pricing or automated scheduling. Chargers can also be programmed to pause or reduce power during peak demand windows. These strategies protect the property from high demand charges, reduce operational costs, and create a more energy-efficient charging environment for both owners and residents.

Demand Response Programs

Many utilities offer demand-response programs that provide financial incentives when properties reduce power usage during periods of grid stress. EV chargers can automatically throttle, pause, or shift charging during these events through the property's Charging Management System. Participation can deliver bill credits, rebate payments, or annual incentive compensation, lowering the overall cost of owning and operating the charging infrastructure. Demand-response integration also supports grid stability, helping properties contribute to broader energy resilience efforts.

Building Management System Integration

Integrating EV charging systems with existing Building Management Systems (BMS) creates a unified view of the property's energy ecosystem. This integration allows building operators to see real-time electrical load, coordinate HVAC and lighting schedules with EV charging demand, and manage energy usage more efficiently across the property. A connected approach helps prevent overloads, improves energy forecasting, and ensures the charging system aligns with the property's overall electrical priorities.

Scalable Electrical Infrastructure

Planning for scalability ensures that the property's EV charging system can grow with resident adoption over time. Installing oversized conduit, adding junction points, and running additional wiring during initial construction significantly reduce future expansion costs. Electrical planning should also evaluate long-term load needs, utility upgrade timelines, and the potential use of battery storage or solar energy to support peak-load reduction. Preparing for expansion from the beginning ensures the charging system remains flexible and cost-effective as demand increases.

Safety, Compliance and Quality Assurance

Safety, compliance, and quality assurance are critical components of every apartment EV charging installation. Meeting electrical code requirements, ensuring proper grounding and protection, providing clear labeling and signage, and following structured inspection procedures all help prevent hazards, support reliable operation, and ensure regulatory approval. Thorough compliance documentation not only protects owners during inspections and audits but also simplifies future maintenance and system expansion. A strong focus on safety and quality ensures chargers operate efficiently, remain code-compliant, and provide long-term value to the property.

Electrical Code Compliance

EV charging installations must comply with national and local electrical codes, with NEC Article 625 serving as a primary standard for EV supply equipment. This includes requirements for properly sized branch circuits, correct conductor ratings, and appropriate overcurrent protection devices. Each charging port typically requires a dedicated circuit, and continuous load calculations must follow the 80% rule to prevent overheating or electrical stress. Ensuring compliance with these standards creates a safe and durable electrical foundation for the entire charging system.

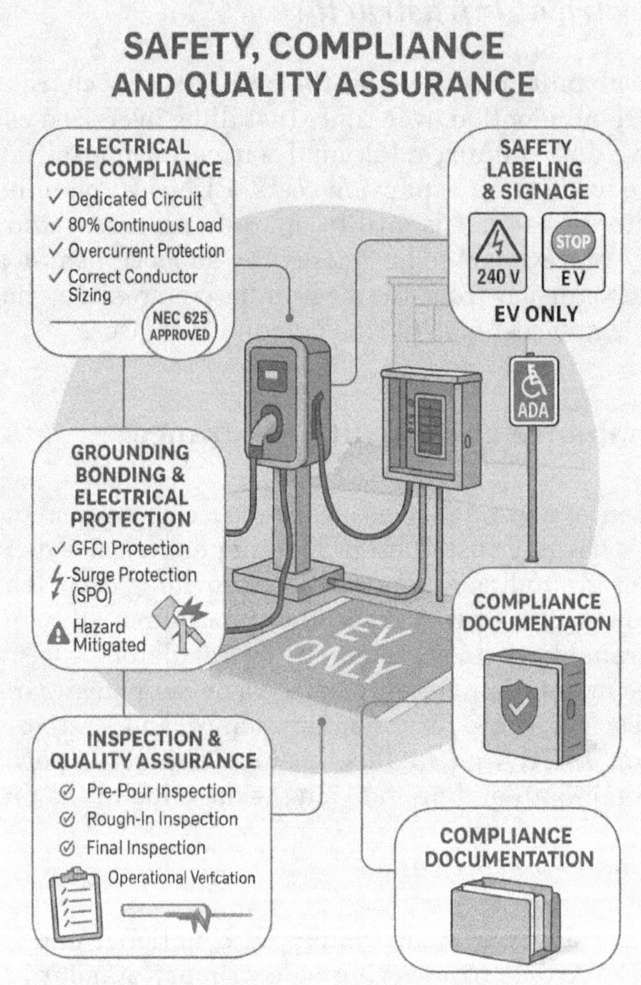

EV Charging System Code Compliance

Grounding, Bonding & Electrical Protection

Proper grounding and bonding are essential to preventing shock hazards, equipment damage, and fire risks. EV charging systems must include effective GFCI protection to shut off power in the event of ground faults and surge protection devices (SPDs) to protect sensitive electronics from voltage spikes. Correctly installed grounding systems also ensure that metal enclosures, conduits, and pedestals remain safe under fault conditions. Strong grounding and protection practices enhance both user safety and equipment longevity.

Labeling, Signage & Safety Markings

Clear labeling and signage support safe operations, smooth inspections, and simplified future maintenance. Installations should include warning labels identifying voltage ratings, disconnect locations, GFCI protection, and emergency shutoff points. ADA-compliant signage and EV-only parking markers help guide users and maintain accessibility standards. Proper markings also help technicians understand system layout during repairs or upgrades, reducing the risk of accidental damage or code violations.

Inspection Checklists & Quality Assurance Procedures

A structured quality assurance process ensures installations meet design specifications and pass inspections the first time. QA procedures should include pre-pour inspections for conduit depth and alignment, rough-in electrical inspections to verify wiring accuracy, and final inspections to confirm proper mounting, labeling, and safety compliance. Apartment owners should verify that contractors follow these steps consistently and maintain detailed checklists. Strong QA practices reduce rework, prevent delays, and improve the long-term reliability of the charging system.

Compliance Documentation

Maintaining thorough compliance documentation protects apartment owners during audits, warranty claims, and future expansion efforts. Documentation typically includes permits, inspection reports, as-built drawings, load calculations, equipment specifications, commissioning records, and manufacturer certifications. Organized records make it easier to troubleshoot issues, plan upgrades, and demonstrate compliance with electrical and safety standards. Proper documentation is an essential long-term asset that supports safe and scalable EV charging operations.

Minimizing Resident Disruption During Installation

Minimizing disruption to residents during EV charger installation requires thoughtful planning, proactive communication, and strong coordination between contractors and property management. By phasing construction activities, keeping tenants informed, planning for temporary parking adjustments, and maintaining clean and safe work areas, apartment owners can ensure a positive experience throughout the installation process. A structured coordination approach prevents confusion, maintains resident trust, and supports the successful rollout of EV charging infrastructure with minimal impact on daily life.

Installation Phasing and Scheduling

Strategic phasing and scheduling of construction activities helps keep most parking and access areas open throughout the installation process. Work can be planned in stages so residents are only affected for short periods, and scheduling during low-traffic times—such as mid-morning on weekdays—reduces interference with departures, arrivals, or peak usage hours. A clear schedule, published in advance, helps residents understand when specific areas will be temporarily closed and when they will reopen. Providing a visual timeline or map further enhances transparency and helps residents prepare accordingly.

Resident Communication and Notifications

Consistent communication is essential to reducing frustration and maintaining tenant satisfaction during installation. Property managers should notify residents well in advance of any planned work, expected noise, or temporary disruptions to parking or access. Effective communication uses multiple channels—emails, text alerts, lobby or garage notices, flyers on affected parking spaces, and temporary signage in work zones. Regular updates on progress, delays, and completion timelines demonstrate professionalism and reassure residents that the project is being carefully managed.

Temporary Parking and Access Planning

During trenching, conduit installation, or charger mounting, some parking stalls may need to be blocked off, requiring temporary relocation plans. Properties should identify alternative parking options ahead of time, such as designated overflow areas, unused guest parking, or short-term arrangements with nearby properties. Clear signage and well-marked temporary spaces help residents easily navigate the changes. Coordinating access routes for pedestrians and vehicles during construction ensures safety and reduces daily inconveniences.

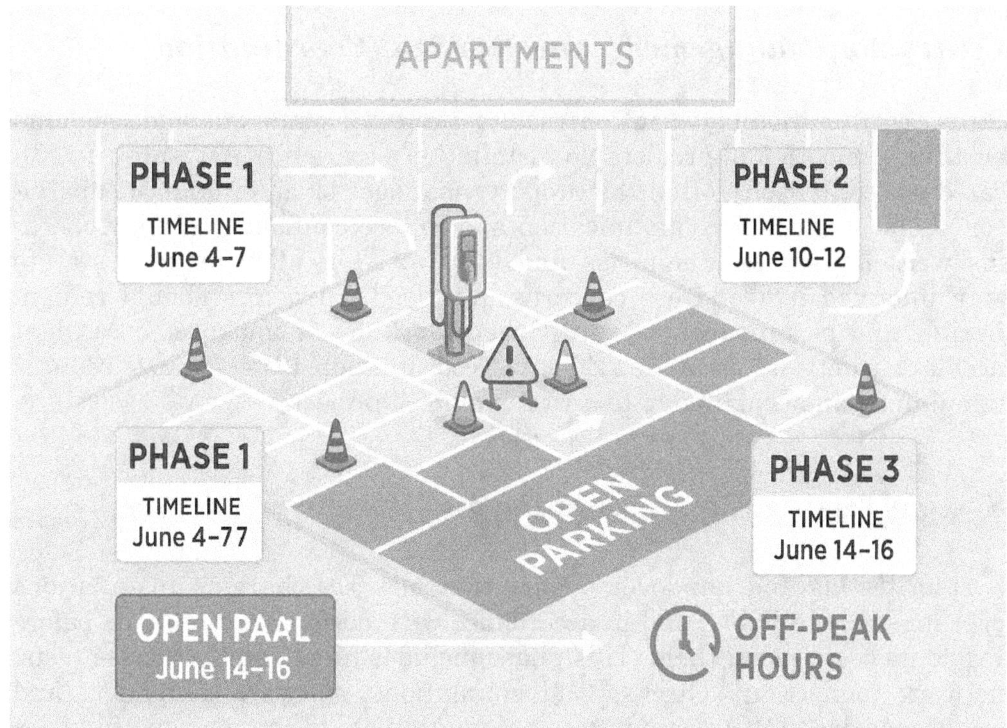

Minimizing Apartment Tenant Resident Disruption During EV Charging System Installation

Safety, Noise, and Dust Management

Maintaining high safety and cleanliness standards is an important element of minimizing disruption. Contractors should use cones, barricades, and clear signage to mark active work zones and protect residents and vehicles. Noise should be managed by limiting work to appropriate hours, maintaining equipment properly, and avoiding unnecessary idle time. Dust and debris should be controlled through barriers, protective coverings, and daily clean-up routines. Keeping work areas clean and secure not only minimizes inconvenience but also enhances resident confidence in the installation process.

Contractor, Management, and Resident Coordination

Strong coordination between contractors, property managers, and residents ensures a smooth and predictable installation experience. Assigning a dedicated project liaison—often the property manager or maintenance supervisor—helps centralize communication and reduce confusion. Weekly check-ins, written progress summaries, and daily work logs allow property staff to stay informed and address concerns quickly. Contractors should remain flexible and be prepared to adjust their workflow if unexpected resident needs or safety issues arise. Effective coordination fosters trust, reduces complaints, and contributes to a well-managed project.

System Testing, Commissioning and Handover

System testing and handover ensure that new EV charging installations operate safely, reliably, and in accordance with design requirements before residents begin using them. This phase includes functional hardware tests, network connectivity checks, load simulations, software activation, and comprehensive staff training. A complete documentation package finalizes the project by providing property owners with all required permits, commissioning records, warranties, and configuration details needed for ongoing management. Thorough testing and a structured handover process ensure a smooth transition from installation to long-term property operations.

Functional Testing

Before going live, every charger and electrical component must undergo detailed functional testing to confirm proper installation and safe operation. Contractors test breakers, wiring connections, conduit terminations, voltage output, and safety devices such as GFCI protection. Chargers are powered on individually to verify that displays, connectors, indicator lights, and internal components operate correctly. This step identifies any installation errors, defective hardware, or wiring issues before the system is put into service, ensuring reliability from day one.

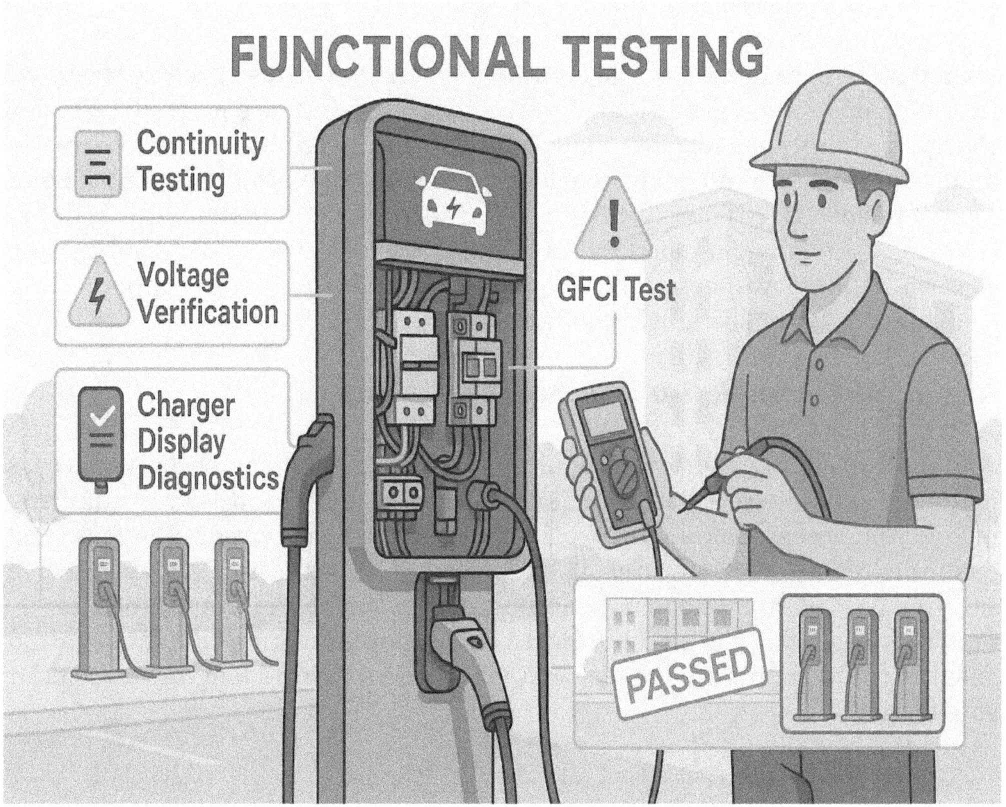

EV Charging System Testing, Commissioning and Handover

Network Connectivity and Software Validation

For networked charging systems, communication with the Charging Management System (CMS) is essential. Installers must verify that each charger successfully transmits session start and stop data, processes remote commands, and reports faults in real time. Firmware updates should be installed to ensure full compatibility with the CMS and to address any manufacturer-issued improvements or security patches. Testing remote monitoring and system alerts helps confirm that property staff can track charger status and manage the system effectively.

Power Management Load Testing

Load testing evaluates how the charging system performs under real or simulated peak demand conditions. Contractors may simulate multiple vehicles charging simultaneously to ensure the system distributes power correctly and that circuits do not overload. Properties using Dynamic Load Management (DLM) must verify that the system automatically reduces charging speeds when electrical demand increases. Successful load testing confirms that the electrical infrastructure and CMS can support daily charging operations safely and efficiently.

Resident Access Setup and Staff Training

A smooth resident experience requires proper setup of user accounts, access methods, and system rules. This includes issuing RFID cards or configuring mobile app access, establishing pricing structures, activating idle fees, and enabling reservation features if supported. Property staff should receive training on how to manage user accounts, respond to charging issues, interpret CMS dashboards, and perform basic troubleshooting. Staff education ensures the system remains well-managed and supports long-term resident satisfaction.

Final Documentation and Handover

A complete handover package ensures that property owners have all the information needed for ongoing operations, maintenance, and future inspections. This documentation typically includes as-built drawings, electrical one-line diagrams, permits, inspection reports, and full commissioning records. Warranty information for equipment and workmanship, CMS configuration details, administrator login credentials, maintenance schedules, and emergency procedures must also be provided. Any utility paperwork related to incentives or interconnection should be included. This final package formalizes project completion and supports long-term operational success.

Post-Installation Operations and Maintenance

Post-installation operations and maintenance (O&M) are essential for keeping apartment EV charging systems reliable, safe, and cost-effective over the long term. Effective O&M programs include routine inspections, preventive maintenance, remote monitoring, troubleshooting processes, and clearly defined service-level agreements. Managing warranties, tracking system uptime, and documenting proof-of-operation also help property owners reduce long-term costs and qualify for utility or government incentives. A proactive approach ensures chargers remain functional, residents receive dependable service, and the property maximizes the return on its EV charging investment.

Operations and Maintenance Procedures

Successful long-term operation of an EV charging system requires structured O&M procedures that include routine inspections, cleaning, and equipment checks. Preventive maintenance tasks—such as verifying connector integrity, inspecting cables for wear, checking for water intrusion, and confirming proper operation of safety features—help prevent unexpected failures. Regular operational reviews ensure chargers are performing within expected parameters and that the Charging Management System

EV Charging System Post-Installation Operations and Maintenance

(CMS) reflects accurate usage data. Establishing a predictable maintenance schedule reduces downtime and keeps the system running safely and efficiently.

Service Support

Service-level agreements define the expectations for support, repair timelines, and system uptime. SLAs often specify remote diagnostics response times, onsite repair requirements, and escalation procedures for critical issues. Many EV charging systems include remote monitoring tools that allow integrators or operators to identify faults, reboot chargers, or apply software updates without needing to visit the property. Clear SLAs and strong remote support capabilities reduce operational disruptions and help apartment owners maintain resident satisfaction.

Troubleshooting Protocols

When issues arise, structured troubleshooting protocols help property staff or service partners quickly identify and resolve problems. Common troubleshooting steps may include verifying network connectivity, checking CMS status notifications, reviewing power delivery, or performing a soft reboot. More advanced issues—such as internal hardware faults, communication failures, or electrical irregularities—may require professional diagnostics. Documented troubleshooting procedures ensure consistent response, minimize downtime, and improve coordination between property staff and service vendors.

Warranty Management

Warranty management plays a key role in reducing repair costs and ensuring long-term system reliability. Property owners should track warranty periods for chargers, mounting hardware, network components, and software services, as well as ensure proper documentation is maintained for claims. In addition, many incentive programs—such as utility rebates or demand-response compensation—require proof-of-operation and uptime reporting. Keeping accurate records helps owners maximize available incentives and optimize long-term operational expenses. Effective warranty and incentive management contributes significantly to overall lifecycle cost savings.

Chapter 6

EV Charging System Operation

EV charging system operations define how apartment owners and property managers manage the daily use, performance, and reliability of their EV charging infrastructure. Effective operations ensure that residents, guests, and staff can easily access chargers, payments are handled fairly, and the system remains dependable through consistent monitoring and maintenance. By establishing clear policies, automated processes, and support systems, properties can ensure reliable service, optimize energy use, and maintain tenant satisfaction while minimizing administrative effort.

User Account Management

User account management defines how residents, guests, and staff access the charging system—whether through RFID cards, mobile apps, keypads, or open-access configurations. Establishing a clear access structure prevents unauthorized use and ensures fair access to shared chargers. Features like user scheduling, time limits, and reservation systems can help reduce congestion and conflicts. Apartment owners should implement transparent access policies and maintain updated user lists to keep the system secure, efficient, and easy to manage.

Billing and Payment Processing

Billing and payment systems automate how charging sessions are measured, billed, and collected. Common billing models include per kilowatt-hour (kWh), per session, or time-based pricing, depending on utility and net-

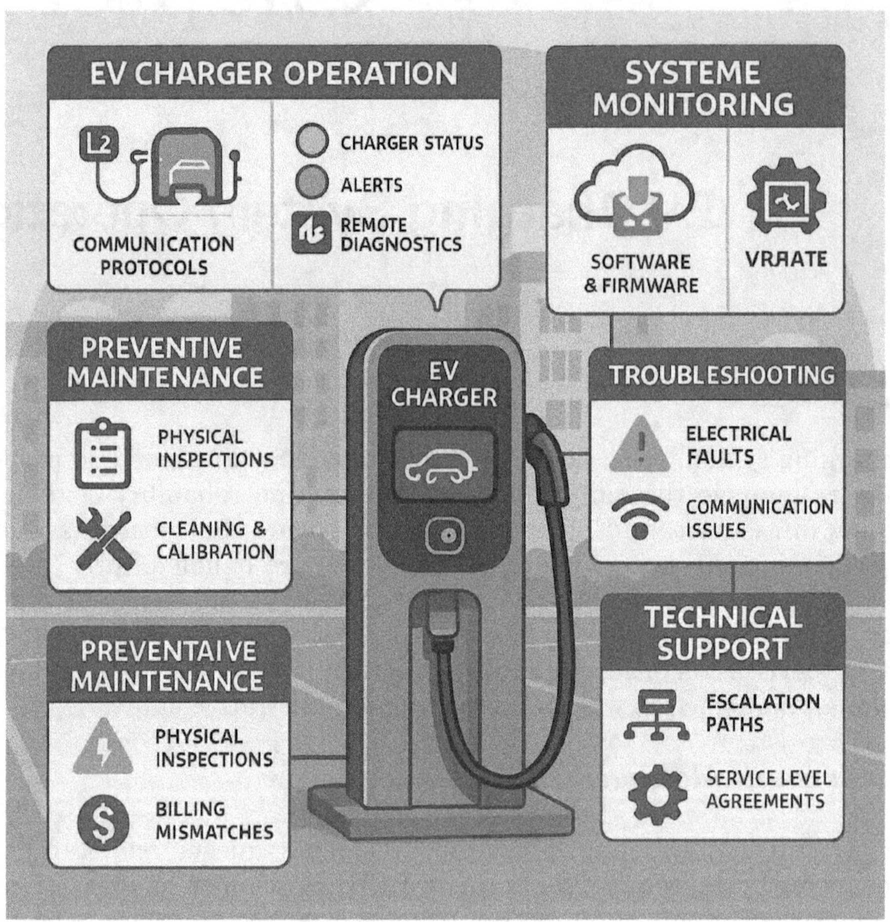

EV Charger Operations

work settings. Apartment owners can use integrated payment platforms that handle electronic transactions, distribute revenue automatically, and generate financial reports. Proper billing setup ensures transparency, fair pricing, and accountability while providing property owners with a predictable income stream and simplified bookkeeping.

Monitoring and Management

Monitoring tools allow property managers and system operators to track charger status, uptime, and energy consumption in real time. Cloud-based dashboards display which chargers are in use, identify faults, and record performance trends that support preventive maintenance planning. Monitoring also helps optimize energy loads across multiple chargers, reducing peak demand and improving efficiency. Reliable system management tools enable quick problem resolution and ensure the charging network operates smoothly for residents and guests.

Maintenance and Servicing

Regular maintenance and servicing are critical to ensuring EV chargers operate safely and efficiently. This includes routine inspections, cleaning connectors, verifying software updates, and responding promptly to repair requests. Apartment owners should establish service level agreements (SLAs) with providers to guarantee response times and uptime targets. Preventive maintenance—performed quarterly or semi-annually—reduces unplanned outages, extends equipment lifespan, and protects the property's investment in EV infrastructure.

Resident Communication and Support

Clear communication and responsive support are essential to maintaining resident satisfaction and operational efficiency. Property owners should provide residents with easy access to help—through signage with QR codes, mobile app support links, or a dedicated helpdesk contact. When issues arise, staff should follow defined escalation procedures for technical and billing problems to ensure quick resolution. Proactive communication about system updates, pricing changes, and maintenance schedules builds trust and helps residents feel confident using the EV charging system as part of their community experience.

System Monitoring, Alerts & Remote Diagnostics

Monitoring, alerts, and remote diagnostics are essential tools for maintaining the reliability, efficiency, and profitability of EV charging systems at apartment complexes. These technologies give property owners and managers real-time insight into how their chargers are performing, help detect and resolve issues before they escalate, and minimize costly downtime or resident complaints. By using these systems effectively, apartment operators can ensure chargers remain available, tenants stay satisfied, and long-term maintenance costs stay under control.

System Monitoring Dashboards

Smart EV charging networks include cloud-based monitoring dashboards that give property owners and operators instant visibility into every charger's status, performance, and energy usage. These dashboards display key metrics such as charger availability, session duration, and total power consumption, allowing managers to quickly identify underperforming or inactive units. Monitoring tools also help detect usage trends—such as peak charging times or resident demand patterns—which can guide decisions on system expansion, pricing, or energy management strategies.
Surprising Fact: EV charging system data at apartment complexes can increase property value by as much as 15%. Usage analytics, uptime logs, and billing history transform charging stations from an amenity into a measurable revenue-producing asset.
Alerts and Notifications

Automatic alerts and notifications are critical for fast issue detection and response. When a charger disconnects from the network, experiences a power fault, or encounters software errors, the system can immediately send notifications via email, text message, or mobile app to designated maintenance staff or vendors. Configuring alerts for key fault categories—like overcurrent, overheating, or network loss—ensures problems are addressed before tenants experience service interruptions. Proactive alert systems shorten downtime and reduce the need for manual system checks.

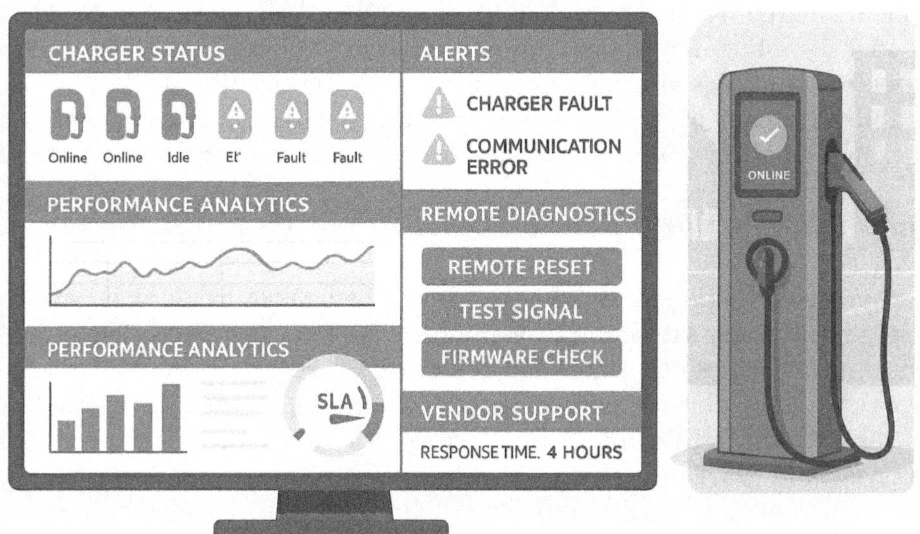

EV Charging System Monitoring, Alerts & Remote Diagnostics

Diagnostics and Reset Capabilities

Remote diagnostic tools allow property managers or service providers to troubleshoot and fix common charger issues without sending a technician on-site. Many networked chargers support remote rebooting, firmware resets, or command-line diagnostics that can restore functionality in minutes. Access to charger logs and error codes through the management platform helps identify root causes—such as communication failures or power interruptions—so that only necessary site visits occur. This capability lowers maintenance costs, minimizes disruptions, and keeps chargers available to residents.

Performance Analytics

Beyond real-time monitoring, performance analytics provide valuable historical insights that support data-driven decision-making. By tracking trends in energy usage, charger uptime, and user behavior, property owners can identify efficiency gaps, plan future expansions, and refine pricing strategies. Analytics also help quantify return on investment (ROI) and sustainability impact by measuring how much electricity is delivered, when peak demand occurs, and how load balancing affects overall energy costs.

Vendor Support and Service-Level Agreements (SLAs)

Effective monitoring and diagnostics should be backed by clear service-level agreements (SLAs) with charger vendors or network providers. These agreements outline response times for resolving alerts, procedures for remote support, and escalation paths for critical faults. A well-structured SLA ensures accountability and defines expectations for uptime, maintenance response, and warranty coverage. Aligning system alerts and diagnostic tools with vendor support workflows helps maintain consistent reliability and simplifies coordination between property staff and external service teams.

Software and Firmware Updates

EV charging system software and firmware updates play a critical role in ensuring that apartment charging infrastructure remains secure, reliable, and compliant with industry standards. Regular updates improve charger performance, enhance security, introduce new capabilities, and keep systems aligned with rapidly advancing technologies and utility programs. A well-defined update strategy—covering scheduling, cybersecurity protections, vendor responsibilities, and documentation—helps property owners maintain consistent charger uptime, reduce risk, and support long-term operational stability.

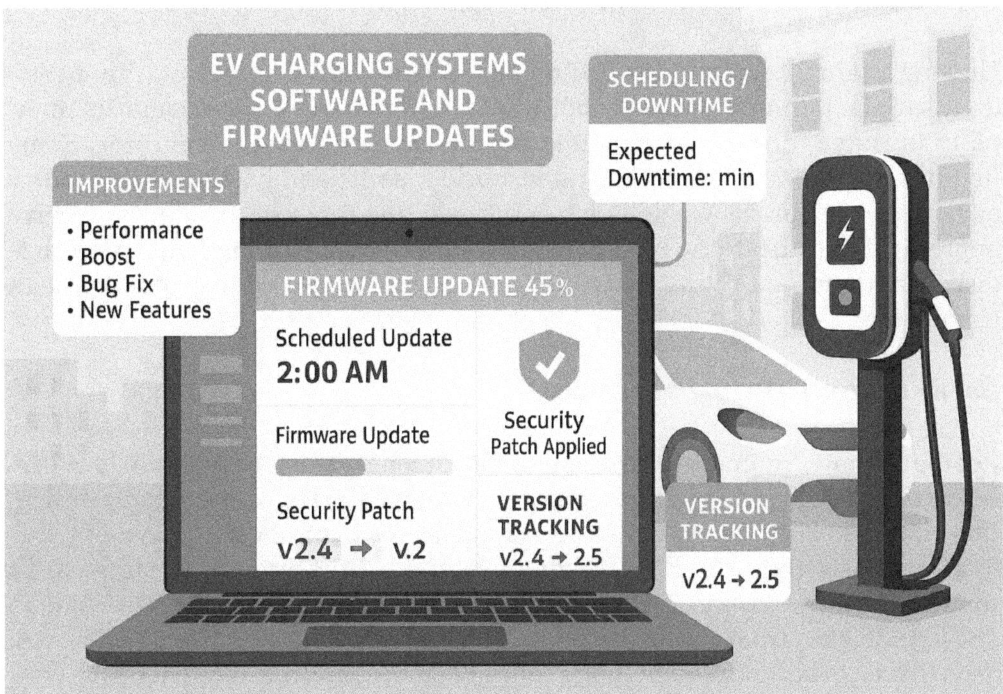

EV Charging Systems Software and Firmware Updates

Importance of Software Updates

Software and firmware updates significantly influence the performance and reliability of EV charging systems. These updates often fix existing bugs, improve charging efficiency, and introduce new features such as dynamic load management or expanded billing options. Updates also ensure ongoing compatibility with evolving standards like OCPP, OCPI, or utility demand response programs. By keeping chargers up to date, property owners ensure that residents experience consistent, safe, and fully supported charging sessions.

Scheduling and Downtime Management

Understanding how updates are deployed is essential to maintaining resident satisfaction and reliable operations. Updates may be automatic, manually initiated, or pushed remotely by the charger network operator. Some updates require a brief service interruption, so it is important for property owners to review downtime expectations and ensure residents receive appropriate notifications in advance. Thoughtful scheduling helps minimize disruption and maintain the availability of charging resources during peak use times.

Security and Data Protection

Regular firmware updates are one of the strongest defenses against cybersecurity threats. These updates patch vulnerabilities, secure communication channels between chargers and cloud servers, and protect payment systems and user data. As EV charging systems increasingly rely on network connectivity, maintaining a rigorous update cadence becomes essential to mitigate risks from malware, unauthorized access, or data breaches. Security-focused updates help preserve both operational integrity and resident trust.

Who Performs the Updates

EV charging updates may be handled by the charger manufacturer, the network operator, or property management—depending on the system architecture and service agreements. Property owners should clarify who is responsible for pushing updates, how frequently updates occur, and what verification processes are used to confirm installation success. These responsibilities should be clearly documented within service-level agreements or maintenance contracts to ensure accountability and avoid operational gaps.

Version Tracking and Documentation

Maintaining detailed records of all software and firmware versions is vital for compliance, warranty protection, and future troubleshooting. Organized logs help track update history, validate installation timelines, and demonstrate compliance during audits or inspections. When issues arise, accurate documentation enables faster diagnosis and resolution, ensuring minimal downtime. Version tracking also supports long-term asset management and helps property owners maintain a predictable update strategy.

Preventive Maintenance

Preventive maintenance is a critical part of ensuring EV charging systems at apartment complexes remain reliable, efficient, and aligned with warranty and performance expectations. Many property owners underestimate the importance of routine inspections and proactive care until unexpected issues begin affecting charger availability and tenant satisfaction. A well-structured preventive maintenance program minimizes downtime, identifies hidden problems, extends equipment life, and protects long-term ROI. By consistently monitoring hardware, electrical systems, software, and operational records, apartment owners can maintain a seamless charging experience while preventing costly emergency repairs.

Routine Inspection and Cleaning

Regular visual inspections and basic cleaning form the foundation of preventive maintenance. These checks ensure that charging connectors, cables, screens, housings, and mounting hardware remain safe, undamaged, and free from debris. Dirt, moisture, vandalism, or environmental exposure can gradually impair charger performance or create safety hazards. By performing scheduled walk-through inspections, property teams can quickly identify early signs of wear, corrosion, cracking, or loose components—preventing small issues from escalating into outages.

Electrical and Network Health Checks

Behind-the-scenes monitoring of electrical systems and network connectivity helps detect hidden problems before they disrupt service. Maintenance teams or integrators evaluate breaker panels, conduit connections, grounding systems, and voltage stability, as well as network signals, cellular strength, and Wi-Fi reliability. These checks ensure chargers maintain consistent communication with the billing platform, cloud management system, and property dashboards. Spotting fluctuations early prevents outages, failed sessions, and billing inaccuracies that could lead to resident complaints.

Firmware Updates

Ensuring that chargers operate on the latest firmware is a critical part of preventive maintenance. Firmware updates optimize performance, fix bugs, patch security vulnerabilities, and improve compatibility with OCPP standards, load management systems, and utility programs. Scheduled update checks verify that each charger is running the correct version and that all newly added features—such as improved diagnostics or upgraded safety protocols—are functioning properly. Staying current with firmware helps maintain uptime and long-term system stability.

Component Replacement and Calibration

Preventive maintenance includes proactive replacement of wear-prone components such as connectors, cable holsters, seals, or cooling elements before they fail. Periodic calibration ensures accurate energy measurement, billing precision, and correct reporting to management platforms. Chargers that are not properly calibrated may underbill, overbill, or misidentify faults, creating both financial and operational risks. Replacing and calibrating components on a planned schedule ensures chargers remain safe, accurate, and compliant with standards.

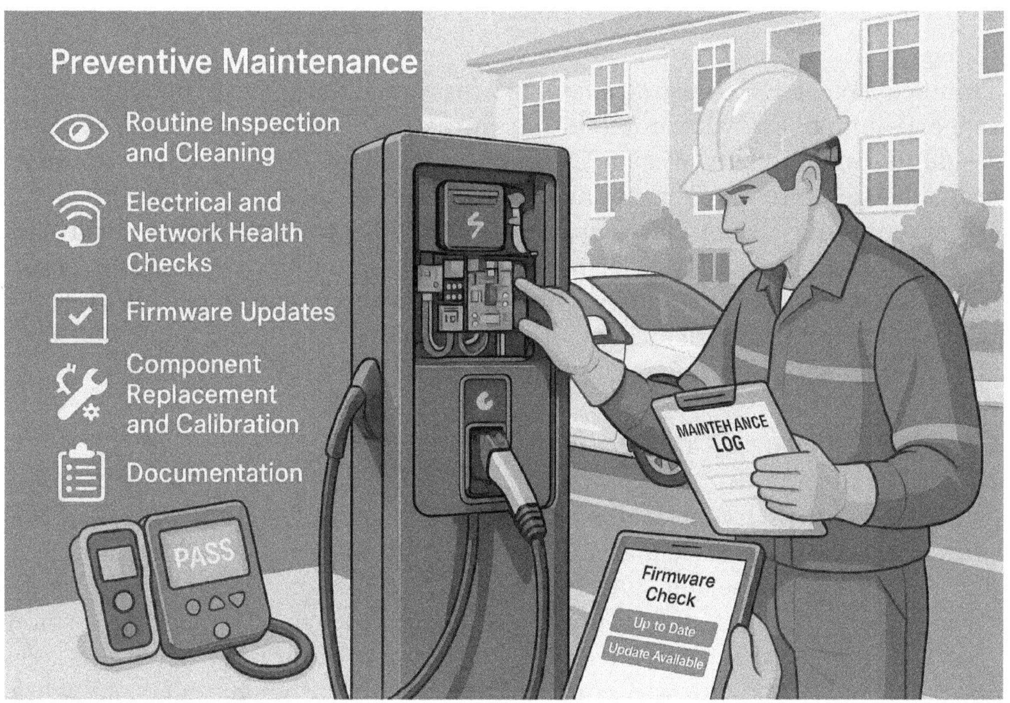

EV Charging System Preventative Maintenance

Maintenance Scheduling and Documentation

A structured preventive maintenance schedule is essential for accountability, warranty protection, and consistent charger uptime. Property owners should maintain written maintenance calendars, assign responsibilities between staff and service providers, and document all inspections, updates, repairs, and part replacements. Organized records help diagnose recurring problems, support warranty claims, simplify audits, and demonstrate adherence to manufacturer or network operator maintenance requirements. Effective documentation strengthens both operational reliability and long-term asset performance.

Troubleshooting Common Issues

Troubleshooting EV charging systems is essential for apartment owners and property managers who must maintain reliable charger uptime, support residents, and quickly resolve issues that disrupt service. Most common problems fall into categories such as network connectivity, access control errors, charging session interruptions, billing mismatches, and hardware or safety faults. By understanding how to systematically diagnose these issues—and knowing when to escalate to network operators or service technicians—owners can ensure smooth operation, reduce downtime, and provide residents with a consistent and dependable charging experience.

Charger Network Connectivity

Network connectivity problems are one of the most frequent causes of EV charger downtime. Issues may involve Wi-Fi interference, weak cellular signal strength, or Ethernet disconnections that prevent chargers from communicating with the network platform. These failures often lead to session errors, offline status, or inaccurate reporting. Troubleshooting includes checking router and gateway connections, rebooting the charger or network hardware, verifying cable integrity, and confirming that service plans or SIM cards are active. If the problem persists, property owners should escalate the issue to the charger manufacturer or network operator for platform-level diagnostics and resolution.

User Access and Authentication Errors

Access problems can prevent residents or guests from initiating a charging session. Common issues include RFID cards not reading, mobile apps failing to authenticate, or user account permissions not syncing correctly across the system. Owners should know how to verify a user's access level, reset or reassign user credentials, confirm that the charger software is current, and check whether communication between the charger and cloud platform is functioning properly. Understanding these troubleshooting steps helps restore access quickly and reduces resident frustration.

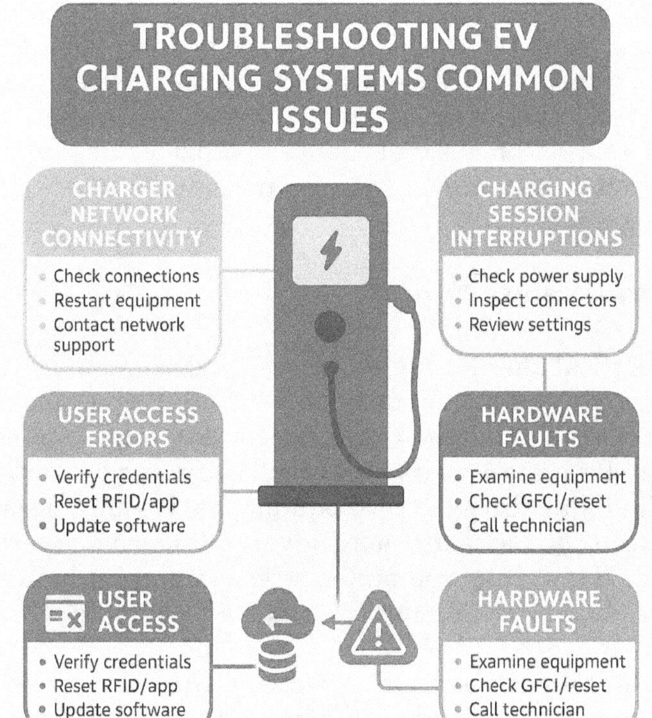

Troubleshooting ev charging systems common issues

Charging Session Interruptions

Unexpected interruptions—such as sessions stopping early, slow charging speeds, or chargers displaying "unavailable" status—may indicate electrical, configuration, or equipment issues. Troubleshooting involves inspecting connectors for wear or contamination, checking circuit breakers for trips, reviewing load management settings for power throttling, and examining session logs to identify error codes. These diagnostics help determine whether the disruption is caused by user error, building electrical limitations, or a charger malfunction requiring professional service.

Billing and Payment Problems

Billing discrepancies can undermine resident trust and complicate cost recovery for the property. Common issues include missing charging sessions, duplicate charges, incorrect energy readings, or delayed payment processing. Effective troubleshooting requires comparing charger logs against cloud platform reports, verifying synchronization between the charger and billing system, and reviewing software versions for compatibility. Owners should be prepared to contact their network provider's billing support team for reconciliation assistance or deeper investigation when system-level adjustments are needed.

Hardware and Safety Faults

Physical or electrical charger faults must be addressed quickly to maintain safety and prevent equipment damage. Warning signs include damaged cables, broken connector heads, overheating alerts, water ingress, or tripped GFCI breakers. Property owners should follow proper lockout/tagout procedures before handling any electrical equipment, visually inspect hardware for obvious defects, and escalate more advanced issues to a certified EV service technician. Rapid response protects residents from hazards and helps return chargers to service promptly.

Surprising Factoid: *Apartment complexes that use EV chargers with remote monitoring and predictive maintenance can reduce operating costs by 18–25% and cut downtime by nearly 50%. These systems detect performance issues early, allowing operators to fix problems before they escalate — meaning fewer service calls, lower repair costs, and better uptime for residents.*

Emergency Response Protocols

Emergency response protocols are essential for ensuring the safety of apartment residents, staff, and property when an EV charging system experiences electrical faults, overheating, fires, or other hazardous conditions. A clear, well-defined plan allows staff to act quickly and confidently, shutting down equipment, isolating danger zones, documenting incidents, and coordinating with service providers and first responders. Proper preparation minimizes risk, protects lives, prevents property damage, and supports efficient recovery after an incident.

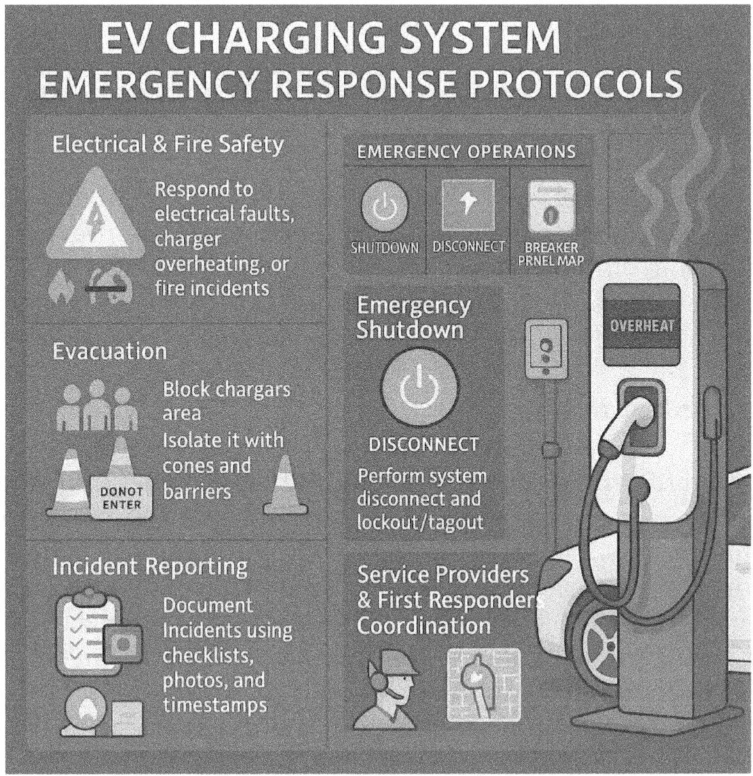

EV Charging System Emergency Response Protocols

Electrical and Fire Safety

Responding to electrical or fire-related incidents requires staff to understand the unique risks associated with high-voltage EV charging equipment. Emergency protocols should specify how to recognize overheating components, smoke, arcing, or unusual odors, and identify when it is necessary to immediately shut off power. Staff must know the exact location of charger disconnect switches, panel breakers, and emergency shutoff hardware. Coordination with local fire departments is critical—responders should be familiar with the property's EV charging layout, electrical shut off points, and any manufacturer-specific safety considerations. Proper training ensures that fires or electrical hazards are managed safely and efficiently.

Evacuation and Isolation Areas

When an EV charging emergency occurs, swift action is needed to isolate the affected area and protect residents and vehicles. Evacuation protocols should define who is responsible for blocking access to the charging zone, placing warning signage, and directing occupants away from danger. Staff should be trained to establish isolation perimeters that prevent residents from approaching malfunctioning chargers or damaged vehicles. Clear communication pathways—such as PA systems, text alerts, or posted instructions—help ensure safe and orderly evacuation when necessary.

Emergency Shutdown

Emergency shutdown procedures provide staff with structured steps to safely disable one charger or the entire charging system during hazardous events. This includes identifying and labeling disconnect points, training staff on how to operate emergency shutoff switches, and following lockout/tagout procedures to prevent accidental re-energization. Regular testing of emergency shutdown systems ensures they function correctly when needed. Understanding these procedures helps staff quickly mitigate risks during electrical failures, equipment malfunctions, or fire incidents.

Incident Reporting

Thorough incident reporting enables property owners to document emergencies accurately and support insurance, service, and regulatory requirements. Reports should include the event timeline, photos or videos of the damage, system logs, witness statements, and any taken actions such as shutdown steps or evacuation orders. Using standardized checklists ensures consistency and helps identify recurring issues or equipment vulnerabilities. Proper documentation also supports future safety improvements and facilitates effective communication with service providers and insurers.

Service Providers and First Responders Coordination

Effective emergency management relies on seamless coordination with charger manufacturers, service contractors, utility companies, and local emergency responders. Property owners should maintain up-to-date contact lists and procedures for escalating urgent technical issues to vendors or integrators. First responders should be provided with system diagrams, electrical shutoff maps, and site layout plans to enable rapid, safe intervention. Establishing these relationships before an emergency occurs improves response times, enhances safety, and minimizes property damage.

EV Charging System Technical Support

EV charging system technical support provides apartment owners and property staff with structured assistance to maintain charger performance, resolve issues quickly, and ensure long-term reliability. Effective support includes multiple communication channels, remote diagnostics, warranty protections, service-level agreements (SLAs), transparent ticket tracking, and access to training resources. Together, these elements help property teams respond efficiently to both everyday issues and urgent problems while preserving uptime, tenant satisfaction, and equipment health.

Support Channel Types

Technical support can typically be reached through multiple channels, including phone hotlines, mobile apps, customer portals, and email-based service desks. Each channel often offers different response times depending on the severity of the issue—for example, safety-related outages may receive immediate escalation, while routine inquiries follow standard business-hour response windows. Understanding which channels to use and how escalation procedures work helps property staff communicate effectively, minimize downtime, and get timely assistance for both residents and building operators.

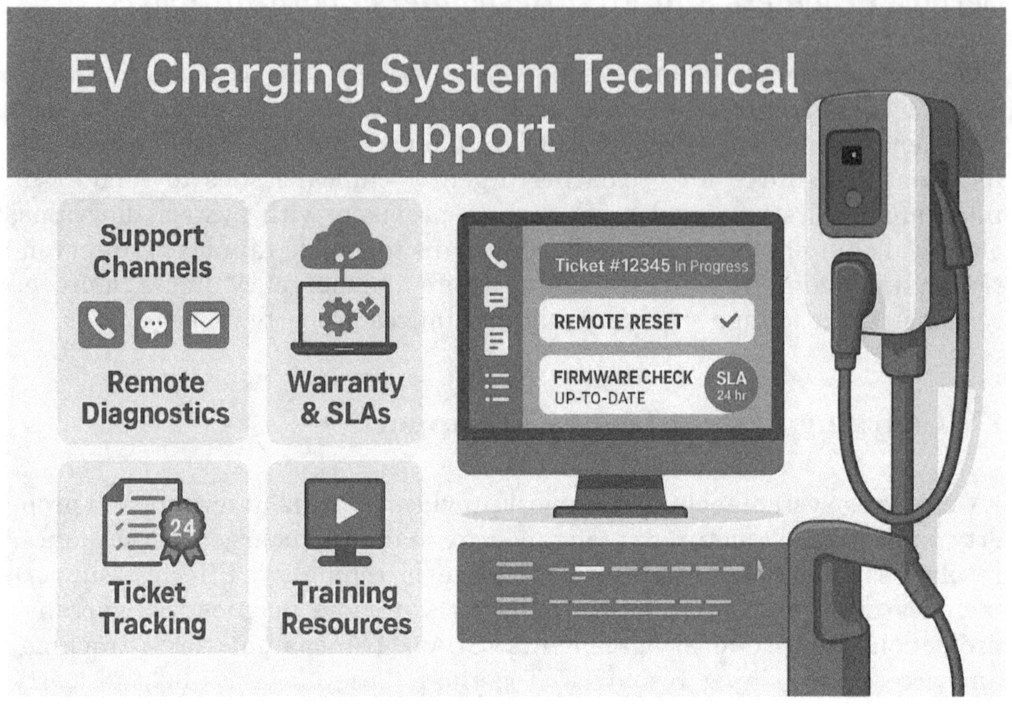

EV Charging System Technical Support

Remote Diagnostics Support

Many EV charging issues can be identified and resolved remotely, eliminating the need for an on-site technician visit. Remote diagnostics often include firmware updates, system restarts, connectivity checks, configuration adjustments, and data log reviews. Support teams can analyze charger activity in real time to pinpoint session failures, communication breakdowns, and hardware warnings. This remote-first approach dramatically improves resolution speed and ensures that most problems are addressed long before they escalate to major service interruptions.

Warranty and Service Level Agreements (SLAs)

Warranty coverage and service-level agreements define the protections, responsibilities, and performance guarantees associated with the EV charging system. SLAs often outline response times, uptime guarantees, included parts replacement, software maintenance, and access to continuous platform updates. These agreements hold vendors accountable for timely repairs and proactive support, while providing property owners with predictable costs and clear expectations. Understanding SLA terms allows owners to ensure adequate coverage and avoid gaps in maintenance or repair obligations.

Trouble Ticketing and Tracking

A transparent ticketing system helps property teams monitor issue progress from initial report to final resolution. Tickets typically include timestamps, problem descriptions, technician notes, and resolution summaries. Property owners can review historical logs to track recurring problems, support warranty claims, and maintain documentation for billing or regulatory purposes. Clear visibility into ticket status enhances accountability and ensures that no issue—large or small—is overlooked during the support process.

Training and Knowledge Resources

Access to training tools such as user guides, troubleshooting videos, FAQ libraries, and live support webinars empowers property staff to resolve minor issues independently. Well-informed personnel can quickly assist residents, perform basic diagnostics, and understand when to escalate problems to technical support. Investing in ongoing training improves operational efficiency, reduces service delays, and enhances tenant satisfaction by ensuring that staff remain knowledgeable and confident in managing the EV charging system.

EV Charging Usage Analytics & Reporting

EV charging system analytics and reporting provide apartment owners with vital insights into charger usage, energy consumption, revenue performance, resident behavior, and system reliability. These data-driven tools enable owners to optimize daily operations, forecast future demand, set equitable pricing, reduce energy costs, and justify long-term investment strategies. By understanding how the charging network performs across technical, financial, and user-behavior dimensions, property managers can maintain a high-quality charging experience while ensuring the system remains efficient, scalable, and profitable.

Charger Utilization Metrics

Tracking charger utilization is essential for understanding how residents use the EV charging system and when demand is highest. Utilization metrics include session counts, average charging durations, energy dispensed per session, and turnover rates. These insights reveal peak charging hours, underutilized chargers, and areas where demand exceeds capacity. By analyzing usage patterns, property managers can decide where to add more chargers, adjust parking assignments, or modify access policies to improve efficiency and reduce congestion.

Energy Cost Analysis

Energy analytics tools help apartment owners monitor total kilowatt-hours delivered, demand peaks, and associated electricity costs. Reviewing this data allows owners to identify opportunities to reduce expenses through strategies such as dynamic load management, demand charge mitigation, or shifting energy use to time-of-use (TOU) rates. Understanding energy cost patterns also supports long-term budgeting, ensuring that the EV charging system remains financially sustainable as resident adoption increases.

Revenue and Billing Reports

Transparent revenue and billing reporting enables owners to track financial performance and verify income generated from the charging system.

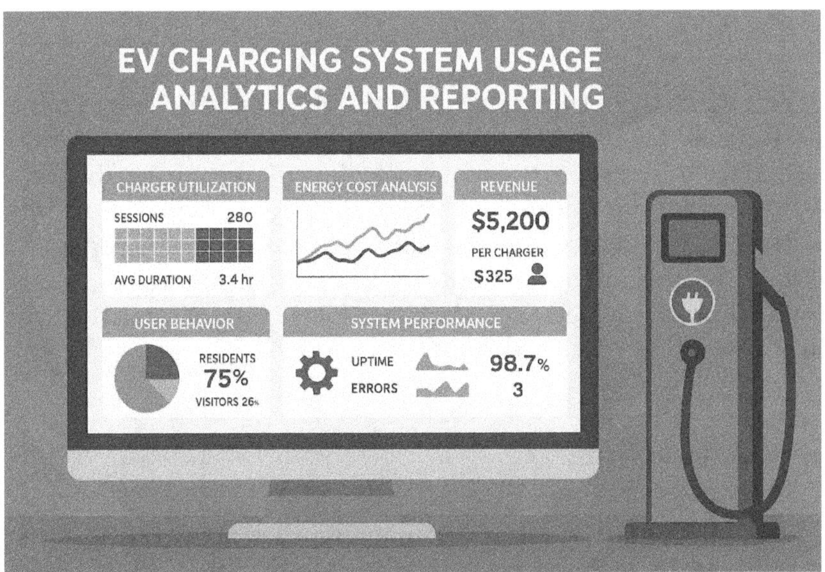

EV Charging System Usage Analytics and Reporting

Reports typically break down revenue per charger, per user, or per time period—such as daily, weekly, or monthly income. These tools help owners reconcile billing discrepancies, validate payment processing accuracy, and evaluate return on investment (ROI). Clear financial insights support strategic decisions about pricing models, subscription offerings, and expansion planning.

User Behavior and Engagement

Analytics related to user behavior reveal which residents charge most frequently, how visitor usage compares to resident demand, and whether pricing or access controls influence participation. These insights help apartment managers shape policies that are fair, transparent, and aligned with resident needs. User engagement data also highlights opportunities for targeted communication—such as encouraging off-peak charging or introducing loyalty programs—to improve system efficiency and resident satisfaction.

System Performance and Reliability

Reliable reporting tools track charger uptime, recurring error codes, maintenance response times, and overall system stability. Monitoring performance trends allows property owners to identify failing hardware, connectivity issues, or software problems before they disrupt operations. Proactive insights from performance reports help reduce downtime, ensure compliance with service-level agreements (SLAs), and maintain a consistent, dependable charging experience that supports tenant retention and confidence in the system.

Resident Onboarding

Resident onboarding is essential for ensuring that tenants and their guests understand how to access, operate, and benefit from the property's EV charging system. A well-structured onboarding process provides clarity on account setup, charging procedures, guest access, support channels, and community policies. By establishing clear expectations and offering easy-to-follow guidance, property owners can reduce confusion, prevent conflicts, and create a smooth, positive charging experience for all users. Effective onboarding promotes safety, fairness, and long-term adoption of the EV charging amenities within the apartment community.

User Account and Access Activation

A successful onboarding process begins with helping residents register their accounts and activate access to the EV charging system. Property staff should provide step-by-step instructions for creating user profiles, downloading required mobile apps, activating RFID cards or key fobs, and linking payment methods when necessary. Ensuring that residents understand how to initiate charging sessions and manage their account settings prevents frustrations and supports consistent usage from the first day of move-in.

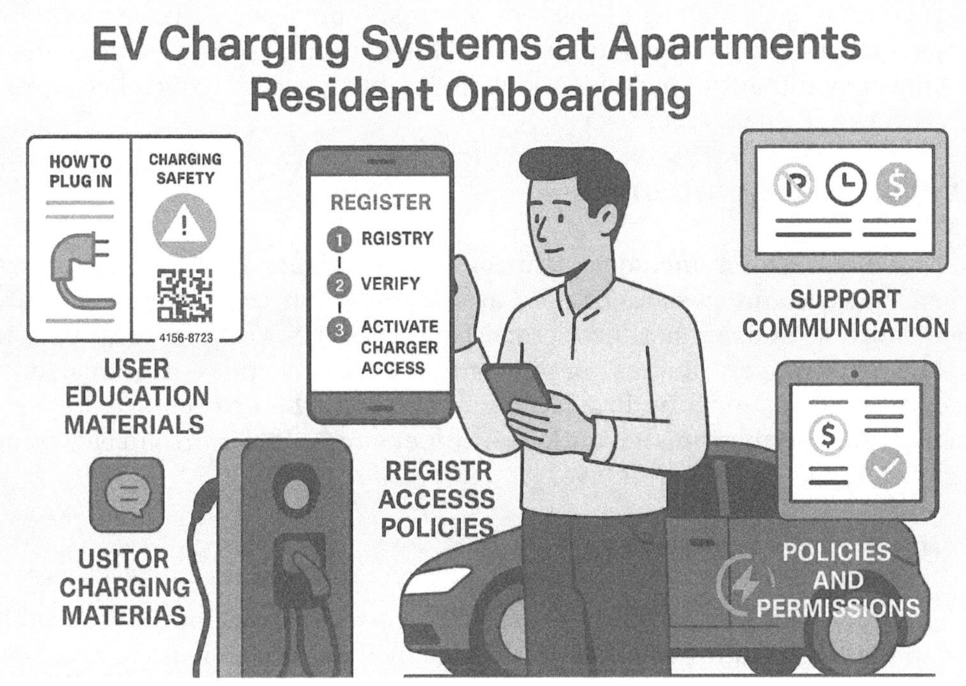

EV Charging Systems at Apartments Resident Onboarding

User Education Materials

Clear and accessible educational materials help residents understand how to safely and properly use the charging equipment. These materials may include quick-start guides, instructional videos, charger signage, safety reminders, and FAQ sheets. Providing visual explanations of cable handling, connector care, session start/stop steps, and etiquette—such as moving vehicles when charging is complete—helps residents avoid errors and contributes to a safe and respectful charging environment.

Visitor Access Policies

Guest charging policies must be clearly defined to maintain fairness and prevent unauthorized usage. Property owners should outline how visitors may request access, any eligibility requirements, time limits, and applicable fees. Options may include guest access codes, temporary RFID credentials, or pay-per-use public charging modes. Transparent visitor guidelines help maintain availability for residents while enabling secure, controlled access for guests and short-term users.

Support Communication

Effective onboarding includes ensuring that residents know where to turn when they encounter issues or need assistance. Clear communication channels—such as support hotlines, property management contact information, mobile app support menus, or customer service portals—help residents resolve problems quickly. Providing guidance on when to contact property staff versus the charging network operator ensures efficient troubleshooting and reduces unnecessary delays.

Policies and Permissions

Community-wide policies help set expectations for responsible and equitable use of the EV charging system. These may include rules about parking limits, charging etiquette, enforcement procedures, ADA stall use, and penalties for misuse. Establishing these expectations early helps prevent conflicts between residents and ensures fair access to the charging infrastructure. Well-defined policies also support long-term system performance, aligning resident behavior with property goals and operational requirements.

Personal Data Storage & Privacy

Personal data storage and privacy management in EV charging systems are essential responsibilities for apartment property owners, ensuring resident information is collected, processed, secured, and deleted in accordance with modern data protection laws and user expectations. Because EV charging platforms gather sensitive data—such as identity details, billing information, charging behavior, and access logs—properties must understand how this information is stored, who can access it, and how it is protected. Transparent policies, strong cybersecurity practices, and well-structured

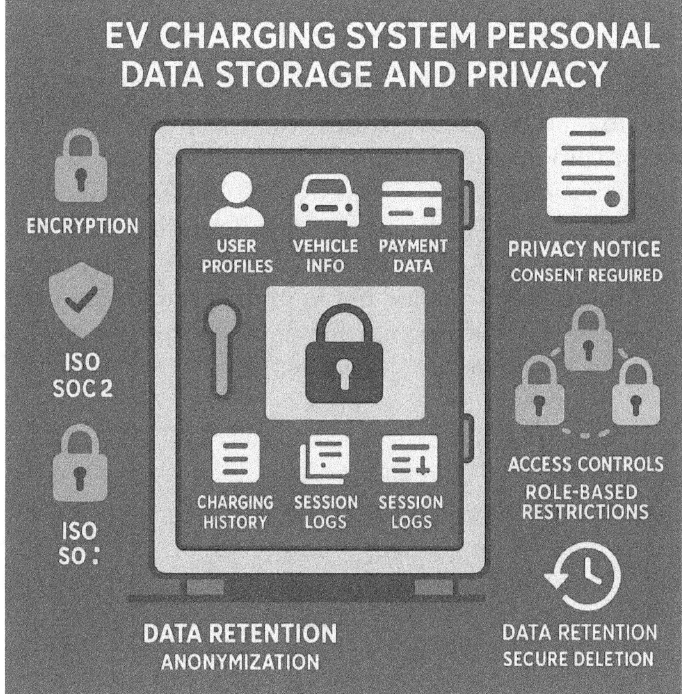

EV Charging System Personal Data Storage and Privacy

data retention procedures help maintain resident trust, reduce liability, and ensure compliance with privacy regulations across local, state, and international frameworks.

Data Collected and Stored

EV charging systems gather a variety of personal and operational data, including user account information, vehicle identifiers, payment methods, session history, energy usage, and access logs. This data may be stored locally on the charger, on the property's internal network, or in the cloud through the charging network operator's platform. Apartment owners should fully understand what information is being collected, where it resides, and how long it is retained. A clear understanding of stored data helps ensure compliance with privacy laws, supports transparent communication with residents, and reduces the risk of improper data handling.

Data Protection and Security

Protecting resident data requires strong cybersecurity measures such as encryption (in transit and at rest), multifactor authentication, secure APIs, firewalls, and continuous system monitoring. EV charging vendors should comply with industry-recognized frameworks like ISO 27001, SOC 2, or similar security certifications, demonstrating adherence to best practices for organizational and technical safeguards. Ensuring chargers and management platforms implement secure network protocols helps defend against unauthorized access, cyberattacks, and data breaches that could compromise resident privacy or disrupt charging system operations.

User Privacy Policies

Transparent user privacy policies help residents understand what data the charging system collects, how it is used, and under what conditions it may be shared with third parties such as billing service providers or utilities. These policies should clearly outline consent requirements, provide easy-to-read disclosures, and comply with relevant regulations such as the GDPR, California Consumer Privacy Act (CCPA), or other U.S. state privacy laws. Incorporating consent prompts into the account registration process ensures residents are informed and provides legally valid authorization for handling their data.

Access Control and Restrictions

Strict access controls must define who within the property's management team, charging vendor organization, or service provider network is allowed to view or modify user data. Access should be limited to authorized personnel based on role and necessity, with all interactions logged for accountability. Clear restrictions help prevent misuse or unauthorized exposure of personal information while ensuring staff and support teams can perform essential troubleshooting and administrative tasks without compromising privacy or security.

Data Retention Policies

Effective data retention policies determine how long personal information is stored, how it is anonymized for usage analytics, and when it should be deleted. Charging networks should provide automated or manual options for secure deletion when residents close accounts or request data removal. Retention timelines must comply with applicable regulations and should balance operational needs with privacy obligations. Clear and consistent data lifecycle management strengthens compliance, reduces liability, and ensures residents that their information is handled responsibly.

Apartment Staff Training Programs

Apartment staff training programs equip property personnel with the knowledge and skills needed to operate EV charging systems safely, support residents, respond to emergencies, and perform basic maintenance tasks. Well-trained staff ensure chargers remain reliable, reduce downtime, improve tenant satisfaction, and contribute to smooth daily operations. By understanding system functionality, troubleshooting basics, guest access workflows, emergency procedures, and maintenance responsibilities, staff become confident and capable partners in managing this important property amenity.

Basic System Operation

Staff should begin their training by learning how the EV charging system works, including the key components such as chargers, communication networks, access systems, and the management platform. Training should cover how to start and stop charging sessions, understand indicator lights, verify charger status through dashboards, and interpret basic system alerts. Familiarity with these fundamentals enables staff to assist residents effectively and recognize when something is not functioning properly.

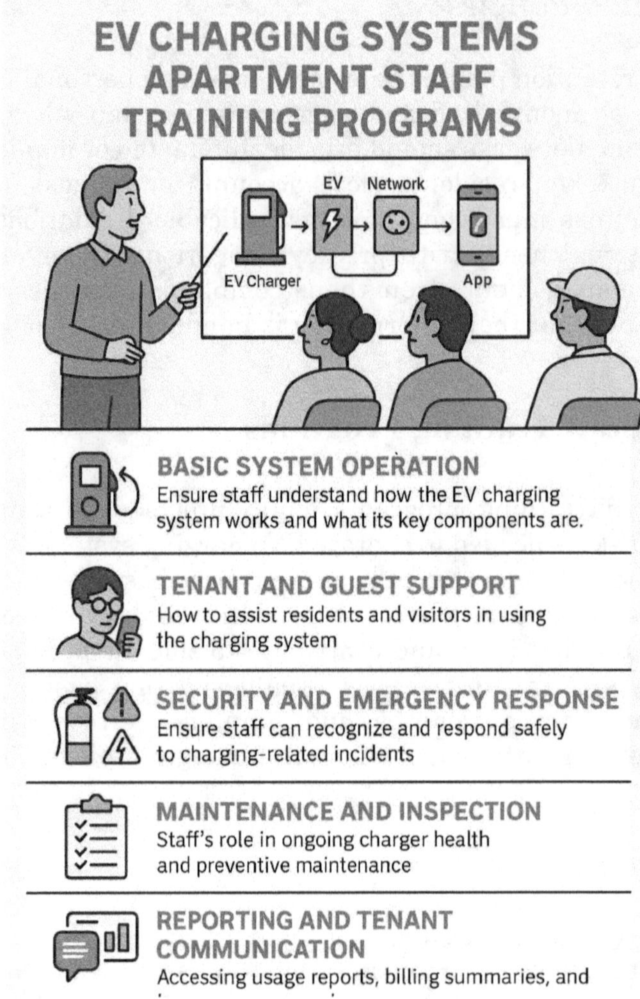

EV Charging Systems Apartment Staff Training Programs

Tenant and Guest Support

A core part of staff training involves learning how to assist residents and visitors in accessing and using the EV charging system. This includes helping new residents register accounts, explaining payment workflows, issuing or reassigning RFID cards, guiding guests through temporary access procedures, and addressing common user questions. Clear communication and helpful support from staff improve resident satisfaction, prevent misunderstandings, and ensure that both residents and guests can confidently use the charging infrastructure.

Surprising Fact: *Automated EV-charging billing systems can reduce administrative costs by 60–80%. With full billing automation, apartment staff spend far less time managing invoices and payments — lowering labor load and operating expenses.*

Security and Emergency Response

Training should also prepare staff to recognize and safely respond to charger-related incidents, including overheating alerts, damaged connectors, suspected electrical faults, or emergencies in the charging area. Staff must know how to initiate emergency shutdown procedures, identify shutoff locations, secure the area, and contact first responders when appropriate. Understanding basic safety protocols ensures quick, effective responses that protect both residents and property while minimizing risk.

Maintenance and Inspection

As part of the property's preventive maintenance program, staff may play a role in performing simple inspections and identifying issues early. Training should cover how to conduct routine visual checks, report damage, clean equipment safely, verify that chargers are online, and log inspection activities. While technical repairs are handled by certified technicians or service providers, trained staff act as the first line of defense—alerting maintenance teams before problems escalate into outages or costly repairs.

Chapter 7

EV Charging System Business

The business foundation of EV charging systems for apartment complexes begins with the critical choice of ownership models. Property owners can select from direct ownership, third-party host arrangements, hybrid partnerships, tenant-owned co-op structures, and subsidized utility or government-funded programs. Each model defines who pays for installation, who controls pricing and access, who manages maintenance, and who earns the revenue. The decision profoundly influences capital requirements, operational responsibilities, and long-term profitability. Direct ownership offers full revenue capture and control but requires higher investment and ongoing management, while third-party and hybrid models reduce risk by distributing costs and responsibilities. Tenant-owned and subsidized programs offer alternative pathways for owners seeking minimal financial exposure while still adding EV charging as an amenity.

There are multiple types of revenue opportunities available through EV charging systems ranging from simple utilities into multi-stream business assets. Beyond user-based charging fees—such as per-kWh billing, per-session pricing, subscriptions, or premium priority-access programs—properties can generate income from higher rental rates, digital advertising, local sponsorships, partnerships, guest charging, and participation in utility energy programs like demand response or managed charging. As more residents adopt EVs, on-site charging increases retention, supports rent premiums, and boosts property value, while smart load management and energy optimization reduce operating costs. Flexible pricing, networked billing, and data insights further enhance financial performance, allowing owners to tailor revenue models to resident needs and market conditions.

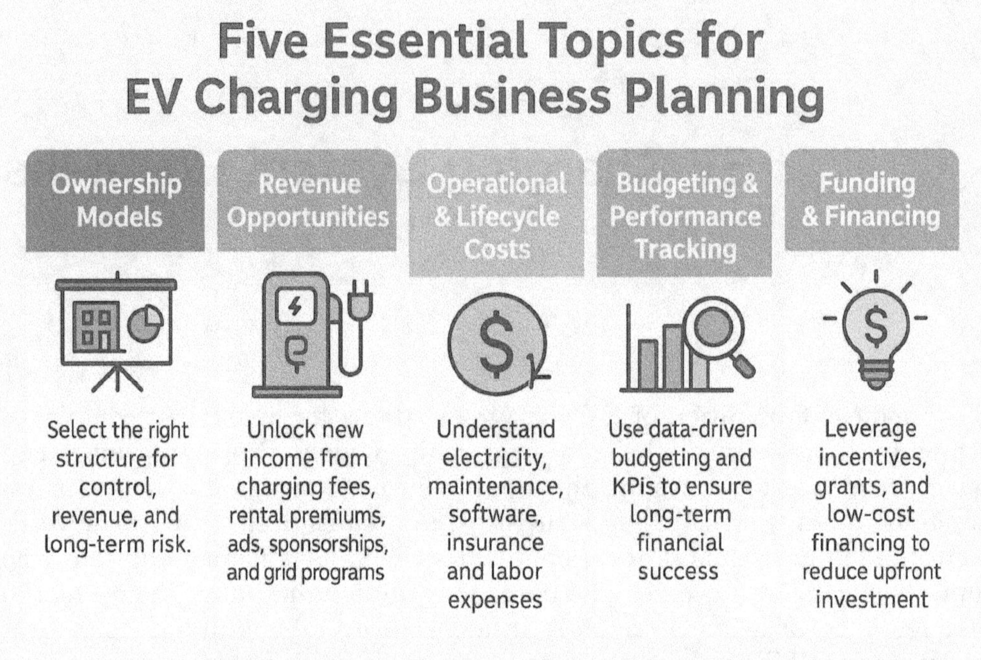

The Business of EV Charging Systems for Apartments

Key EV charging system costs include electricity and demand charges, software and network fees, payment processing, maintenance, repairs, warranties, insurance, and administrative labor. Effective budgeting—supported by monitoring tools, maintenance plans, and long-term upgrade strategies—ensures system reliability and profitability. By combining incentives, cost-recovery mechanisms, energy management, and diversified revenue streams, apartment owners can achieve typical ROI within two to four years, while building a resilient charging infrastructure that supports future growth, sustainability goals, and competitive differentiation in the multifamily housing market.

Ownership Models

EV charging ownership models are one of the most strategic decisions apartment complex owners must make. Ownership defines who pays for installation, who earns the revenue, who controls access and pricing, and who is responsible for maintenance, upgrades, and compliance. Selecting the right model can mean the difference between creating a profitable resident amenity and assuming an ongoing financial or operational burden.

Direct Ownership (Property-Owned)

In the direct ownership model, the apartment complex purchases, installs, and operates the EV charging equipment. The property retains full control over pricing, user access, and maintenance schedules while capturing 100% of the revenue from charging fees. However, this approach also carries the highest upfront cost and long-term responsibility for service contracts, repairs, and equipment upgrades. It is ideal for owners who want to maximize revenue and maintain complete control over the resident charging experience.

Third-Party Owned (Host Model)

Under the third-party ownership or host model, an external company installs, owns, and manages the charging infrastructure on the property. The apartment complex provides the parking spaces and electrical access, while the third-party partner handles installation, network management, and ongoing maintenance. In return, the property may receive a share of the revenue or benefit from having EV charging as a no-cost amenity. This model reduces financial risk but limits control over pricing and service terms.

Third party control can be a friction point for residents. Some third-party owned system operators may provide poor support and change pricing. When chargers break down and tennants tell the office, nothing may get done. This can do brand damage to the complex. Also the 3rd party controls the price and the complex may not be able to do anything thing about it. They can rasie it and the complex or owner has limited or ZERO control to adjust the pricing.

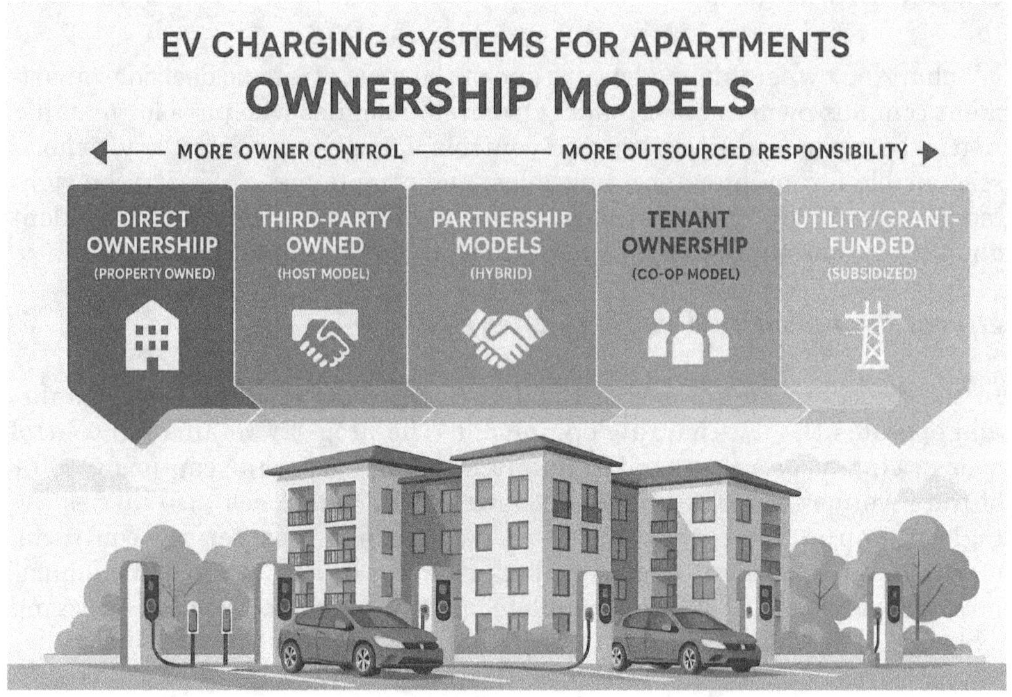

EV Charging Systems for Apartments Ownership Models

Partnership Models (Hybrid)

Hybrid or partnership ownership models combine elements of both direct and third-party ownership. The apartment complex and vendor share costs, revenues, and responsibilities according to a negotiated agreement. For example, the property may fund site preparation and electrical work, while the vendor supplies and operates the chargers. These shared-risk, shared-reward arrangements can balance investment and control, making them attractive for owners seeking financial flexibility and operational support.

Tenant Ownership (Co-op Model)

In a tenant or cooperative ownership model, residents, homeowner associations (HOAs), or tenant groups invest directly in EV chargers for their exclusive use. This structure shifts installation and maintenance costs to end users while allowing them to control charging schedules and fees. Property owners benefit by offering charging amenities without managing daily operations or capital expenses, though they must still ensure proper permitting, safety compliance, and electrical access.

Utility or Grant-Funded (Subsidized)

Some apartment complexes may qualify for utility- or government-funded EV charging programs. In these cases, utilities, energy service companies (ESCOs), or public agencies may cover part or all of the installation costs and retain partial ownership or operational oversight. Subsidized ownership models reduce capital expenditures and accelerate deployment, though they may include restrictions on pricing, usage, or reporting. These programs are well suited for properties looking to expand EV infrastructure while minimizing financial risk.

EV Charging System Revenue Types

Apartment complexes can generate multiple revenue streams from EV charging systems—including higher rental rates, user fees, advertising, partnerships, and energy program incentives—transforming charging infrastructure from a cost center into a profitable, value-adding amenity. By strategically combining these sources, property owners can improve returns, enhance tenant satisfaction, and position their communities as modern, sustainable, and future-ready.

Increased Rental Rates

EV charging amenities have become a strong differentiator in the multifamily housing market. Offering convenient, on-site charging attracts higher-income and environmentally conscious tenants willing to pay a premium for sustainable living options. Tennants with EVs may have desirable high income and more stable profiles. Properties with EV charging can justify higher rental rates or premium unit pricing, improve tenant retention, and

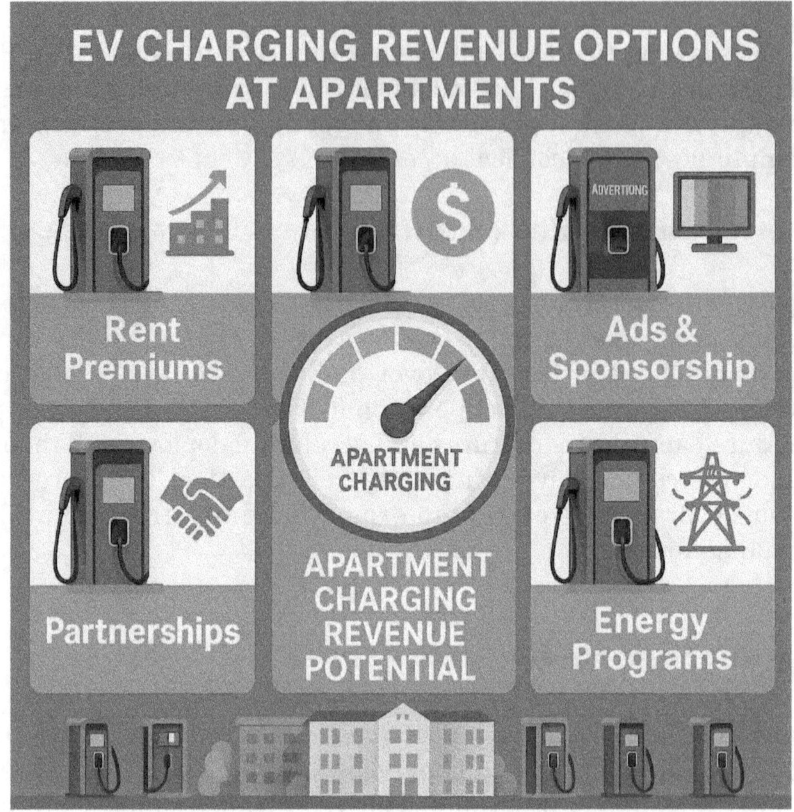

EV Charging System Revenue Types at Apartments

increase overall property value. This indirect revenue stream often provides one of the fastest returns on investment.

User-Based Charging Fees

Direct revenue can be generated through a variety of user-based fee models, including resident subscription plans, pay-per-session pricing, or premium fees for priority access or guest usage. These options allow property owners to recover operating costs such as electricity, maintenance, and software fees while also generating profit. Dynamic pricing can be applied based on time of day, demand, or energy cost to further optimize revenue and promote efficient charger usage.

Advertising & Sponsorships

EV charging stations can serve as digital or physical advertising platforms. Charger screens, mobile apps, and nearby signage can feature sponsorships, co-branding, or paid promotions from local businesses or national advertisers. This model turns everyday charging sessions into a monetizable media channel. Advertising and sponsorship revenue can also be used to subsidize system costs, reducing the owner's financial burden while enhancing community engagement.

Partnerships & Barter Programs

Strategic partnerships and barter agreements with charger vendors, utilities, or local businesses can offset installation costs and provide additional value. For example, a charger manufacturer might provide discounted equipment in exchange for brand exposure, or a local utility might share revenue in return for data on energy usage. These collaborations reduce out-of-pocket expenses and create win-win scenarios that strengthen the property's sustainability profile and market appeal.

Energy & Grid Participation Income

Advanced EV charging systems can participate in energy optimization programs that generate additional income. Through demand response initiatives, load management incentives, or vehicle-to-grid (V2G) capabilities, properties can receive payments or credits from utilities for helping balance grid demand. This emerging revenue stream rewards properties for smart energy behavior, further enhancing ROI and supporting long-term energy resilience. Apartment complexes equipped with V2B systems can maintain power during outages, improving resilience and helping ensure residents remain comfortable and happy.

Apartment Rental Rates

Apartment complexes that add EV charging can increase rental rates by 4–6%, while also improving tenant retention and property value by offering a modern, high-demand amenity. As electric vehicle adoption grows, on-site charging has become a key differentiator that attracts tech-savvy, environmentally conscious residents and strengthens a property's competitive position in the multifamily market.

Amenity & Necessity

What was once viewed as a luxury perk has quickly become an expected feature for modern apartment communities. EV charging has shifted from an amenity to essential infrastructure, similar to high-speed internet or fitness centers. Properties that offer it signal forward-thinking management and environmental responsibility—qualities that resonate strongly with today's renters and position the property ahead of market demand.

Premium Rent Potential

Apartments with EV-capable parking spaces can command $50–$150 more per month per space, depending on local market demand and charger availability. These premiums reflect both the added convenience for EV drivers and the scarcity of charging access at competing properties. Even partial deployment—such as designating a small percentage of parking spots as EV-ready—can significantly increase the property's perceived value and monthly revenue potential.

Tenant Retention

Adding EV charging supports long-term tenant satisfaction and retention. Residents with electric vehicles are more likely to renew their leases when they have convenient, reliable charging access at home. On-site charging fosters a sense of community investment and convenience that enhances the overall living experience, reducing vacancy rates and turnover costs for property owners.

EV Charging at Higher Apartment Rental Rates

Infrastructure Readiness

To support sustainable growth, apartment complexes must ensure proper electrical infrastructure and load management. Installing Level 2 chargers with intelligent load balancing and individual metering enables safe, scalable implementation that meets both current and future tenant needs. Future-proofing the property in this way helps maintain its competitiveness as EV adoption accelerates.

EV Charger Subscription Fees

EV charging subscription programs transform a one-time tenant amenity into a predictable, recurring revenue stream that enhances tenant satisfaction, strengthens financial stability, and increases property value. By offering residents consistent access to convenient charging, property owners can create long-term engagement and a steady source of income that supports ongoing operations and future system expansion.

Recurring Income

Subscription-based charging creates steady monthly revenue and predictable cash flow compared to fluctuating per-use models. This approach allows property owners to forecast income, budget for maintenance and software costs, and demonstrate consistent returns for investors. Predictable revenue also helps offset initial installation costs while supporting long-term operational sustainability.

Tenant Retention

Offering a subscription model strengthens tenant loyalty and retention by providing reserved or priority charging access for subscribers. Residents value the convenience and reliability of a personal charging plan, especially when spaces are limited. Subscription-based systems reinforce the property's image as a forward-thinking, resident-focused community—one that supports tenants' evolving mobility needs and lifestyles.

Pricing Strategy

Establishing the right subscription pricing structure is key to balancing tenant affordability and owner profitability. Typical rates range from \$40–\$60 per month, depending on local electricity costs, charger access, and amenities included. Transparent pricing, paired with clear service benefits (such as guaranteed access or premium charging speeds), ensures residents view the subscription as a valuable, fair-priced service rather than a surcharge.

Operational Readiness

To run an effective subscription program, properties must implement integrated billing, access control, usage tracking, and monitoring systems.

EV Charger at Apartment Subscription Fee Revenues

Reliable network management ensures chargers remain available and functioning at all times, while automated billing systems simplify management for both owners and tenants. Consistent uptime and support are critical for maintaining trust and satisfaction among paying subscribers.

Scalable Growth

Subscription programs can be introduced gradually—starting with a small pilot group of early EV adopters—and expanded as demand grows. This approach minimizes financial risk, provides valuable performance data, and allows owners to refine pricing and management processes over time. As EV adoption accelerates, scalable subscription programs position apartment complexes to meet future resident needs while steadily improving ROI.

EV Charger Per Session Fees

Per-use EV charging fees transform apartment complex chargers into a transparent, usage-based revenue stream that aligns directly with tenant and guest charging behavior. This model provides flexibility, fairness, and measurable return on investment—typically within 2–4 years—when integrated with smart billing systems and supported by available incentives.

Idle session fees—charges applied when a vehicle remains plugged in after charging has finished—help encourage drivers to move their vehicles promptly, improving charger availability and maximizing utilization of the charging infrastructure for the property owner.

Usage-Based Revenue

Implementing per-session or per-kilowatt-hour (kWh) billing ensures fair and transparent pricing tied directly to actual charger utilization. Tenants and guests pay only for the energy they consume, making the system equitable while helping property owners recover costs proportionally. This usage-based approach also encourages responsible charging behavior and discourages charger "hogging," leading to higher overall efficiency and satisfaction.

Flexible Fee Options

Apartment owners can choose from several fee structures—per-kWh, time-based (per hour), or flat-fee per session—depending on local utility rules and tenant preferences. Per-kWh billing aligns with most state regulations and energy fairness principles, while time-based models can help manage dwell time and turnover. The flexibility to adjust pricing over time allows property managers to respond to energy costs, charger utilization trends, and resident feedback.

Smart Billing Systems

Modern networked billing platforms automate the entire process of metering, invoicing, and reporting. These systems integrate with mobile apps or

EV Charging at Apartment Per Session Fees

RFID cards for seamless user authentication and payment, eliminating the need for staff involvement. Automated reporting also provides valuable insights into energy use, revenue trends, and charger performance—critical data for scaling or optimizing the system.

Guest & Fleet Pricing

EV charger networks can apply tiered pricing to capture additional value from guest users, delivery fleets, or rideshare vehicles. Non-residents may be charged premium rates for access, helping to offset infrastructure costs while keeping resident fees lower. This approach maximizes charger utilization, improves revenue per port, and positions the property as a local charging hub for both residents and visitors.

ROI & Incentives

When combined with utility rebates, tax incentives, and smart load management, per-use charging models typically achieve payback within two to four years. The combination of recurring revenue, cost recovery through incentives, and reduced administrative burden makes per-session billing a financially sound strategy for apartment owners seeking sustainable, long-term returns from their EV charging infrastructure.

Surprising Fact *— Public-access Type 2 EV chargers can generate 3-5x or more revenue than apartment resident-only chargers. A typical private, resident-only Type 2 charger at an apartment property earns roughly $50 per month ($300–$600 per year). When EV chargers are opened for public access in a high-traffic urban area, a similar Type 2 charger can earn $500–$1,500 per month — or about $6,000–$18,000 annually per charger. Public EV charging fees commonly range from $0.20–$0.30 per kWh, or $1–$5 per hour when billed by time. This means that allowing public usage — even part-time, during off-peak hours, or with controlled access — can transform a low-yield resident amenity into a meaningful recurring revenue generator for the property.*

Priority Usage Fees

Priority usage fees allow apartment complexes to charge extra for premium EV charging access—including faster charging speeds, reserved spaces, or guaranteed charger availability. This approach creates a high-margin revenue stream while enhancing convenience and satisfaction for residents who value reliable, priority charging access. By offering differentiated service levels, properties can boost profitability and tenant appeal without significant infrastructure expansion.

Premium Access

Providing reserved parking spaces or guaranteed charger availability transforms EV charging into an exclusive amenity. Tenants are often willing to pay more for the assurance that a charger will be open when they need it. This "VIP access" model mirrors reserved parking programs and adds perceived value to the property while ensuring that priority users always have access to critical charging resources.

EV Charging Priority Access Options

Faster Charging

Apartment properties can offer high-output Level 2 chargers (11–22 kW) or even limited-access DC fast chargers for residents who need quicker turn-around times. Faster charging capability justifies premium pricing and appeals to commuters, professionals, and residents with higher daily driving needs. These premium options can operate alongside standard chargers, giving tenants flexibility to choose between cost and convenience.

Tiered Pricing

Using software-based access controls and smart billing systems, property owners can easily manage tiered pricing structures that distinguish between standard and premium users. This model automatically enforces pricing, scheduling, and priority access rules within the network management platform. Tiered pricing introduces flexibility for both tenants and management, allowing price adjustments based on usage data, demand, and feedback over time.

Revenue Growth

Priority charging programs can deliver meaningful incremental income. Studies and market trials show that renters are willing to pay $25–$40 per month extra for premium EV charging access, especially in properties with limited parking or shared charger availability. These additional fees contribute directly to operating income, supporting faster cost recovery and higher overall property valuation.

Pilot & Scale

The most effective approach is to start small, launching a pilot with four to six premium-designated chargers. This allows property owners to measure usage, satisfaction, and revenue impact before expanding. Based on pilot results, the program can be scaled to meet growing demand, ensuring optimal return on investment and long-term tenant satisfaction.

Guest User Fees

Allowing guest access to apartment EV chargers transforms unused charging capacity into a new revenue source while positioning the property as a visible, community-friendly mobility hub. With proper pricing, access control, and safety measures, guest charging programs can enhance utilization rates, generate recurring income, and strengthen the property's role in local EV infrastructure networks.

Idle Capacity ROI

Most apartment EV chargers sit idle 75–85% of the time, particularly during work hours or when residents are away. Opening these chargers to guest users—such as visitors, delivery drivers, or nearby EV owners—turns that

EV Charging at Apartment Guest User Fees

downtime into profit. By monetizing underutilized capacity, properties can earn consistent incremental revenue while improving charger efficiency and justifying the system's overall investment.

Access Control Tools

Smart EV charging management platforms like AmpUp, ChargeLab, and SWTCH make it easy to manage secure, time-limited, or pay-per-use guest access. These systems allow property managers to issue digital access codes, set usage windows, or enable public visibility through major charging networks. Automated authentication and billing ensure that guest charging remains convenient while maintaining control and accountability.

Dynamic Pricing

To optimize revenue and manage demand, properties can implement dynamic pricing models for guest users. Common fee structures range from $0.25–$0.45 per kWh or $3–$8 per session, with higher rates applied during evenings, weekends, or peak occupancy times. Variable pricing encourages off-peak charging and maximizes earnings from guests who value convenience and location proximity.

Time of Use Pricing (TOU)

Time-of-Use (TOU) pricing aligns EV charging rates with the utility's electricity cost schedule, allowing property owners to manage energy costs while encouraging residents to charge during lower-demand periods. Under TOU pricing, electricity rates vary depending on the time of day, reflecting how much demand is placed on the power grid.

Charging rates are typically highest during peak hours, usually in the late afternoon and early evening when residents return home and overall electricity usage increases due to cooking, heating or cooling, and other household activities.

During off-peak hours, such as overnight, early morning, or midday when demand on the grid is lower, electricity prices are reduced, making charging more economical. Some utilities also offer super off-peak periods, typically late at night, when electricity is cheapest and EV charging is strongly encouraged.

By integrating TOU pricing into EV charging systems, apartment properties can lower operating costs, reduce strain on building electrical infrastructure, and encourage residents to charge vehicles during the most efficient times.

Security & Liability

Opening chargers to the public requires enhanced safety and liability management. Installing clear "Guest Charging Only" signage, ensuring proper lighting and video surveillance, and confirming insurance coverage are essential steps. Guest usage policies should be clearly communicated to avoid conflicts with residents and to protect the property from potential claims or misuse.

Hybrid Models

Many apartment complexes find success using hybrid charging models that combine resident subscriptions with guest per-use access. This approach maximizes utilization, diversifies revenue streams, and accelerates ROI timelines. Guests fill charging gaps during off-peak periods, while residents enjoy priority or discounted access—creating a balanced, efficient system that benefits both the property and its tenants.

EV Charging System Advertising Revenues

EV charging systems equipped with digital screens, mobile apps, and connected platforms create new income opportunities by transforming chargers into monetizable media assets. Each charging session, app interaction, or notification can become a revenue-generating touchpoint through local, programmatic, and sponsorship-based advertising—turning everyday energy use into an ongoing marketing and profit channel for property owners.

The EV charging advertising model has been validated by companies such as Volta and Blink. Volta, founded on the concept of offering free or subsidized EV charging funded by digital advertising, deployed chargers with large-format screens in high-traffic retail locations throughout the late 2010s and early 2020s. In 2023, Shell Recharge acquired Volta's network and media platform, further integrating charging infrastructure with retail media and out-of-home (DOOH) advertising strategies.

EV Charging System Advertising Revenues

In 2024, the Volta network was acquired by JOLT (often referenced as Jolta), continuing the model of combining free charging with advertiser-funded revenue. Blink Charging has also expanded into advertising-supported charging, introducing chargers with digital displays and media capabilities to generate additional revenue streams beyond energy sales. These developments demonstrate how EV charging infrastructure is evolving into a hybrid utility and media platform, creating new monetization opportunities for site hosts and network operators.

Digital Ad Screens

Many EV chargers now feature built-in LCD or LED displays that function as high-visibility digital-out-of-home (DOOH) advertising units. These screens display short video ads, static graphics, or property-branded messages while vehicles charge, capturing a captive audience of drivers and pedestrians. Apartment complexes can sell screen time directly to local businesses, sponsors, or property amenities (such as gyms or cafes), creating a steady and scalable revenue stream.

In-App Promotions

Most EV charging networks use companion mobile apps or web portals for user access and payment. These digital interfaces provide prime space for banner ads, sponsored coupons, and promotional offers. Properties can collaborate with local restaurants, retailers, or service providers to deliver targeted ads to tenants or visitors. In-app promotions not only generate ad income but also add perceived value by connecting residents to neighborhood businesses.

Station Branding

EV charging stations themselves can double as branding real estate. Custom wraps, decals, or signage offer advertisers long-term exposure and provide the property with an upgraded, professional look. These sponsorship-based branding opportunities can be sold as flat monthly or annual contracts, generating predictable ad revenue while improving the site's visual appeal and sustainability image.

Programmatic Ad Revenue

Advanced EV charging platforms can integrate with programmatic ad networks such as Vistar Media or Broadsign, enabling automated ad placement and reporting. Through these systems, ad inventory is sold dynamically to national or regional advertisers based on audience data, location, and time of day. This automation allows property owners to earn passive ad revenue with minimal effort while maintaining control over ad categories and display frequency.

Local Advertising

Beyond digital ads, properties can build relationships through local advertising programs. Partnering with nearby businesses—like auto dealers, coffee shops, or insurance agencies—for flat monthly sponsorships helps stabilize revenue and strengthen community ties.

EV chargers equipped with digital displays can also serve as community communication platforms, allowing property managers to share timely and relevant announcements with residents and visitors. These screens can be used to display messages such as upcoming community events, maintenance notices, safety alerts, or local happenings.

For example, a common and effective use is promoting resident events like community gatherings, holiday celebrations, or pool openings, helping increase participation and engagement. By combining advertising with community messaging, charging stations become not only revenue-generating assets but also valuable tools for improving resident communication and strengthening the sense of community within the property.

Surprising Fact *– Advertising revenue from EV charger displays and their mobile apps can actually exceed the income from selling electricity. Standard EV charger screens typically earn $10–$22 CPM (cost per thousand impressions), compared to just $2–$15 CPM for most digital out-of-home (DOOH) advertising. This means the typical advertising revenue earned per EV Charger display is roughly $1–$3 per hour. The potential grows dramatically with interactive displays, which can generate 10x or more when drivers engage directly with ads. For instance, a streaming subscription sign-up can deliver $5–$20 per customer, while auto test drive bookings can earn $25–$75 per qualified lead.*

EV Charging System Sponsorships

Sponsorships transform apartment EV charging systems into recurring revenue channels by allowing local and corporate partners to feature their branding across chargers, mobile apps, and resident communications. These partnerships provide consistent income with minimal operational effort

EV Charging at Apartment Sponsorships

while enhancing community engagement and sustainability visibility. Sponsorships can be structured as one-time campaigns or ongoing programs, creating both short-term and long-term financial value for property owners.

Sponsorship Types

Apartment properties can offer tiered sponsorship packages that bundle multiple forms of brand exposure. Options may include physical charger branding, digital placements within charging apps or websites, co-branded signage, and event co-sponsorships. Many properties use structured tiers such as Bronze, Silver, and Gold packages, allowing sponsors to choose their level of visibility and engagement. This approach standardizes offerings and simplifies sales while giving sponsors flexibility in how they reach residents and visitors.

Revenue Potential

Sponsorship programs can be highly profitable, often generating $400 to $3,500 per month per property, depending on factors such as location, resident demographics, and charger utilization. High-traffic properties or those located in urban areas with strong EV adoption rates typically command higher rates. The recurring nature of sponsorship income provides financial stability and can offset software, maintenance, or utility costs associated with the EV charging system.

Audience Value

Apartment EV drivers represent a premium, sustainability-minded demographic that sponsors are eager to reach. These residents tend to have higher incomes, longer tenancy, and a strong interest in green living and technology. Ideal sponsors include auto dealerships, insurance companies, energy providers, and local retailers seeking targeted exposure to an environmentally conscious audience. This alignment of values increases sponsor appeal and strengthens property branding as a sustainable, forward-thinking community.

Operational Setup

Launching a sponsorship program is straightforward using existing property assets. Chargers can feature branded wraps, decals, or digital screens; apps and web portals can host sponsored content or banner ads; and resident newsletters or emails can include sponsor messages. Tracking performance through QR code scans, session counts, or digital impressions provides proof-of-play for sponsors, ensuring transparency and accountability while supporting renewal discussions.

Sponsorship Models

Property owners can choose from several sponsorship models to fit their goals and capabilities. Local direct sales—selling sponsorships to nearby businesses—typically offer the highest profit margins but require some outreach. Alternatively, programmatic digital-out-of-home (DOOH) or platform-assisted sponsorships automate the process by integrating with advertising networks, offering scalable long-term revenue with less management. Many successful programs use a hybrid approach, combining local relationships with automated national ad placements for maximum yield and efficiency.

EV Charging System Partnerships & Bartering

EV Charger System Partnerships and Bartering at Apartment Properties Strategic partnerships and barter agreements transform apartment EV charging systems into community marketing and collaboration platforms, generating new revenue streams or in-kind value through local business relationships. By aligning with service providers, sustainability brands, and

EV Charging at Apartments Barter Exchange

EV ecosystem partners, apartment owners can turn charging infrastructure into an asset that drives engagement, visibility, and long-term financial return while enhancing community identity.

Partnership Models

Apartment properties can develop integrated partnership programs that combine branding, resident events, and digital exposure. Local businesses and corporate sponsors value access to sustainability-minded renters who represent a growing and influential audience. These partnerships may include charger co-branding, event sponsorships, app-based promotions, or resident engagement campaigns, offering win-win opportunities for both property owners and partners seeking to align with clean energy initiatives.

Barter Value Exchange

Not all partnerships need to involve direct payments—many can be structured as barter or in-kind value exchanges. For example, a local car wash might offer resident discounts or free detailing services in return for branding on the chargers or inclusion in tenant communications. Similarly, technology vendors could provide upgraded charging equipment or maintenance services in exchange for visibility or pilot program participation. These creative value exchanges enhance amenities, reduce operating costs, and strengthen local business relationships.

Tiered Packages

To simplify sales and management, properties can offer tiered partnership packages such as Bronze, Silver, and Gold levels. Each tier provides different levels of exposure—ranging from charger wraps and mobile app placement to co-branded signage, digital communications, and event sponsorships. Tiered packages make it easy for businesses to choose a level that fits their marketing budget while ensuring predictable and scalable income or barter value for the property.

Revenue & ROI

Well-structured partnership and barter programs can generate $1,000 to $3,000 per month in direct cash or equivalent in-kind value, depending on property size, visibility, and local business participation. Beyond the monetary return, these programs contribute to measurable community benefits such as resident engagement, sustainability branding, and local economic collaboration—all of which enhance the property's market appeal and long-term value.

Key Requirements

To maximize partnership success, EV charging systems and management platforms must be customizable, compliant, and data-enabled. Chargers, apps, and resident communications should allow sponsor integration without violating advertising or utility regulations. Properties should also provide proof-of-performance reporting—such as ad impressions, QR scans, or session counts—to validate value for sponsors and support renewals. A well-managed system ensures transparency, credibility, and sustained partnership growth.

Energy Management & Grid Revenue Streams

Apartment complexes can turn EV charging systems into active energy assets by participating in smart grid and energy management programs. Through strategic integration with utility demand response, load management, and Vehicle-to-Grid (V2G) services, properties can earn new revenue, lower electricity costs, and contribute to renewable energy adoption. This approach transforms EV charging from a cost center into a dynamic, grid-connected opportunity that strengthens both sustainability and financial performance.

Smart Load Management

Implementing smart load management systems allows apartment complexes to optimize energy usage by controlling when and how EV chargers draw

EV Charging at Apartments Grid Energy Revenue Stream

power. Advanced software can balance charging schedules, prioritize off-peak hours, and prevent simultaneous high-load events. By reducing monthly demand charges by up to 20–40%, properties not only lower utility bills but also extend the capacity of existing electrical infrastructure without costly upgrades.

Demand Response Programs

Utilities across the country offer demand response programs that pay participants to temporarily reduce power consumption during peak demand periods. Apartment complexes can enroll EV chargers or other building loads in these programs to receive financial incentives or bill credits. Automated load reduction—such as delaying or throttling charger output for a short duration—provides passive income while supporting grid stability and reducing the risk of blackouts.

Vehicle-to-Grid (V2G)

With the emergence of bi-directional charging technology, electric vehicles can serve as both energy consumers and providers. Vehicle-to-Grid (V2G) systems enable EVs to discharge stored energy back to the grid or supply power to the property during peak hours. This capability allows owners to earn energy credits or direct payments from utilities while improving local energy resilience. As more vehicles and chargers become V2G-compatible, this model offers a powerful new revenue stream for multifamily communities.

Renewable Integration

Integrating solar panels, battery storage, and EV charging systems creates a closed-loop energy ecosystem where excess solar energy can be stored, used for charging, or sold back to the grid. Smart energy management platforms can automatically shift charging to align with time-of-use (TOU) rates, ensuring maximum financial benefit. This combination not only reduces dependence on grid electricity but also enhances the property's sustainability credentials and long-term energy independence.

V2G Vehicle and Charging System Requirements

Vehicle-to-Grid (V2G) functionality requires both bi-directional chargers and bi-directional capable vehicles. Standard EV chargers are designed only to deliver power to the vehicle and cannot draw energy back from the battery. To enable V2G operation, the charging system must support two-way power flow, and the vehicle must be equipped with compatible hardware and software to safely export energy back to the grid or building.

Long-Term Potential

As utilities transition toward flexible, distributed grid models, managed charging and V2G participation will become increasingly valuable. Apartment complexes that invest now in smart, grid-ready EV infrastructure will be positioned to capitalize on future incentive programs and energy markets. Beyond revenue, these technologies contribute to cleaner grids, lower emissions, and greater property resilience—establishing a competitive advantage in the evolving energy economy.

EV Charging System Costs

Operating costs are a critical part of managing an EV charging system at apartment properties. These expenses include electricity and demand charges, software subscriptions, maintenance, payment processing, and administrative labor—all of which influence long-term affordability, reliability, and profitability. Understanding and managing these recurring costs allows owners to maximize return on investment while maintaining dependable service for residents and guests.

Electricity and Utility Demand Charges

The largest ongoing expense for apartment EV charging systems is electricity consumption. In addition to the cost of energy used, properties must account for utility demand charges, which are based on peak power usage during billing periods. Apartment owners can reduce these expenses by implementing load management systems and taking advantage of time-of-use (TOU) rates that lower costs during off-peak hours. Careful planning of charging schedules and system controls can cut monthly electricity bills by as much as 20–40%.

Network and Software Subscription Fees

Most modern EV chargers rely on networked software platforms for essential functions like monitoring, payment processing, access control, and system reporting. These services typically come with annual or monthly fees—averaging $150–$400 per charger per year, depending on vendor, features, and data services. While these fees add to operational costs, they are vital for maintaining secure, reliable, and revenue-generating charging operations. Owners should also review contract terms for renewals, updates, and bundled service options to ensure long-term cost efficiency.

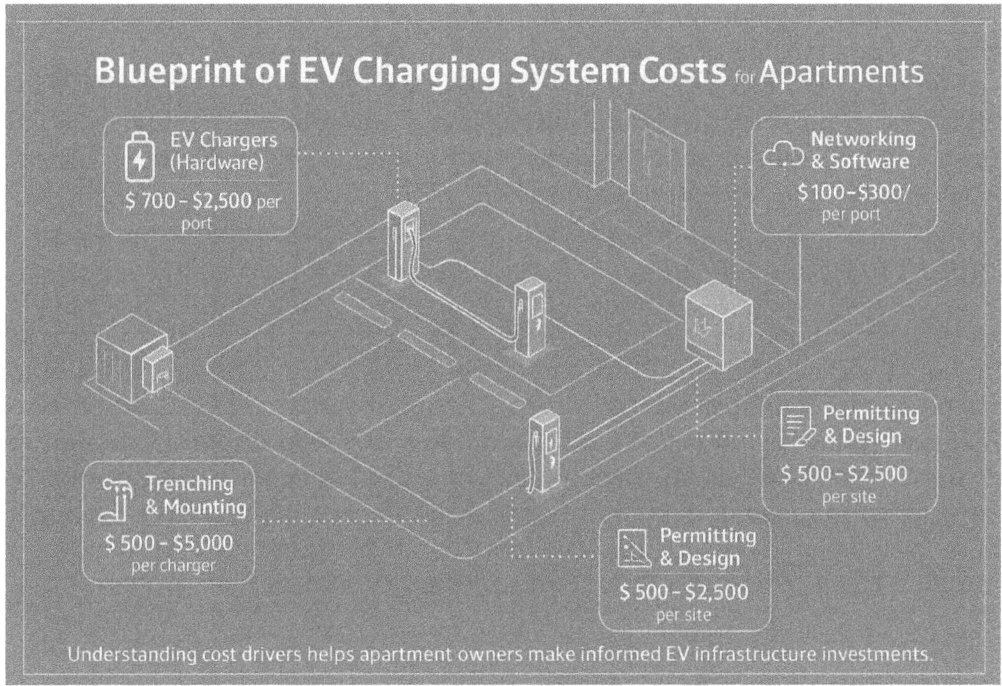

EV Charging Systems for Apartments Costs

Maintenance, Repairs, and Service Contracts

Like any mechanical and electrical system, EV chargers require routine maintenance and occasional repairs to ensure consistent performance. Service contracts can help stabilize costs by including preventive inspections, firmware updates, and technical support. Apartment owners should confirm what's covered—such as replacement parts, cables, and labor—and plan for annual maintenance expenses of roughly 3–5% of equipment value. Investing in proactive maintenance reduces downtime, extends equipment lifespan, and helps retain resident satisfaction.

Payment Processing and Transaction Fees

For properties that charge users per session or per kWh, payment processing and transaction fees are an unavoidable cost. Most credit card processors and digital payment platforms charge 2.5–3.5% per transaction, sometimes with additional flat fees. These costs can accumulate over time, particularly at high-use properties. Apartment owners should compare vendor offerings, explore integrated billing solutions, and consider bulk transaction processing to minimize fees while maintaining smooth, secure payment experiences for residents and guests.

Administrative Labor

Even with automation, operating an EV charging system requires ongoing administrative oversight. Property staff or third-party managers must handle reporting, tenant inquiries, billing discrepancies, and maintenance coordination. While cloud-based dashboards and automated alerts can significantly reduce labor needs, owners should still budget for some internal or outsourced management time. Investing in efficient management tools not only cuts labor costs but also ensures that the charging system operates seamlessly—protecting both revenue and tenant satisfaction.

Maintenance Costs

Effective EV charging maintenance management combines preventive care, service contracts, smart monitoring, and strategic budgeting to minimize downtime, control expenses, and plan for long-term system reliability. A well-structured maintenance program ensures chargers remain safe, compliant, and fully operational—protecting both resident satisfaction and the property's investment.

Routine Maintenance & Inspections

Preventive maintenance is the foundation of a cost-effective EV charging program. Regular inspections help identify wear, corrosion, or loose connections before they lead to costly failures. Typical tasks include checking cables and connectors, cleaning equipment, verifying signage and accessibility, and confirming that safety features such as GFCI protection function correctly. Scheduled preventive care reduces unexpected downtime, extends equipment lifespan, and ensures continued compliance with electrical and safety codes.

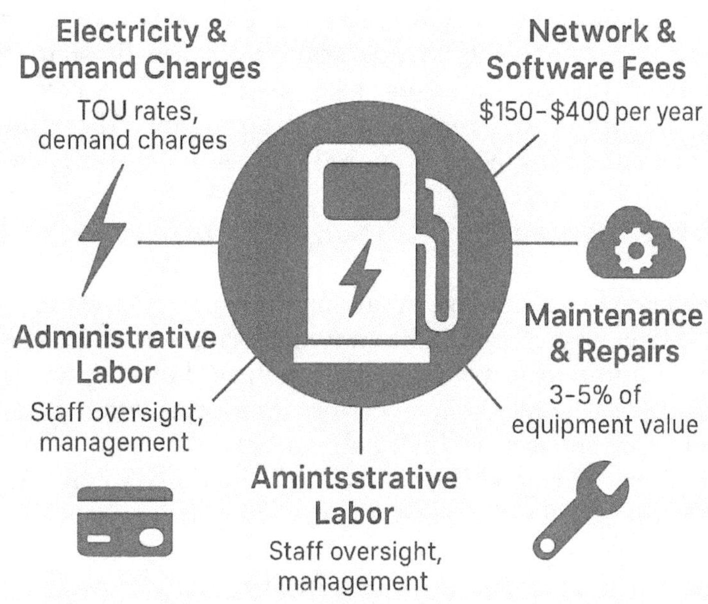

EV Charging System at Apartments Maintenance Costs

Service Contracts and Maintenance Plans

Many property owners choose to purchase service contracts or maintenance plans from charger manufacturers or network providers. These agreements can stabilize maintenance costs by bundling routine inspections, software updates, and technical support into a predictable annual fee. However, contract terms vary widely—some include parts and labor, while others only cover diagnostics or remote support. Owners should review service-level agreements carefully, confirming response times, warranty coverage, and any limits on repair services.

Repair and Replacement Lifespan Costs

Every charger component has a defined service life, and planning for repairs or replacements is essential for long-term budgeting. Connectors and cables may need replacement every 3–5 years, while control boards and payment modules may last 7–10 years. Understanding these lifespan cycles helps owners forecast future expenses and avoid large, unexpected costs. Factoring depreciation and replacement reserves into the annual maintenance budget ensures financial preparedness as the system ages.

Monitoring, Diagnostics, and Support Costs

Smart EV charging systems use smart monitoring software to detect issues before they affect operations. Automated alerts, remote diagnostics, and data-driven maintenance tracking can reduce labor costs and prevent unnecessary service calls. Many network platforms offer 24/7 monitoring and remote troubleshooting, which helps property owners resolve problems quickly and minimize downtime. Investing in these smart support tools improves efficiency and enhances the reliability of the charging network.

Budgeting, Cost Tracking, and Contingency Funds

A comprehensive maintenance budget should include predictable costs—such as service contracts, labor, and monitoring fees—as well as contingency funds for unexpected repairs or component failures. Effective cost tracking through maintenance logs and performance reports enables property managers to identify spending trends and refine budgets over time. Allocating reserves for emergencies ensures chargers remain operational even when unplanned issues arise, protecting both tenant trust and long-term ROI.

Software Costs

EV charging software costs include licensing, connectivity, feature upgrades, integration, and support—key factors that shape total operating expenses, scalability, and long-term system value. The software layer is what enables access control, billing, monitoring, and performance optimiza-

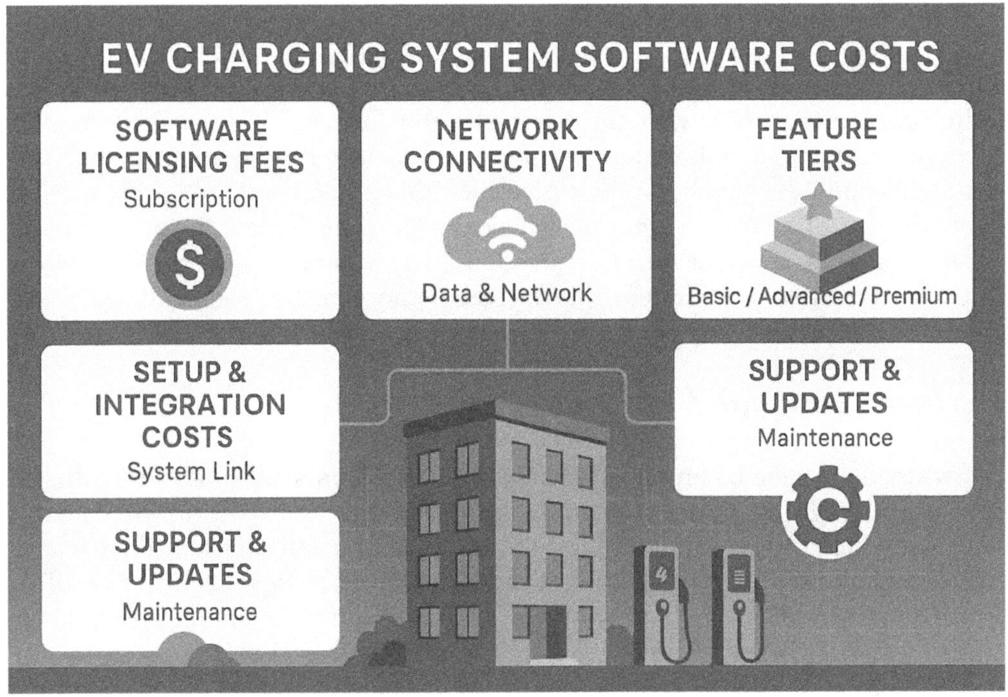

EV Charging Systems for Apartments Software Costs

tion, making it a critical part of any apartment charging system's operational strategy. Understanding how these costs are structured helps property owners budget effectively and avoid unexpected expenses over time.

Software Licensing Fees

Most EV charging management platforms operate under software licensing models that may charge per charger, per site, or per user. Licensing fees can be billed monthly or annually and often bundle essential services such as network access, data storage, reporting tools, and technical support. While these recurring costs can range significantly depending on the vendor and features, they are vital for maintaining reliable system performance, user authentication, and payment processing. Owners should confirm whether licensing fees scale with charger quantity or user volume to plan for future expansion.

Network Connectivity Costs

Network connectivity fees cover the infrastructure that keeps chargers online and integrated with management platforms. These costs typically include real-time data hosting, payment processing, remote monitoring, and firmware updates. Some vendors also include access to mobile apps or web dashboards, allowing residents to locate and activate chargers easily. Owners should confirm what's included in the service—such as network uptime guarantees or SIM card data costs—and whether the provider offers redundant communication options to ensure reliability.

Feature Tiers and Add-Ons

Software platforms often provide tiered service levels that define available functionality. Basic plans may include monitoring and user access control, while advanced tiers add load management, billing automation, fleet tracking, or reporting analytics. Property owners should review each tier carefully to understand which features are standard and which require add-on licenses or upgrades. Recognizing these distinctions early helps prevent unplanned cost escalation as operational needs evolve or as resident demand for additional services increases.

Setup and Integration Costs

Beyond licensing, apartment owners must consider the initial setup and integration expenses for connecting EV charging software with property management systems, smart meters, and energy management platforms. These integrations can streamline billing, automate reporting, and align charging usage with tenant accounts. However, additional configuration work or custom development may be required. It's also important to assess scalability—whether adding more chargers or sites will trigger extra software fees, new licensing, or per-port activation charges.

Support, Updates, and Renewals

Ongoing software maintenance and support are essential to ensure system security and performance. Annual or monthly fees may include bug fixes, software updates, cybersecurity enhancements, and customer support access. Owners should verify the specifics of their support package, including response times and update frequency. Renewal terms, cancellation policies, and potential price adjustments after the first contract period should be reviewed in advance to maintain predictable costs and prevent unexpected increases.

Network Service Fees

Network service fees represent the ongoing operational costs required to keep EV charging systems connected, secure, and functioning efficiently. These fees typically cover essential services such as monitoring, payment processing, data analytics, and software updates. Because pricing models and service quality can vary widely among vendors, apartment owners must evaluate fee structures, uptime guarantees, and contract terms carefully to ensure they're getting reliable performance and fair value.

EV Charging Network Services

A comprehensive EV charging network service supports the day-to-day operation of chargers by enabling remote monitoring, payment processing, data analytics, user authentication, and system updates. These cloud-based services allow property managers to track usage, manage access for residents and guests, and receive automated maintenance alerts. Reliable network connectivity is critical to maintaining charger uptime, ensuring smooth user experiences, and enabling revenue collection without manual oversight.

Customer Support

Customer support is critical for EV charging in apartment communities because it keeps residents informed, reduces frustration, and ensures issues are resolved quickly. Without proper support, residents often become confused about charging procedures, payment issues, or equipment behavior, and they end up calling or visiting the front office for help. This disrupts property operations and creates unnecessary stress for both staff and resi-

EV Charging Systems at Apartments Network and Service Fees

dents. A platform such as Chargemate.ai provides direct support for residents, answers common questions, and resolves many problems automatically, which keeps users satisfied and prevents front office staff from being overwhelmed with EV related issues. Reliable support improves the overall charging experience, increases resident confidence in the system, and protects the property team from repeated interruptions.

Network Service Fee Structures

Network fee structures depend heavily on the vendor's business model and the scope of services included. Common options include per-charger, per-site, or per-user pricing, billed on a monthly or annual basis. Some providers offer multi-year discounts for long-term commitments, while others may include variable or hidden charges such as activation fees, reactivation costs, or communication SIM card data expenses. Understanding these details upfront helps apartment owners avoid unexpected increases and ensures accurate budgeting for the full lifecycle of the system.

Revenue Systems Fee Integration

Network service fees are often tied to how payment and revenue systems are integrated. Many platforms bundle transaction processing costs—covering credit card or app-based payment fees—into their network subscriptions. Property owners should clarify whether revenue is distributed directly to the owner, through a vendor wallet, or via a third-party processor, as this affects both payout timelines and transparency. Integration with property management systems can streamline resident billing and access control, reducing administrative labor and improving financial tracking.

Network Service Quality

The value of network service fees depends largely on the quality and reliability of the network itself. Key performance indicators include uptime guarantees—often stated as a percentage (e.g., 98–99.9%)—and response times under Service Level Agreements (SLAs). High-quality networks ensure continuous charger availability, fast troubleshooting, and responsive support. Properties should review SLAs carefully to confirm what service levels are guaranteed and what remedies are provided in cases of extended downtime or service interruption.

Service Terms and Exit Clauses

Because network service fees are recurring operational costs, it's essential to review contract duration, renewal conditions, and exit clauses before signing. Some agreements automatically renew or include escalating fees after the first term. Others may impose penalties for early termination or equipment transfer. Apartment owners should ensure contracts provide flexibility to switch providers if performance or pricing becomes unfavorable. Transparent terms and clear exit options help maintain control over long-term operating costs and service quality.

EV Charging System Insurance Costs

EV charging system insurance costs depend on multiple factors including coverage type, liability protection, and compliance with safety and maintenance standards. These elements influence overall premiums, deductibles, and the availability of business interruption protection. For apartment complex owners, understanding insurance requirements and cost drivers is essential to protect both the property and residents while maintaining long-term financial stability.

Coverage Types and Policy Integration

Apartment owners must first determine how EV charging systems are classified under existing property and liability insurance policies. In some cases, chargers are covered as part of general building equipment, while in others they may require a standalone equipment or technology policy to protect against damage, theft, vandalism, or malfunction. Reviewing coverage with an insurer ensures that the EV infrastructure is properly listed and valued, preventing gaps in protection and ensuring claims are handled smoothly in the event of loss.

Surprising Fact - *EV charging stations introduce new insurance risks, but smart mitigation may lower premiums. Because chargers add exposure to vandalism, fire, and user injury, many standard property insurance policies do not automatically cover EVSE infrastructure, and premiums may increase when chargers are installed. However, properties that implement documented safety protocols, add real-time equipment monitoring, and use the charger's existing network to support video surveillance and well-lit charging zones may actually qualify for reduced insurance costs — turning a potential risk into a risk-controlled asset.*

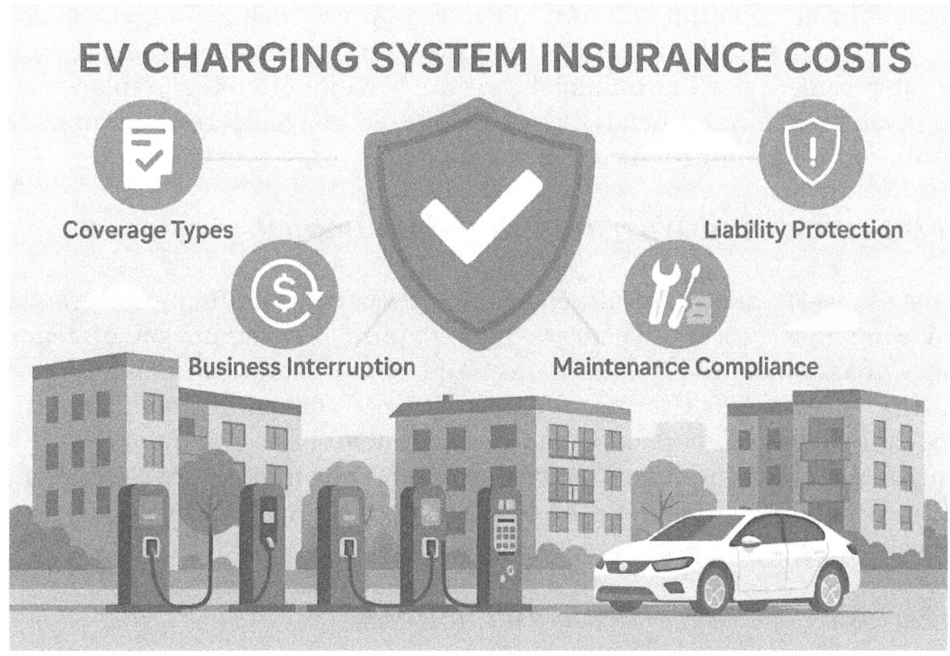

EV Charging System at Apartments Insurance Costs

Liability and Accident Coverage

Because EV chargers are interactive, electrical devices used by the public, they introduce new potential risks that standard property insurance may not fully address. These include electrical shock, trip hazards, equipment misuse, or vehicle damage during charging. Apartment owners should confirm that their general liability coverage extends to these risks and that limits are sufficient to cover potential claims involving residents, guests, or service personnel. Having comprehensive liability protection helps safeguard both the property and ownership from financial exposure.

Business Interruption Protection

An unexpected charger outage, power failure, or equipment malfunction can temporarily halt operations and reduce revenue from usage fees or rental premiums. Business interruption insurance provides compensation for lost income during downtime related to covered events such as fire, storm damage, or vandalism. This coverage can also extend to income loss from halted EV operations, ensuring financial continuity while repairs or replacements are completed. For properties that depend on charging revenue or brand reputation, this protection can be invaluable.

Maintenance and Warranty Premium Impact

Insurance costs are often influenced by a property's maintenance practices and compliance record. Insurers may require documentation of regular inspections, preventive maintenance, and compliance with standards such as NEC Article 625 (Electric Vehicle Power Transfer System) and ADA accessibility requirements. Demonstrating adherence to manufacturer warranties and code compliance can reduce premiums and improve claim eligibility. Well-documented maintenance practices show insurers that risks are actively managed, leading to lower rates and more favorable terms.

Premium Cost Drivers and Deductibles

EV charger insurance premiums are calculated based on equipment value, installation environment, usage frequency, and overall risk exposure. Chargers located outdoors or in high-traffic public areas typically have higher premiums due to increased risk of impact, vandalism, or weather damage. Policies may include deductibles that balance premium cost and claim responsibility. Owners should work with insurers to identify the right coverage limits and deductible levels that protect against major losses without inflating annual costs.

Budgets

Creating a comprehensive EV charging system budget is essential for apartment property owners seeking to ensure financial sustainability and measurable return on investment (ROI). Effective budgeting must consider total ownership costs, available funding, revenue opportunities, maintenance needs, and data tracking. By proactively planning for both predictable and

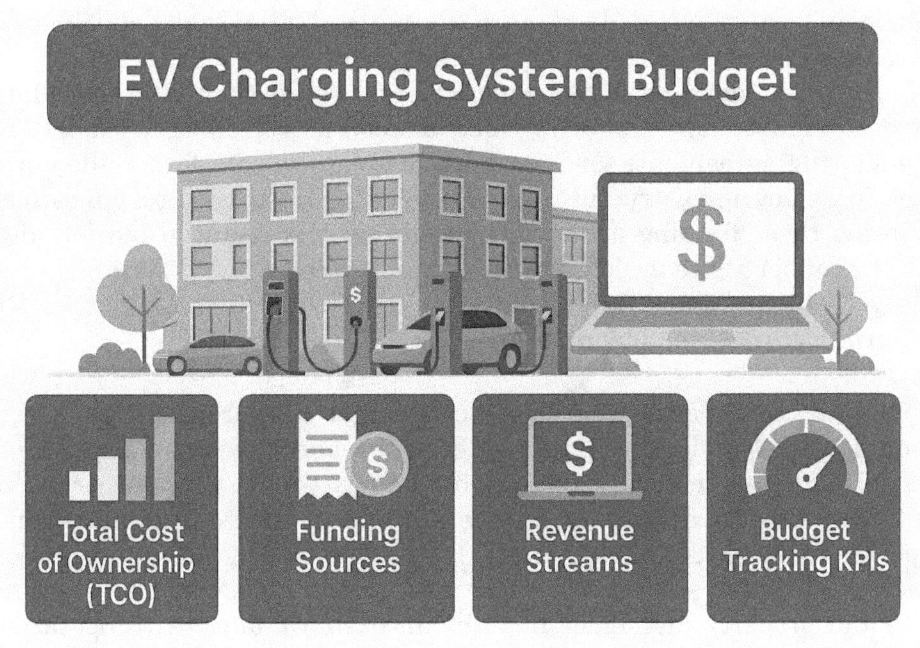

EV Charging System at Apartments Budget

variable expenses, owners can maintain system reliability, maximize efficiency, and align costs with long-term property goals.

Total Cost of Ownership (TCO)

The total cost of ownership encompasses all financial components of an EV charging system throughout its lifecycle. This includes initial hardware and installation costs—such as chargers, trenching, wiring, and electrical upgrades—along with network setup, permitting, and inspection fees. Ongoing operational costs like software subscriptions, connectivity, and preventive maintenance must also be factored in. Over time, owners should plan for depreciation, component replacements, and technology upgrades to maintain performance and compliance as systems evolve.

Funding and Financing Options

Apartment owners can reduce upfront costs and accelerate deployment by leveraging a mix of funding and financing programs. These may include utility incentives, federal or state grants, and tax credits that offset installation expenses. Additionally, financing models such as EV charger leasing, revenue-sharing agreements, or "charging-as-a-service" platforms allow properties to deploy infrastructure with little or no initial capital investment. Exploring these funding avenues ensures that the financial burden aligns with the property's cash flow and investment strategy.

Revenues and Cost Recovery

EV charging can operate as either a cost center or a profit center, depending on how it is managed. To recover costs, property owners can implement user-based pricing models—charging per kilowatt-hour, per hour, or per session—supported by automated billing systems. Strategic load management helps reduce peak demand charges, further improving profitability. Some owners also choose shared cost structures, dividing expenses between residents and property management to balance affordability with operational sustainability.

Maintenance, Monitoring, and Upgrades

A well-maintained EV charging system supports both reliability and budget stability. Apartment properties should plan for annual maintenance contracts, software license renewals, and monitoring tools that prevent costly downtime. Over time, budgeting for component replacements, firmware updates, and potential system expansion—such as adding more chargers or upgrading to faster models—ensures long-term adaptability. Including these items in annual budgets prevents financial surprises and extends the system's useful life.

Budget Tracking and Reporting

Continuous budget tracking and performance reporting are key to optimizing EV charging investments. Collecting data on usage rates, cost per kilowatt-hour, revenue per port, and system uptime allows owners to identify inefficiencies and refine future budgets. Setting measurable key performance indicators (KPIs) helps evaluate the program's success and supports ROI justification to stakeholders. Accurate, data-driven reporting ensures transparency and enables better financial forecasting for future EV infrastructure projects.

Chapter 8

EV Charging System Funding, Grants and Incentives

EV charging system funding types help apartment owners reduce upfront installation costs, improve project feasibility, and accelerate deployment by leveraging financial support such as grants, incentives, tax credits, partnerships, and flexible financing options. Understanding these funding categories allows owners to design a cost-effective project strategy that maximizes external support while minimizing the financial burden on the property.

Grants

Grants are non-repayable funds provided by federal, state, local, or utility programs to support EV charger adoption. These programs often target multifamily housing, underserved communities, or sustainable infrastructure projects. Grants can significantly reduce upfront expenses by covering portions of equipment purchases, installation work, or electrical upgrades. Because grants are competitive and require detailed applications, property owners benefit from early planning, proper documentation, and partnering with experienced integrators to increase approval success.

Incentives

Incentives are programs offered by utilities, manufacturers, and occasionally state agencies to encourage EV charging deployment. These may include

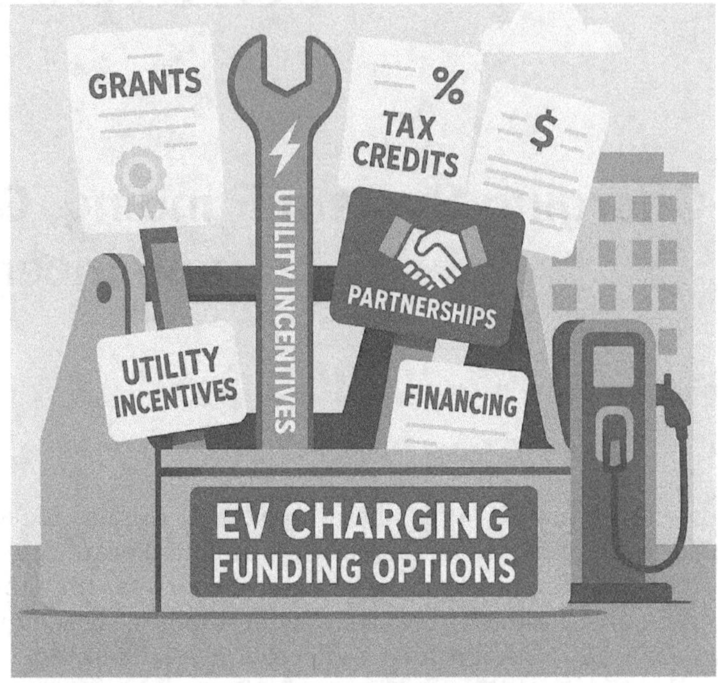

EV Charging System for Apartment Complexes Funding Options

equipment discounts, reduced electric rates for EV charging, bill credits, or rebates tied to participation in demand-response programs. Incentives help offset ongoing operational costs and can reduce the long-term cost of energy delivered through the chargers. Understanding available utility incentive programs—and their technical requirements—ensures owners capture the full financial advantage.

Tax Credits and Rebates

Tax credits and rebates return a percentage of EV charging project costs to property owners either through tax reductions or cash reimbursements after installation. Federal tax credits (such as the 30C credit in the U.S.) and various state and municipal rebate programs can significantly lower net project expenses. Owners must meet certain eligibility, installation, and documentation requirements to qualify. Proper coordination with accountants and installers ensures that all qualifying expenses—equipment, labor, and electrical upgrades—are captured for maximum benefit.

Partnerships

Partnerships allow apartment owners to collaborate with charger operators, utilities, advertisers, or EV service companies to share installation or operating costs. In some cases, third-party operators may cover most or all of the expenses in exchange for managing the chargers, setting pricing, or retaining a portion of revenue. Other partnerships may include shared ownership, branding opportunities, or pilot programs with utilities seeking to expand EV infrastructure. These arrangements reduce financial risk and provide professional management support.

Financing

Financing options allow property owners to spread the cost of EV charging projects over time, making installations more affordable without large upfront expenditures. Common financing models include traditional loans, equipment leases, on-bill financing through the utility, or energy-as-a-service agreements that bundle installation, maintenance, and operations into a predictable monthly payment. Financing helps match project expenses with long-term revenue from charging fees or amenity value, improving return on investment and budgeting flexibility.

EV Charging Funding Experts

EV charging funding experts play a crucial role in helping apartment owners navigate the complex landscape of incentives, financing options, compliance reporting, and utility coordination. Their specialized knowledge ensures properties maximize available funding opportunities, reduce capital expenses, maintain regulatory compliance, and achieve stronger long-term financial performance. By leveraging expert guidance, owners can avoid common mistakes, accelerate project timelines, and secure significantly higher returns on their EV charging investments.

EV Charging System Funding Experts

Complex Incentive Programs

Funding consultants are highly skilled at identifying and securing the wide range of federal, state, local, and utility incentive programs that many property owners may not know exist. These incentives often have strict eligibility criteria, application deadlines, and documentation requirements that change frequently. Experts track program updates, prepare application materials, and ensure compliance with all procedural rules. Their familiarity with program scoring criteria and submission standards dramatically increases approval success rates and maximizes the total incentive value captured by the property.

***Surprising Fact** — EV charging grant and incentive consultants can find and help stack incentives to slash installation costs by 50–70% or more. By using a specialized grants and incentives consultant, apartment properties can unlock multiple overlapping funding sources — federal infrastructure grants, utility rebates, make-ready credits, state/local programs, and federal tax incentives. When combined strategically, this layered funding approach can reduce the out-of-pocket cost of each charging port by half to more than two-thirds, turning a high-capital project into a financially accessible investment.*

Financing and Ownership Options

EV charging funding experts help owners evaluate multiple project financing and ownership structures, such as lease-to-own, energy-as-a-service, revenue-sharing partnerships, or fully third-party-funded installations. These models can significantly reduce or even eliminate upfront capital expenditures, shifting costs into predictable monthly payments or shared revenue arrangements. By analyzing property-specific needs—such as cash flow, ownership preferences, and operational responsibilities—experts recommend the best structure to minimize financial risk and deliver optimal long-term value.

Grant Compliance and Reporting

Once grants or incentives are awarded, properties must meet strict compliance requirements to maintain eligibility and avoid repayment risks. Funding experts manage these administrative responsibilities by organizing documentation, tracking energy-usage reports, documenting charger uptime, and completing post-installation verification. They ensure properties remain compliant with program conditions such as community-access rules, sustainability commitments, or ongoing maintenance standards. This consistent oversight protects funding, supports audits, and reduces administrative burdens on property staff.

Utility and Vendor Coordination

Funding consultants often act as project liaisons between property owners, utilities, installation contractors, and EV charging vendors. Their role includes aligning the project with utility interconnection rules, optimizing electric rate structures, coordinating transformer or panel upgrades, and advising on load-management or smart-charging strategies. By handling technical and administrative coordination across multiple organizations, experts streamline communication, minimize delays, and keep the project on schedule and within budget.

Optimizing ROI

By strategically combining grants, rebates, incentives, financing tools, and efficient project management, EV funding experts significantly shorten the project's payback period and increase overall return on investment. They ensure that no available funding source is overlooked and that all cost-reduction strategies are layered effectively. Their financial modeling tools help property owners forecast revenues, operational costs, utilization trends, and long-term asset value, enabling informed decision-making and stronger financial outcomes.

Grants

EV charging grants help apartment owners significantly reduce installation and upgrade costs by leveraging federal, state, local, and utility funding. However, success requires understanding which grants apply to multifamily properties, adhering to complex eligibility requirements, submitting detailed applications, and maintaining long-term compliance with post-award obligations. Careful planning and expert guidance can help properties maximize available funding while avoiding administrative pitfalls.

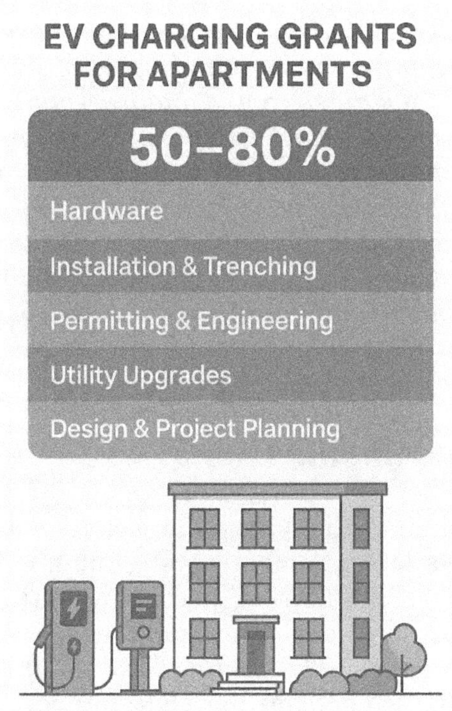

EV Charging Systems for Apartment Grants

Grant Types and Eligibility

Not all EV charging grants are available to every apartment property, making it essential for owners to understand which programs apply to multifamily housing. Eligible programs may include federal initiatives such as NEVI (National Electric Vehicle Infrastructure), EPA and DOE clean transportation grants, state energy office programs, municipal sustainability grants, and utility-administered rebates. Eligibility often depends on factors such as the number of residents served, property type, affordability levels, public accessibility, geographic location, income-qualified housing requirements, or proximity to designated transportation corridors. Properly identifying applicable programs ensures owners pursue opportunities that align with their property profile.

Surprising Fact *- EV charging grants and incentives tend to shrink as adoption rises. Globally, early EV growth is often fueled by generous subsidies for both charging infrastructure and vehicles. But as EVs move from emerging technology to mainstream standard, many governments begin reducing or phasing out financial incentives. This pattern is already visible in several advanced markets. Norway, for example, saw EV market share jump from ~3% of new vehicles in 2012 to nearly 89% in 2024, after which policymakers started rolling back key incentives — including VAT exemptions, toll and ferry discounts, and purchase-tax waivers. (ev.com) Across Europe, multiple countries have similarly reduced or eliminated EV purchase bonuses and charging-infrastructure grants, shifting funding instead to grid upgrades and heavy-transport electrification.*

Covered Costs and Funding Limits

Each grant program defines the types of project costs it will support and the maximum funding available. Some grants reimburse hardware purchases only, while others cover installation, permitting, utility service upgrades, design engineering, or even long-term maintenance. Many programs offer partial cost coverage—commonly funding 50% to 80% of the total eligible project cost—and may include caps per charging port or per property site. Understanding these limits helps owners build accurate financial models and determine how much of the project budget will remain out-of-pocket.

Application Process and Timeline

Grant applications often require extensive documentation, including site plans, charger specifications, contractor cost estimates, proof of property ownership, and explanations of tenant or community benefits. Some applications must include letters of support, environmental assessments, or utility interconnection plans. Timelines vary significantly, ranging from just a few months to more than a year from submission to award. Owners must plan project schedules carefully, ensuring that application preparation, review periods, and award cycles align with installation timelines and property goals.

Compliance, Reporting and Obligations

Most EV charging grants require long-term compliance after funds are awarded. Obligations may include maintaining uptime or reliability thresholds (e.g., 97% availability), providing public access to chargers, posting required signage, reporting usage data to government agencies, or participating in open-data networks. Some programs require multi-year commitments of 5–10 years, during which owners must demonstrate ongoing compliance through annual or quarterly reports. Failure to meet these requirements can trigger penalties or repayment (clawbacks) of grant funds, making it essential to plan for ongoing administrative responsibilities.

Grant Writers and Consultants

Because EV charging grants are competitive and technically complex, many apartment owners benefit from partnering with grant writers, energy consultants, or EV funding specialists. These professionals help identify the most financially beneficial programs, prepare compelling applications, create compliant documentation packages, and coordinate with utilities, vendors, and contractors to ensure all technical specifications meet grant requirements. Their expertise significantly improves approval rates and helps owners avoid costly mistakes or missed opportunities.

Incentives

EV charging incentives help apartment owners significantly reduce both installation and operating costs by leveraging utility rebates, time-of-use rate programs, renewable energy credits, and manufacturer or network partner discounts. These incentives complement grants and financing programs, enabling properties to deploy EV charging infrastructure more affordably while improving long-term operational efficiency and ROI.

Utility Rebates

Electric utilities often provide substantial rebates and infrastructure support programs specifically for EV charging installations. Unlike grants,

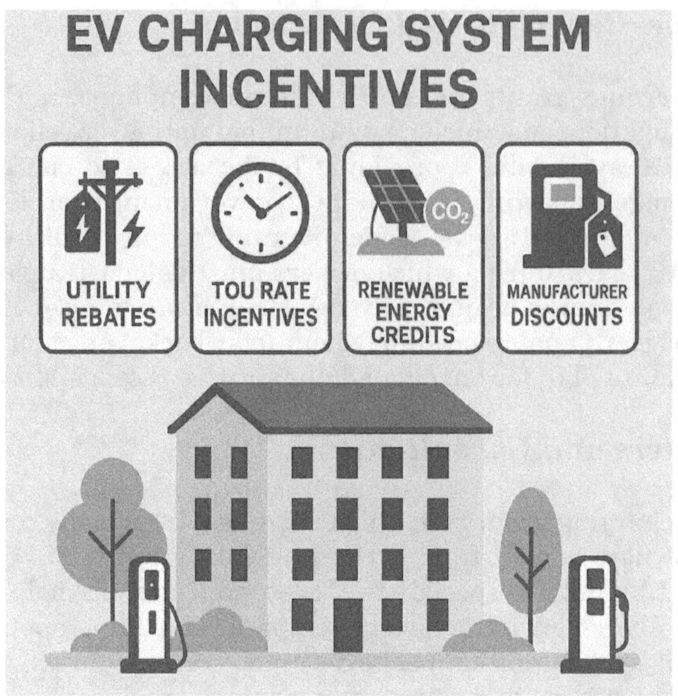

EV Charging System Incentives

these incentives are typically easier to qualify for and are designed to encourage electrification within the utility's service area. Programs may cover partial or full equipment costs, reimburse installation expenses, or include "make-ready" contributions such as upgrading transformers, panels, conduit, or wiring to charger locations. Utility rebates can significantly reduce upfront capital requirements and accelerate project timelines, making EV charging installations more accessible for multifamily properties.

Time-of-Use (TOU) Rates Mitigation

Many utilities now offer preferential EV charging rate plans that reduce electricity costs during off-peak hours—sometimes by 20–40%. These Time-of-Use (TOU) programs encourage lower-cost, grid-friendly charging behavior. Some utilities also provide demand charge reduction incentives for properties using smart load management or dynamic load balancing systems. By adopting TOU-optimized charging schedules and intelligent energy controls, apartment complexes can dramatically lower operational expenses long-term, improving cost predictability without relying on direct grant funding.

Renewable Energy Incentives

Apartment properties that integrate EV charging with solar generation, battery storage, or microgrid systems may qualify for renewable energy incentives and sustainability-based financial programs. These benefits may include state or utility renewable energy rebates, Investment Tax Credit (ITC) enhancements, or participation in carbon credit programs where property-generated renewable energy is monetized. In some regions, third-party aggregators purchase carbon credits or renewable energy certificates (RECs), creating a recurring revenue stream that helps offset system operating costs.

Manufacturer and Company Incentives

EV charger manufacturers, network operators, and energy service companies frequently offer additional incentives to encourage adoption. These may include promotional discounts, free or discounted hardware with multi-year service contracts, reduced network or subscription fees, revenue-sharing programs, or co-branded marketing partnerships that increase property value. These offers can greatly reduce startup costs or ongoing operational fees while providing enhanced features, improved support, or premium services at minimal additional expense.

Tax Credits

EV charging system tax credits can significantly reduce project costs through federal, state, and local incentives—combined with accelerated depreciation, credit transferability options, and proper documentation and timing requirements—to maximize financial benefits for apartment property owners.

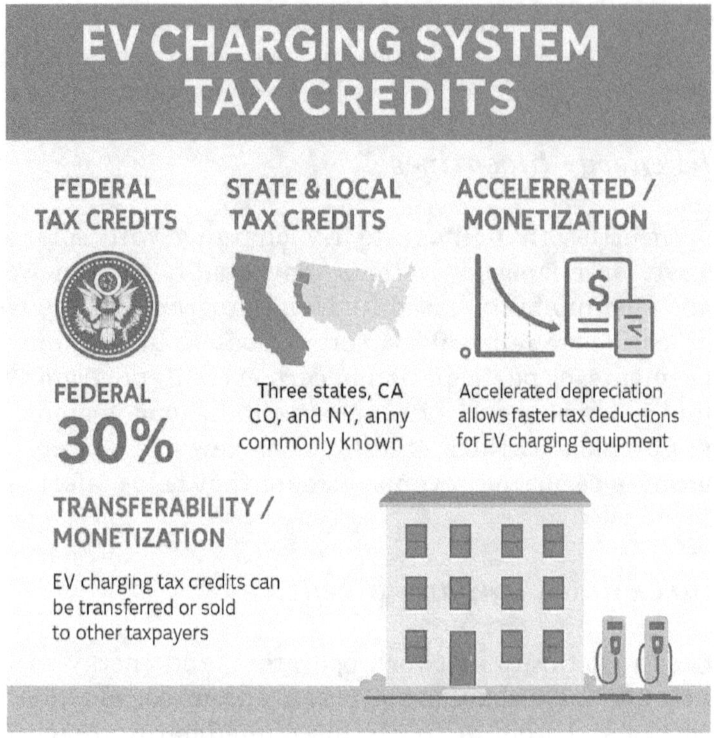

EV Charging System Tax Credits

Federal and National Tax Credits

Federal and national tax credits provide some of the most substantial financial benefits for apartment properties installing EV charging systems. In the United States, programs like the IRS Section 30C Alternative Fuel Vehicle Refueling Property Credit can cover up to 30% of eligible project costs, including equipment, installation, and electrical upgrades. These credits help lower the effective cost of deploying charging infrastructure and serve as foundational incentives that can be combined with state or utility programs to significantly reduce out-of-pocket expenses.

State, Province, and Local Tax Credits

Many states, provinces, and local governments offer their own EV charging tax credit programs to further encourage sustainable transportation and multifamily EV adoption. These regional incentives often provide an additional 10–35% of eligible project costs, with states like Colorado, New York, and California offering particularly strong support. Local credits can target specific property types, income-qualified housing, or public-access chargers, allowing owners to layer multiple incentives for deeper savings.

Accelerated Depreciation

In addition to direct tax credits, apartment owners can use accelerated depreciation provisions to reduce taxable income more quickly. Under tax regulations, EV charging equipment can often be depreciated over five years rather than longer asset schedules. In some cases, the equipment may qualify for immediate expensing under Section 179 or bonus depreciation rules. Accelerated depreciation provides substantial early-year tax benefits, improving project cash flow and strengthening overall ROI.

Credit Monetization and Transferability

For property owners who lack sufficient tax liability to fully use EV charging tax credits, monetization or transferability programs can create immediate financial value. Certain clean energy credits can be transferred or sold to other taxpayers, converting the credit into cash that can be reinvested into the project or used to offset other property expenses. Credit transferability expands access to tax incentives, especially for nonprofit housing providers or properties with limited taxable income.

Documentation, Timing, and Compliance

Claiming EV charging tax credits requires thorough documentation and adherence to strict timing rules. Owners must maintain detailed records such as itemized invoices, receipts, equipment certifications, contractor documentation, and proof that the chargers are fully operational. Tax credits must generally be claimed in the year the charging system is placed in service, making coordination with installers, accountants, and property managers essential. Proper documentation ensures compliance and protects the owner during audits or incentive verification reviews.

Shocking Factoid *- An entire EV charging tax credit can disappear over a single missed detail. Even a fully installed, operational, and compliant charging system can be denied if paperwork is incomplete or eligibility rules are misunderstood. A missing prevailing-wage declaration, an incorrectly identified census-tract GEOID, or incomplete installation records is enough to void the claim entirely. For multi-port apartment deployments, that could mean hundreds of thousands of dollars in lost tax credit value. Some consultants have errors and omissions insurance (E&O insurance) that could cover legal defense costs or client losses and damages.*

Preparing Grant Applications

Preparing grant applications requires careful eligibility assessment, detailed documentation, accurate budgeting, and a structured compliance plan to improve the chances of securing EV charging funds and successfully managing post-award obligations. Apartment owners who understand these requirements and prepare proactively are far more likely to win competitive funding and keep projects on schedule.

Grant Eligibility and Preparation

Before beginning an application, apartment owners must confirm that their property and project meet the eligibility requirements for the specific grant program. Eligibility factors may include property type (multifamily residential versus commercial), geographic location within qualifying census tracts, minimum or maximum property size, or whether chargers must provide public access. Some grants require installations in disadvantaged or low-income communities or mandate compliance with local zoning, building codes, or permitting standards. Establishing eligibility early prevents wasted effort and ensures the project aligns with program goals.

Required Documentation and Estimates

Most EV charging grants require extensive technical and financial documentation, often including site plans, electrical designs, equipment specifications, contractor bids, utility interconnection details, and detailed cost

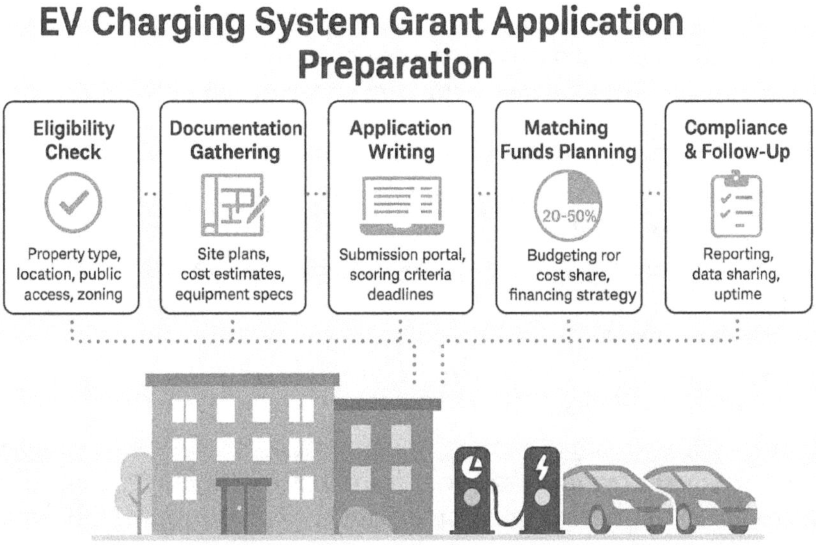

EV Charging System Grant Application Preparation

estimates. Providing accurate, clearly referenced information strengthens the application and demonstrates project readiness—a key criterion in many competitive programs. Collecting this documentation early also ensures consistency across project partners, including contractors, utilities, and design engineers.

Application Writing and Submission

Each grant program has specific formatting rules, scoring criteria, and submission processes that must be followed precisely. Federal programs like NEVI or DOE grants often require narrative responses, community impact statements, and detailed technical appendices. State and utility-administered programs may use standardized online portals with strict word limits or upload requirements. Some programs require a sponsoring entity—such as a utility, city, consultant, or nonprofit partner—to submit the application on behalf of the property. Understanding these rules helps owners prepare complete, compliant applications that maximize scoring potential.

Matching Funds and Budget Planning

Most EV charging grant programs require cost-sharing or matching contributions from the property owner, typically covering 20–50% of total project costs. Apartment owners must develop a clear budget that accounts for both grant-covered and owner-funded portions, including equipment, installation, electrical upgrades, engineering design, and long-term operational costs. Well-structured budgets increase application strength and demonstrate financial readiness—often a critical scoring factor in competitive funding programs.

Post-Submission Follow-Up and Compliance

After submitting a grant application, apartment owners should be prepared for follow-up requests from program administrators, including clarification questions, revision requests, or supplemental documentation. If awarded, the grant will include ongoing compliance requirements such as performance reporting, uptime tracking, energy-use data sharing, signage installation, and long-term operational commitments. Many programs also require periodic inspections or documentation updates. Establishing a compliance plan early helps ensure the property meets all post-award obligations and avoids penalties or funding clawbacks.

Future Grants and Incentive Trends

Future EV charging grants and incentives are expected to shift from broad installation subsidies to performance-based, equity-focused, and smart-grid-integrated programs—making early adoption and strategic partnerships increasingly critical for apartment owners who want to maximize funding opportunities before support declines.

Declining Incentives as EV Adoption Increases

As EV adoption accelerates, incentives in many regions are beginning to phase out, following patterns seen in mature EV markets like Norway and parts of Europe. Early government programs often prioritize rapid infra-

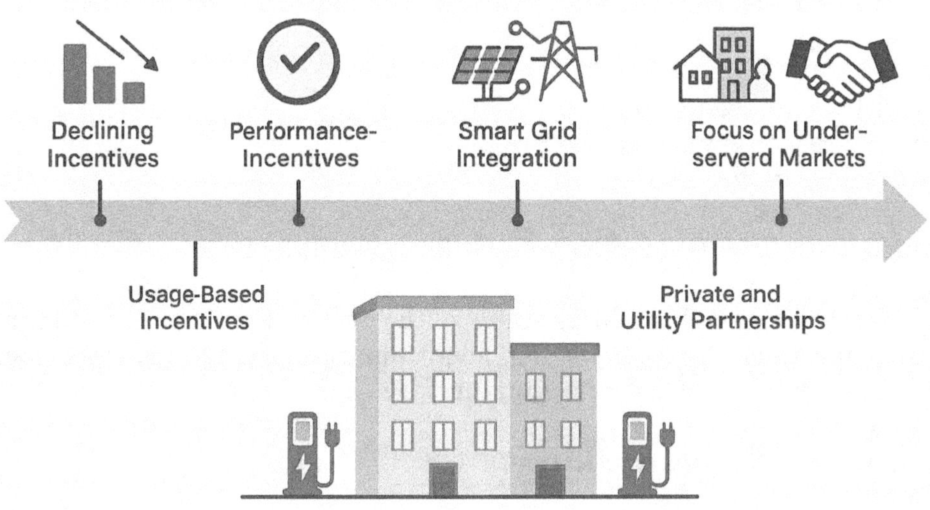

EV Charging Systems Future Grants and Incentive Trends

structure growth by subsidizing equipment and installation costs, but these subsidies typically taper as market adoption reaches critical mass. For apartment owners, this means the strongest financial support is available now, and waiting may lead to higher out-of-pocket costs and fewer rebate opportunities.

Shift to Performance-Based Incentives

Future funding programs are expected to shift toward performance-based models that reward measurable results—such as high charger uptime, efficient energy use, compliance with open standards, or verified carbon reduction. Instead of simply paying for chargers to be installed, agencies may compensate properties for demonstrating real operational impact. This shift encourages apartment owners to choose reliable equipment, implement strong maintenance plans, and use data-driven systems that allow for transparent reporting.

Smart Grid and Energy Program Integration

Grants and incentives will increasingly be tied to smart-grid capabilities and advanced energy management. Programs may prioritize properties that utilize:

- Smart load management
- Demand-response participation
- Solar integration
- Battery storage
- Vehicle-to-grid (V2G) or vehicle-to-building (V2B) technology

These integrations help utilities stabilize the grid and reduce peak demand, making apartment properties that adopt smart-charging strategies more attractive candidates for future funding.

Focus on Underserved Markets

As EV infrastructure becomes more common in commercial and single-family sectors, policymakers are redirecting resources toward underserved segments—including multifamily housing, low-income communities, and rural regions. Future incentives will likely reward projects that address these infrastructure gaps, improve equitable access to EV charging, and support environmental justice goals. Apartment properties located in disadvantaged census tracts may receive priority scoring, enhanced rebates, or simplified application processes.

Increased Private Funding and Utility Partnerships

With government incentive programs expected to taper over time, utilities, automakers, charging networks, and private investors are likely to play a larger role in EV infrastructure funding. Co-funded programs, infrastructure credits, revenue-sharing models, and turnkey operator-funded installations will become more common. For apartment owners, these partnerships can offset capital costs, simplify operations, and provide long-term financial stability even as public funding declines.

Chapter 9

EV Charging System Regulations

EV charging system regulations ensure that apartment installations are safe, accessible, grid-compatible, and legally compliant. These rules span electrical and building codes, accessibility requirements, zoning and permitting standards, utility interconnection procedures, and environmental and safety mandates. Together, they define how chargers must be installed, labeled, powered, and maintained—while protecting residents, property owners, and local infrastructure from risks associated with improper installation or operation.

Electrical and Building Codes

EV charging systems in apartment complexes must comply with national, state, and local electrical and building codes, with NEC Article 625 serving as the primary standard governing electric vehicle power transfer systems. These requirements address critical design and installation details such as circuit sizing, grounding, conduit sealing, overcurrent protection, wiring methods, load management, and GFCI protection. Compliance ensures the electrical infrastructure supporting the chargers is safe, reliable, and capable of supporting sustained EV charging loads without creating fire or shock hazards.

Disabilities Accessibility Requirements

Federal and local accessibility regulations, including ADA-related rules, require that a defined percentage of EV charging spaces be accessible to users with disabilities. These requirements typically include wider parking spaces, accessible routes, proper curb heights, and reachable charging interfaces that

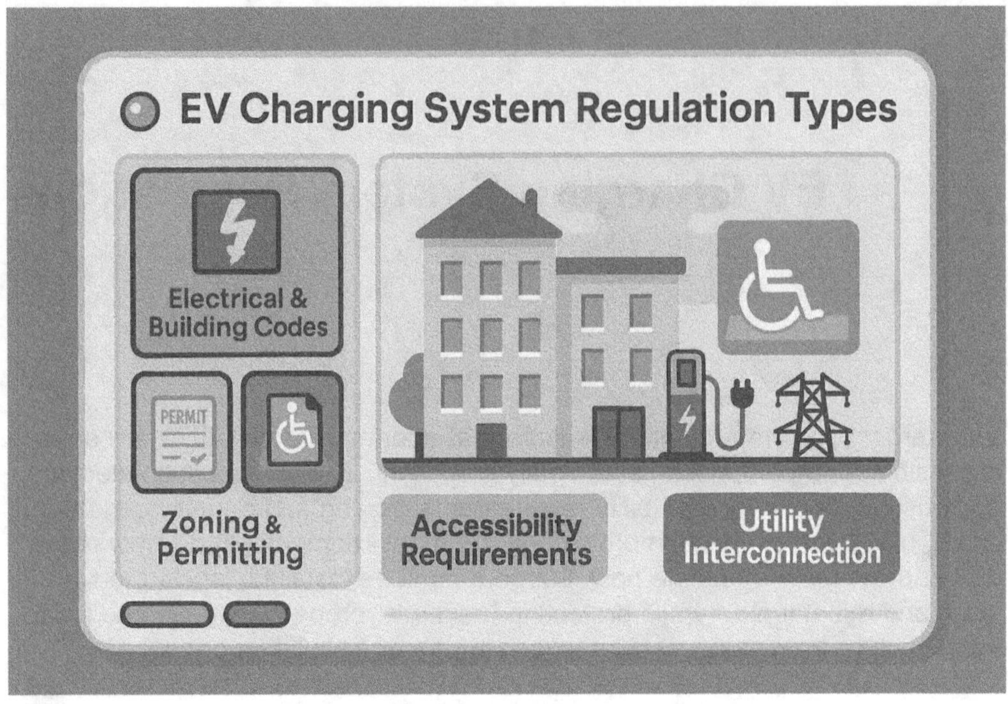

EV Charging System Regulation Types

accommodate wheelchair users and individuals with limited mobility. Ensuring accessibility compliance not only avoids penalties but also supports equitable access to charging resources for all residents and visitors.

Zoning, Permitting, and Local Ordinances

Local governments maintain zoning regulations and permitting processes that dictate where and how EV charging infrastructure can be installed. These rules may influence equipment placement, signage, parking space designation, and lighting, and may impose restrictions on modifications in historic or environmentally sensitive zones. Some cities now mandate a minimum number of EV-ready or EV-capable spaces for multifamily housing, requiring builders and property managers to integrate EV charging infrastructure into long-term development plans.

Utility Interconnection Regulations

Utilities often require EV chargers to meet specific interconnection standards to protect grid stability and ensure adequate service capacity. These standards may include load studies, transformer capacity assessments, panel reviews, and specific metering configurations depending on the charging power level and number of units installed. Utility approval is frequently a critical path item in the project timeline, making early coordination essential for avoiding delays and ensuring chargers operate safely within local grid constraints.

Environmental, Fire, and Safety Standards

Environmental and safety regulations govern how EV charging systems are installed, labeled, operated, and maintained. These include requirements for equipment testing and product certification, often through nationally recognized testing laboratories such as UL or ETL, as well as rules for proper grounding, bollard protection, signage, fire safety clearances, and emergency shutoff labeling. Environmental rules may also cover site disturbance, hazardous materials handling, and stormwater protection during construction, ensuring that installation activities do not negatively impact the surrounding environment.

Federal and National EV Charging Regulations

Federal and national regulations for EV charging systems ensure that apartment properties meet uniform safety, accessibility, environmental, cybersecurity, and tax compliance requirements across the country. These regulations establish baseline standards for how EV chargers must be wired, installed, labeled, protected, and operated. They also define accessibility rules for disabled users, set energy-efficiency and environmental expectations, govern how user data must be secured, and outline the criteria required for tax credits and federal incentive programs. Understanding and adhering to these nationwide requirements helps apartment owners avoid compliance issues, reduce risk, and qualify for substantial financial benefits.

National Electrical Code (NEC) Requirements

The National Electrical Code (NEC) is the primary federal reference standard governing the installation of EV charging equipment in the United States. NEC Article 625 outlines requirements for wiring methods, overcurrent protection, grounding, ventilation, conduit sizing, and general EV supply equipment (EVSE) safety. It establishes the minimum acceptable practices that ensure EV chargers operate safely under varying load conditions and protects residents, property owners, and maintenance personnel from electrical hazards. Compliance with NEC standards is mandatory nationwide and is enforced through permitting and inspection processes.

Disabilities Accessibility Standards

Federal disabilities accessibility standards—including the principles established by the Americans with Disabilities Act (ADA)—ensure equitable access to EV charging stations for individuals with disabilities. These rules require accessible parking spaces, adequate aisle widths, clear and unobstructed routes to the charger, and proper placement of operable parts so that controls, screens, and cables are reachable from a seated or wheelchair position. Many countries have their own versions of ADA-like laws, making accessibility a global regulatory requirement. Apartment owners must integrate these standards into site planning to ensure compliance and to support inclusive charging access.

Energy and Environmental Regulations

National agencies such as the Department of Energy (DOE), Environmental Protection Agency (EPA), and Federal Highway Administration (FHWA) establish environmental and energy-efficiency standards that influence EV charging installations at multifamily properties. These regulations may govern emissions reductions, sustainable design practices, and energy consumption monitoring. Federally funded programs such as the NEVI (National Electric Vehicle Infrastructure) initiative require chargers—especially publicly accessible ones—to meet specific reliability, uptime, and interoperability requirements. These national guidelines help ensure EV charging contributes to broader environmental and climate goals while providing owners access to federal funding opportunities.

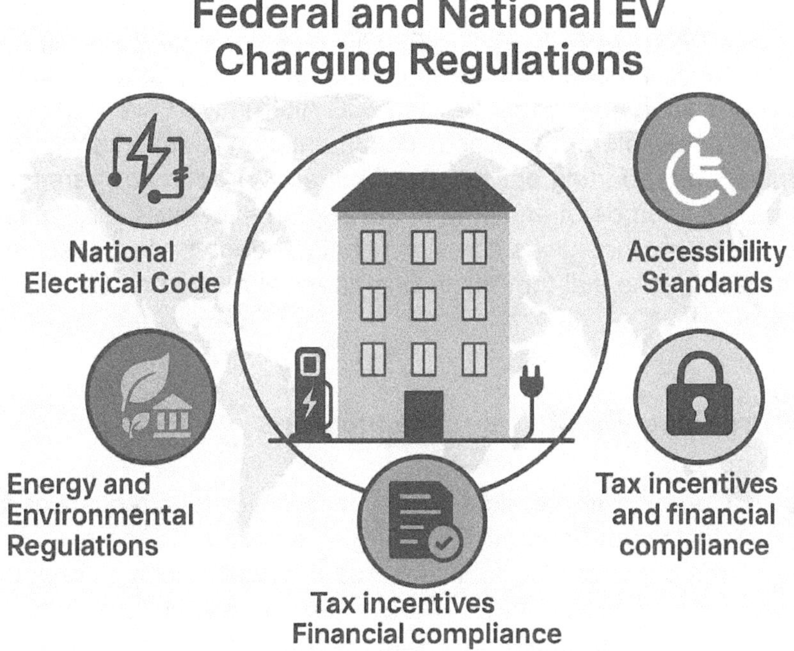

Federal and National EV Charging Regulations

Data Privacy and Cybersecurity Requirements

Federal privacy and cybersecurity standards regulate how EV charging systems must store, transmit, and protect user information. Agencies and frameworks such as the Federal Trade Commission (FTC) and the NIST Cybersecurity Framework require secure data handling practices, including encryption, access controls, vulnerability management, and breach reporting. Because EV chargers collect sensitive data—such as payment credentials, charging behavior, and user identities—multifamily property owners must ensure their charging networks and vendors meet federal cybersecurity expectations to minimize liability and maintain user trust.

Tax and Financial Compliance Standards

Federal tax regulations provide major financial incentives for installing EV charging systems, but these benefits come with strict compliance requirements. Programs such as the IRS Section 30C Alternative Fuel Infrastructure Tax Credit outline eligible project costs, documentation requirements, prevailing wage rules, and reporting obligations. To qualify, property owners must maintain accurate records of equipment, installation expenses, and supporting paperwork. These tax incentives can significantly reduce project costs, making proper compliance essential for maximizing financial returns on EV charging investments.

State and Province EV Charging Regulations

State, provincial, and territorial regulations play a major role in how apartment owners design, install, and operate EV charging systems. These rules build on national standards but introduce additional requirements, such as regional electrical code amendments, EV-ready mandates for new construction, public utility commission rules for metering and load management, environmental policies tied to clean-transportation goals, and incentive eligibility standards for grants and rebates. Understanding these region-specific regulations helps apartment owners avoid compliance issues, qualify for funding, and build EV charging infrastructure that aligns with long-term state or provincial sustainability and transportation objectives.

State Electrical and Building Codes

Many states and provinces adopt their own versions of electrical and building codes, often based on the National Electrical Code (NEC) or national building standards but modified to reflect local conditions, priorities, or enforcement practices. These amendments may affect wiring methods, overcurrent protection requirements, inspection procedures, or the technical specifications required for EV supply equipment. Apartment owners must understand these regional differences because they determine the exact permitting, inspection, and installation requirements for EV charging systems within each jurisdiction.

***Shocking Fact** - Around the world, national and regional energy-transition laws increasingly override private bylaws, HOA rules, and building-association restrictions that would otherwise block residents from installing EV-charging systems. Many countries have introduced "right-to-charge" regulations that legally supersede community covenants, meaning private associations cannot prohibit or unreasonably delay EV-charger approval if minimum safety and installation standards are met.*

EV-Ready Infrastructure Mandates

A growing number of states and provinces require new or significantly renovated multifamily buildings to include a minimum percentage of EV-ready or EV-capable parking spaces. EV-ready mandates typically require installed conduit, wiring, or panel capacity so that chargers can be added later without major construction. EV-capable requirements may only call for future-ready infrastructure or reserved electrical capacity. These mandates ensure new buildings can support future EV adoption and reduce retrofit costs for property owners over time.

Utility Commission Regulations

Public utility commissions at the state or provincial level regulate key aspects of EV charging, including electricity rate structures, demand-response programs, time-of-use pricing requirements, and interconnection standards. These rules influence how apartment owners meter electricity, manage load across multiple chargers, and participate in grid-support programs. In some areas, commissions also regulate whether property owners may resell electricity by the kilowatt-hour, shaping how owners set pricing and billing policies for residents.

State Environmental Policies

Many state and provincial governments implement environmental policies that support transportation electrification, such as clean transportation acts, emissions-reduction mandates, or zero-emission vehicle (ZEV) targets. These programs may provide funding or impose compliance requirements related to EV infrastructure. For apartment owners, this can influence eligibility for grants,

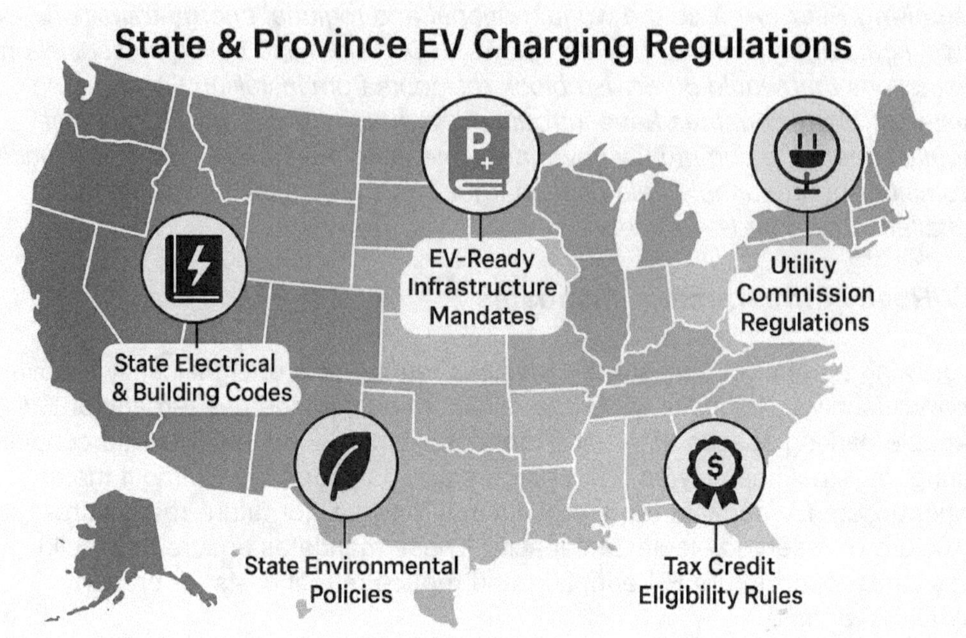

State and Province EV Charging Regulations

preferred design standards, or reporting requirements tied to sustainability metrics. Understanding these environmental policies helps properties align their EV charging projects with state-level climate and air-quality goals.

Tax Credit and Incentive Eligibility Rules

State-level EV infrastructure grants, rebates, and tax incentives often come with detailed application processes, reporting requirements, and operational rules that differ significantly by region. These may include project timelines, approved equipment lists, installation standards, maintenance obligations, and documentation of energy usage or resident benefits. To maximize available funding, apartment owners must follow these state or provincial requirements closely to avoid application rejection or loss of incentive eligibility after installation.

Local and Municipal EV Charging Regulations

Local, municipal, and city regulations shape nearly every on-the-ground aspect of installing EV charging systems at apartment complexes. These rules determine how permits are issued, where chargers may be located, how parking and accessibility must be configured, how local utilities coordinate interconnection, and what incentives or fees may apply. Because cities enforce their own zoning, inspection, and compliance processes, early engagement with local authorities is essential to avoid delays, meet design and accessibility standards, and ensure long-term regulatory compliance.

Permitting and Inspections

Local governments generally oversee the full permitting and inspection process for EV charging installations, making them a critical authority for apartment owners. Municipal permitting offices may require electrical permits, building permits, zoning permits, or combinations of all three depending on the project scope. Inspectors verify that installations comply with electrical codes, safety requirements, and construction standards before the chargers can be energized. Timely submission of accurate documentation and plans is essential because local permitting timelines often define the project's overall schedule.

Surprising Fact - *Many cities now classify EV charging system installations including those at commercial and multifamily apartment properties as priority sustainability projects, which means permits can move through approval pipelines significantly faster than standard building or electrical permits. In areas that have adopted "streamlined EV-charger permitting," developers who once waited months for approval are now getting green-lighted in a matter of weeks, accelerating deployment and reducing project delays.*
Land Use Regulations

Municipal zoning codes dictate how land can be used and may impose restrictions or design requirements for EV charging placements. These rules can influence setback distances, equipment enclosure locations, parking space reallocation, lighting, landscaping, and even aesthetic guidelines to maintain neighborhood character. Some municipalities require signage, screening, or specific design features for EV chargers located in visible public or residential areas. Understanding and complying with these land use rules is key to ensuring approvals and avoiding costly redesigns.

Parking and Accessibility Requirements

Cities often enforce their own versions of accessibility standards that mirror or supplement national ADA-style rules. These may require a specific number of accessible EV charging spaces, defined striping patterns, curb markings, signage, and unobstructed pathways from parking spaces to charger interfaces. Local rules may also address how many spaces can be reserved exclusively for EV charging and what enforcement methods apply to non-EV vehicles parked in those spaces. Proper compliance ensures chargers are accessible to all residents and reduces the risk of municipal fines or complaints.

Electrical Utility Coordination

In many cities, local municipal utility departments or city-managed utility franchises control grid interconnection requirements for EV chargers. They may impose transformer capacity limits, trenching or conduit installation standards, specific meter configurations, or review and approval of load studies before work can begin. Each utility may also have its own timelines and inspection processes. Early coordination with the local utility helps apartment owners avoid delays and ensures the site's electrical infrastructure can safely support EV charging loads.

Local Incentives, Fees, and Enforcement Policies

Many municipalities offer their own EV-friendly programs such as rebates, permit fee reductions, expedited permitting, or sustainability grants for properties installing EV infrastructure. Conversely, some cities impose parking enforcement policies, usage fees, or penalties related to improper charger installation or non-compliant signage. Understanding these local incentives and enforcement mechanisms helps apartment owners budget accurately and leverage available benefits while avoiding fines or operational disruptions.

Building Code & Fire Safety Considerations

Building code and fire safety regulations ensure that EV charging systems in apartment complexes are designed and installed to protect residents, property, and first responders. These rules govern electrical design, equipment placement, hazardous location protections, emergency access controls, and material requirements. By adhering to these standards—such as NEC Article 625, NFPA codes, ventilation rules, and structural safety guidelines—property owners can minimize fire risks, prevent electrical hazards, and ensure the charging installation meets all safety and emergency response expectations.

Electrical Code and Installation Standards

EV charging systems must comply with electrical requirements outlined in NEC Article 625, which governs electric vehicle power transfer systems. These standards specify acceptable wiring methods, grounding techniques,

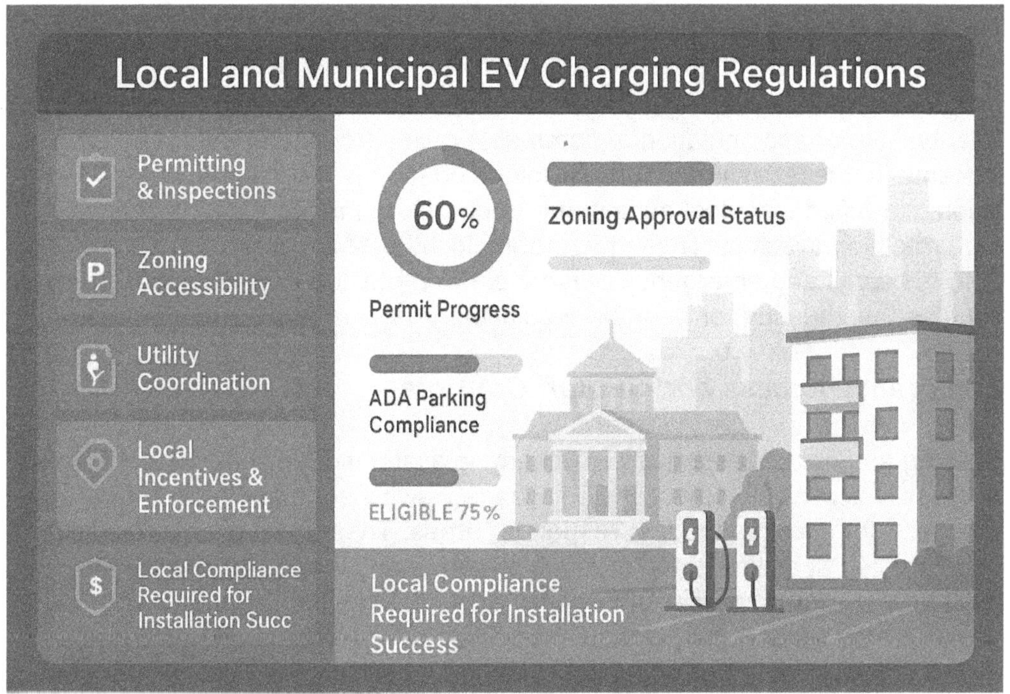

Local and Municipal EV Charging Regulations

conduit sealing, overcurrent protection, and ventilation requirements depending on charger type and location. Adhering to NEC guidelines ensures chargers operate safely, prevents electrical faults, and provides inspectors with clear evidence that the installation meets national electrical safety expectations.

Fire Safety Codes and Equipment Placement

Fire marshals apply fire safety regulations that dictate how EV chargers should be spaced and installed to prevent fire spread and ensure safe operation. Codes such as NFPA 70 (electrical safety) and NFPA 855 (stationary energy storage systems) may require specific clearances from walls, adjacent vehicles, structural elements, and other equipment. Proper signage, bollards, and clear emergency shutoff access are often mandated to help first responders quickly control an incident. Following these standards reduces fire risks and ensures installations pass fire department inspections.

Hazardous Location Requirements

Indoor or enclosed parking garages may introduce additional risks, including heat buildup or accumulation of flammable gases from vehicles or charging systems. In these environments, building codes may require mechanical ventilation, classified electrical equipment, temperature monitoring, or enhanced fire protection systems. These hazardous location requirements ensure that both residents and emergency personnel are protected from potential ignition sources, overheating, or poor air circulation.

Emergency Access and Shutoff Controls

Building and fire codes require EV charging systems to include clearly labeled and easily accessible emergency disconnect switches, often located near the chargers or in designated first-responder areas. These controls must remain unobstructed at all times and must be tested during inspections to confirm functionality. Having proper emergency access and shutoff systems in place allows fire crews to rapidly depower equipment, reducing response time during an electrical or fire emergency.

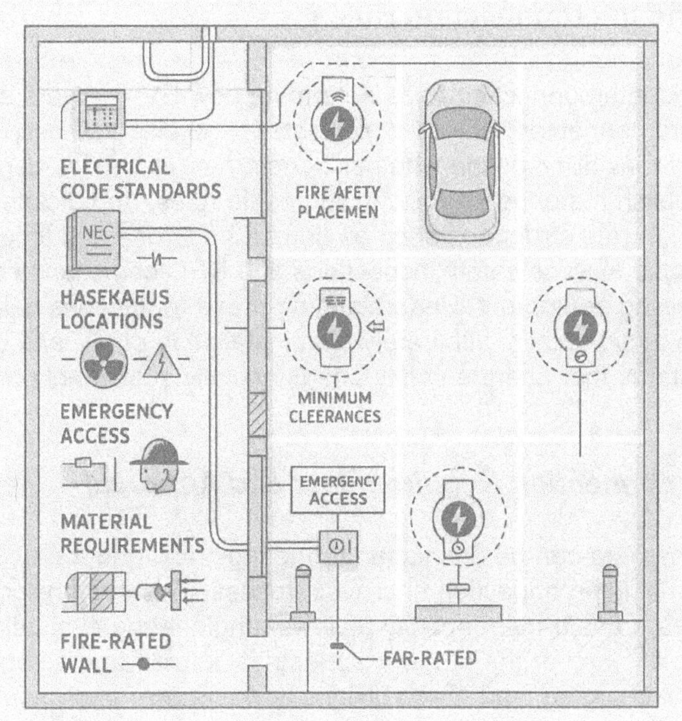

EV Charging System Building Code and Fire Safety Considerations

Material Ratings and Construction Modifications

Installing EV chargers may require structural assessments or construction modifications to meet building and fire code standards. These can include the use of fire-rated materials, properly sealed wall penetrations, metal conduits, and protective barriers such as bollards to prevent vehicle impact damage. Compliance with these material and construction requirements ensures the installation is durable, safe, and compatible with long-term building operations. Early coordination with building officials helps prevent redesigns, cost over-runs, and approval delays.

Utility & Grid Interconnection Rules

Utility and grid interconnection rules determine how EV chargers at apartment complexes are connected, powered, regulated, and billed. These requirements shape project feasibility, define whether transformer or service upgrades are needed, establish metering and electricity resale rules, and dictate how usage is billed through rate structures such as demand charges and time-of-use pricing. Utilities also enforce safety inspections and NEC compliance checks before energizing equipment. Understanding these regulations helps apartment owners avoid delays, accurately plan installation costs, and build EV charging systems that operate safely and financially sustainably over the long term.

Utility Interconnection Requirements and Approval

Before EV chargers can be connected to the electrical grid, utility companies require a formal interconnection approval process. This may include load impact studies, transformer capacity reviews, engineering evaluations, and assessments of whether the property's electrical infrastructure can safely support additional charging load. Each utility follows its own application, review, and approval timeline, making early coordination essential. Interconnection approval is often the longest and most critical path step in an EV charging project.

Transformer Capacity and Required Upgrades

EV chargers—especially when installed in groups—can place significant load on existing electrical infrastructure. Utilities may require upgrades to onsite transformers, service drops, switchgear, or feeder lines to ensure safe and reliable operation. These upgrades can significantly affect project cost and timeline, so owners must factor transformer availability, lead times, and utility construction schedules into planning. In some cases, load management software can reduce or eliminate the need for transformer upgrades.

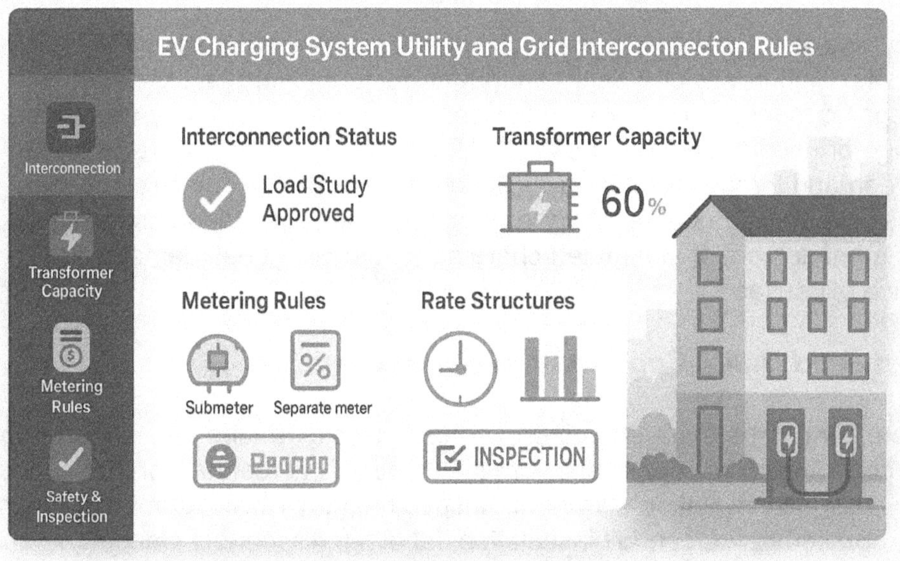

EV Charging System Utility and Grid Interconnection Rules

Metering and Electricity Resale Rules

Utilities establish clear rules for how EV charging electricity must be metered, measured, and billed. Depending on the region, apartment owners may need to install:

- Dedicated meters for charging equipment
- Submeters tied to specific resident usage
- Shared or whole-building meters with load allocation

Utilities and state commissions also regulate electricity resale, determining whether property owners may charge residents per-kWh or whether they must use alternative billing methods such as time-based or session-based pricing. Understanding these rules is essential for designing compliant billing practices.

Electric Usage, Demand Charges, and Time-of-Use Pricing

Utility rate structures play a major role in the operational cost of EV charging stations. High-power chargers can trigger demand charges, significantly increasing monthly utility bills during peak usage periods. Many utilities also require or encourage time-of-use (TOU) pricing, which adjusts rates based on grid demand throughout the day. Apartment owners must understand how these rate structures affect long-term operational costs and consider using load management or scheduled charging to minimize peak demand and reduce expenses.

Safety and Utility Coordination Requirements

Before EV chargers are energized, utilities typically require safety inspections and confirmation of compliance with NEC codes, interconnection rules, and utility-specific installation standards. Inspectors may review grounding methods, breaker sizing, conduit installation, labeling, disconnect placement, and load management configurations. Utilities also coordinate with local authorities to verify that all permits and jurisdictional approvals have been completed. This final coordination step ensures chargers operate safely and meet all regulatory and technical requirements.

Disabilities Accessibility Standards

Disability access regulations ensure that EV charging systems in apartment communities provide safe, convenient, and independently usable charging options for all drivers, including those with mobility limitations. These standards define how many accessible spaces must be provided, how the equipment must be positioned for ease of use, and how pathways and signage must be designed to support safe navigation from parking areas to chargers. By following ADA-compliant requirements for design, reach ranges, pathways, and labeling, apartment owners ensure equitable access while avoiding compliance violations.

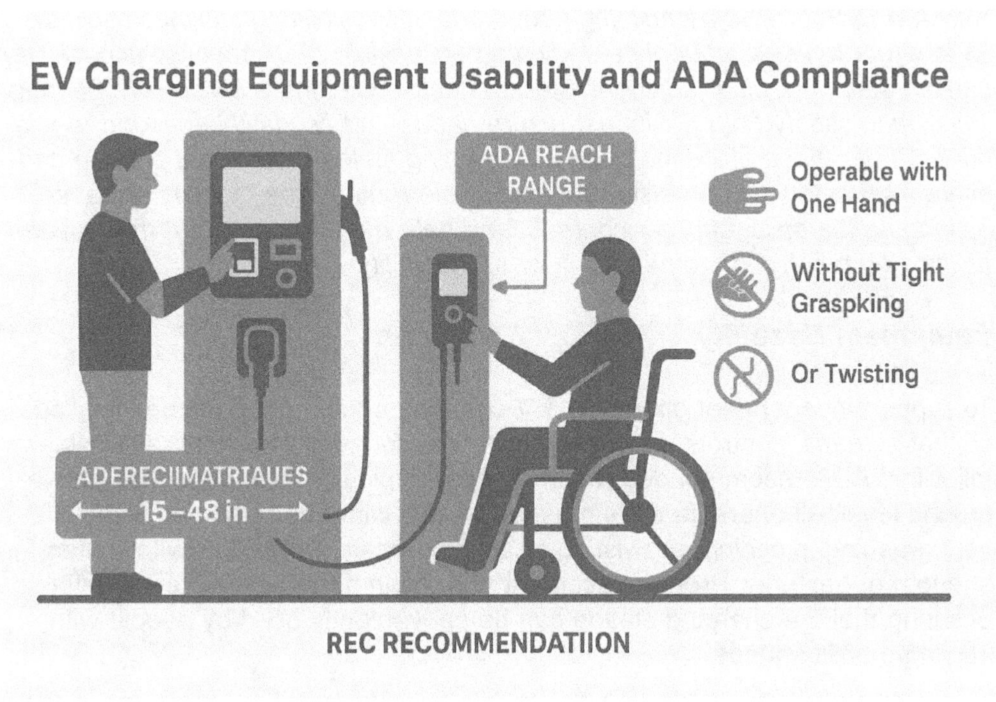

EV Charging Systems Disabilities Accessibility Regulations

EV Charger Accessibility Requirements

EV charging installations must comply with the Americans with Disabilities Act (ADA) and any local accessibility regulations, which mandate that a designated number of EV charging spaces be accessible to people with disabilities. These requirements define parking space width, access aisles, ground surface conditions, maximum allowable slope, and clear floor space needed for safe and independent maneuvering. Compliance with these guidelines ensures that residents with disabilities can access charging spaces safely and reliably without additional assistance.

Surprising Fact - *Some building codes and accessibility guidelines allow an EV charger to serve not only a dedicated accessible (ADA/mobility-accessible) parking stall - but also "adjacent" stalls, effectively letting a single EV-charging installation satisfy both EV-infrastructure needs and accessible-parking regulations. Under these guidelines, the EV-charging stall and adjacent parking can share a common access-aisle and accessible route to the building entrance, as long as the aisle, charger controls, and path meet the spacing, maneuverability, and reach requirements set for accessibility.*

Equipment Usability

To support independent operation, EV charging equipment must be installed so that screens, controls, payment interfaces, connector holsters, and cables fall within ADA-recommended reach ranges—typically 15 to 48 inches above ground level. All operable parts must be usable with one hand and without tight grasping, pinching, or twisting to accommodate individuals with limited strength or dexterity. Proper placement and equipment choice are essential to ensuring that the charging station can be conveniently used by people with varying mobility needs.

Accessible Pathways and Signage

Accessible EV charging spaces must connect to building entrances or common areas through a continuous, unobstructed pathway that includes properly graded surfaces, curb ramps, and, where required, tactile warning strips. Clear, visible signage identifying accessible EV charging spaces is necessary for enforcement and helps prevent misuse by non-disabled drivers. Proper markings, symbols, and wayfinding signs enhance safety, improve visibility, and ensure that accessible charging resources remain available to those who need them most.

Environmental & Sustainability Regulations

Environmental and sustainability regulations for apartment EV charging projects require owners to evaluate and mitigate site impacts, comply with energy-efficient construction standards, integrate renewable energy where applicable, responsibly manage equipment end-of-life materials, and meet reporting or certification requirements tied to sustainability goals. These rules help ensure that EV charging installations support long-term environmental stewardship, reduce carbon emissions, and avoid regulatory penalties while aligning with state, municipal, and federal sustainability initiatives.

Site Disturbance and Environmental Impact

EV charging installations often require trenching, conduit installation, and electrical upgrades, all of which may trigger environmental review requirements depending on local or state regulations. Property owners must evaluate how construction activities affect soil disturbance, stormwater runoff, existing landscaping, and the handling of potentially hazardous materials such as old transformers, soil contamination, or legacy electrical equipment. Following proper environmental practices helps protect surrounding ecosystems, reduces liability, and ensures compliance with environmental protection standards.

Sustainable Infrastructure Requirements

Many states and municipalities have adopted sustainability mandates that reward or require the use of energy-efficient equipment, smart load management systems, and environmentally responsible installation practices. These may include standards for reducing energy waste, using low-impact construction techniques, incorporating energy-efficient lighting or signage, and designing EV infrastructure that aligns with broader sustainability and building-performance goals. Compliance helps properties reduce operational energy costs while meeting local environmental expectations.

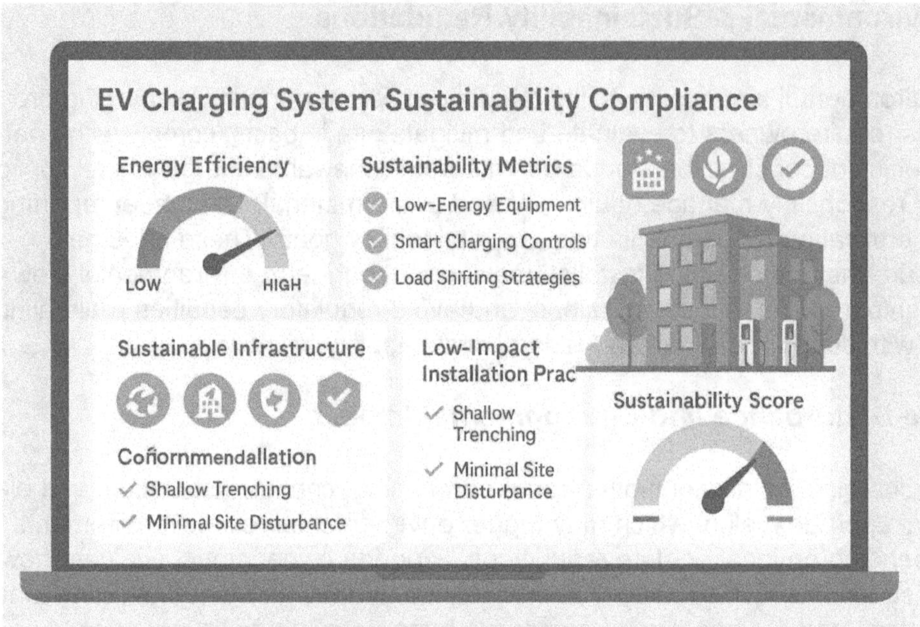

EV Charging System Environmental and Sustainability Regulations

Renewable Energy Regulations

Environmental regulations increasingly encourage—or in some cases require—multifamily properties to integrate EV charging with renewable energy sources such as solar power. This may involve incentives for solar-EV pairing, requirements for future solar readiness, or standards for utilizing clean energy programs offered by local utilities. Integrating renewable energy can reduce carbon footprints, lower long-term electricity costs, and improve eligibility for sustainability certifications and incentive programs.

Waste, Recycling, and End-of-Life Management

EV chargers, cables, and electrical components must be managed responsibly at the end of their service life. Regulations often define how electronic waste (e-waste), metals, packaging materials, and hazardous components must be recycled, refurbished, or disposed of. Owners may need to use certified recycling partners or follow specific disposal protocols. Planning for environmentally compliant end-of-life practices ensures long-term sustainability and minimizes environmental harm.

Certifications and Sustainability Reporting

Some jurisdictions and sustainability programs require apartment owners to document energy usage, emissions reductions, renewable energy integration, and overall environmental performance tied to their EV charging infrastructure. This may include compliance with programs such as LEED, Green Globes, or regional sustainability certifications. Accurate reporting not only supports regulatory compliance but may also unlock incentives, enhance property value, and demonstrate commitment to sustainable operations.

Data Privacy and Cybersecurity Regulations

EV charging systems in apartment communities must protect sensitive resident information through comprehensive data privacy policies, secure data storage and retention practices, strong cybersecurity frameworks, tightly managed access controls, and clear breach-notification procedures. Because charging systems process personal and financial data—including payment information, user profiles, charging history, and sometimes vehicle identifiers—property owners must ensure that vendors, software platforms, and internal teams follow strict security standards to prevent unauthorized access and comply with federal and state privacy regulations.

Data Collection, Storage, and Privacy Requirements

EV charging systems collect a wide range of personal data, including resident names, payment methods, RFID card identifiers, charging history, usage patterns, and in some cases vehicle identification numbers. Regulations require apartment owners and their vendors to protect this information through encrypted data storage, secure transmission, and formal privacy policies that clearly disclose what data is collected and how it is used. Transparency and security in data handling help maintain resident trust and ensure compliance with privacy laws.

Data Retention, Anonymization, and Deletion Rules

Because EV charging platforms store user data for billing, authentication, diagnostics, and performance analytics, properties must establish policies governing how long this data is stored and when it must be anonymized or deleted. Regulations may require data minimization—keeping only the information necessary for operations—and secure deletion procedures after retention periods expire. Clear retention and anonymization policies reduce liability exposure and ensure compliance with emerging data-protection standards.

Cybersecurity Standard Requirements

Property owners must ensure that EV charger manufacturers, software providers, and network operators follow recognized cybersecurity frameworks such as ISO 27001, SOC 2, and NIST guidelines. These frameworks mandate controls including secure data handling, encryption, role-based access, vulnerability management, penetration testing, secure firmware updates, and documented incident-response procedures. Compliance with established cybersecurity standards greatly reduces the risk of cyberattacks targeting chargers, user data, or backend systems.

Access Control Rules and Permissions

Strong access control policies ensure that only authorized individuals can view, modify, or export sensitive user data. Regulations require apartment owners to define which internal team members—such as property managers, billing administrators, or maintenance personnel—may access specific data types, and under what conditions. External vendor personnel must also be governed through contracts and technical restrictions such as role-based accounts, multifactor authentication, and audit logs. Proper access controls help prevent unauthorized data exposure or internal misuse.

Data Breach Notifications and Incident Response Requirements

Most state privacy laws mandate that properties notify affected residents and relevant authorities within a defined timeframe if a data breach occurs. EV charging systems are no exception: owners must have formal incident-response plans that include breach detection procedures, reporting protocols, documentation requirements, and communication strategies. Failure to follow breach-notification laws can result in fines, liability, reputational damage, and loss of resident trust. Preparing an incident-response framework ensures faster, compliant action in the event of a security incident.

Payment and Metering Regulations

Payment and metering regulations for apartment EV charging systems ensure that property owners comply with electricity resale laws, follow utility-approved metering configurations, meet secure payment processing standards, uphold consumer-protection billing rules, and accurately report financial and energy data required for tax credits and incentive programs. These rules affect how owners price charging sessions, recover costs, structure billing systems, and maintain long-term regulatory compliance across both energy and financial reporting channels.

Electricity Resale Laws and Legal Billing Restrictions

In many states, property owners cannot legally resell electricity by the kilowatt-hour unless their EV charging equipment and billing systems meet specific state or utility requirements. Some jurisdictions restrict per-kWh billing to regulated utilities, while others allow resale if equipment meets approved accuracy standards or if certain disclosures are provided. Apartment owners must understand their state's electricity resale rules to avoid violations and ensure that pricing models—whether per-kWh, per-hour, per-session, or flat-fee—are legally compliant.

Utility Metering Requirements

Utilities determine how electricity used for EV charging must be metered, monitored, and billed, which may involve dedicated EV meters, shared building meters, or submeters assigned to specific residents or charging locations. Each configuration affects cost allocation, tenant billing, and eligibility for incentives or demand-response programs. Early coordination with the utility helps property owners select the correct metering arrangement and avoid

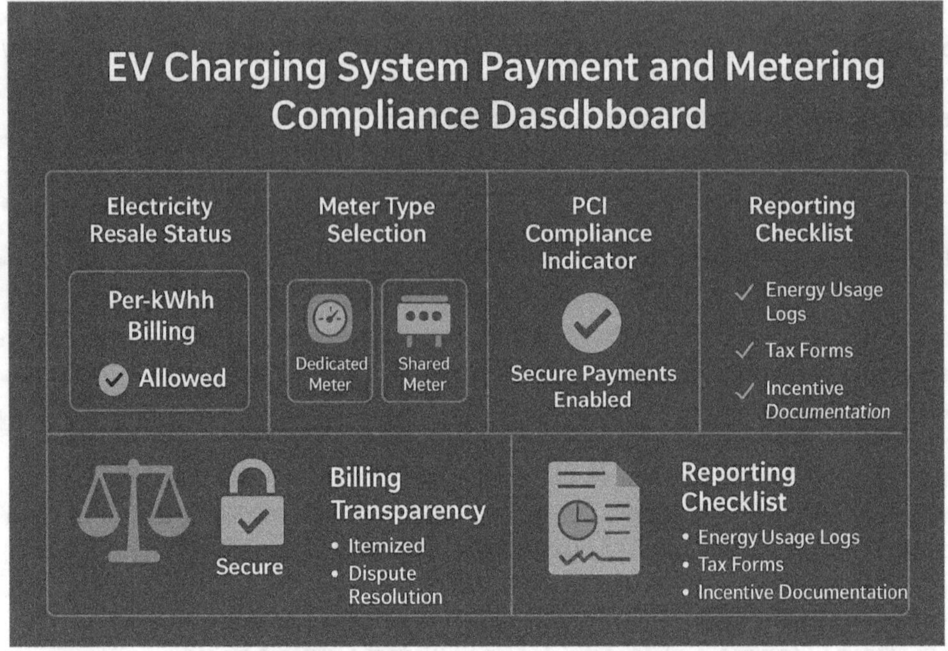

EV Charging System Payment and Metering Regulations

delays stemming from meter availability, inspection requirements, or utility approval processes.

Payment Method Compliance and Data Security Standards

EV charging systems that process payments must comply with PCI DSS (Payment Card Industry Data Security Standards) and other financial-security regulations to protect user payment information. This includes encrypted transactions, secure card readers, masked payment data, strong authentication methods, and vendor adherence to cybersecurity frameworks. Compliance ensures not only legal protection but also resident trust in the charging system's financial security.

Billing Practices, Dispute Handling, and Consumer Rights

State consumer-protection laws often regulate how EV charging sessions must be priced, displayed, and billed to residents. Requirements may include transparent pricing, itemized receipts, dispute-resolution procedures, refund policies, and accurate session reporting. Clear billing practices reduce complaints, prevent misunderstandings, and ensure compliance with state consumer-rights laws, which increasingly apply to EV charging services in multifamily settings.

Tax, Incentive, and Utility Reporting Requirements

Many EV charging incentives—including grants, rebates, and tax credits—require properties to maintain detailed energy-use records, revenue reports, commissioning documentation, and operational data. Programs such as federal tax credits or state-level rebates may also require periodic reporting or proof that the chargers remain operational for a specified period. Accurate data collection and reporting ensure compliance, prevent clawbacks of incentives, and support ongoing financial benefits tied to EV charging infrastructure.

EV Charger Certification and Labeling Standards

EV charger certification and labeling standards ensure that equipment installed in multifamily properties meets nationally recognized safety requirements, complies with electrical codes, follows required labeling rules, supports reliable communication and cybersecurity protocols, and satisfies the criteria needed to qualify for rebates and utility incentives. These standards protect residents, simplify inspections, ensure equipment interoperability, and help property owners avoid regulatory issues while unlocking financial benefits tied to certified EV charging hardware.

Testing Laboratory Certifications

EV chargers installed in apartment communities must be certified by a Nationally Recognized Testing Laboratory (NRTL) to verify that they meet established product safety and performance standards. Common NRTL certifications include UL (Underwriters Laboratories) and ETL (Intertek) marks, which confirm that chargers have been tested for electrical safety, temperature performance, structural durability, and protection against electrical faults.

These certifications are often required by permitting authorities, insurance providers, and incentive programs.

Electrical Code Compliance Requirements

To ensure safe operation, EV charging equipment must comply with NEC Article 625, which defines installation requirements such as equipment ratings, wiring methods, grounding, conduit sealing, GFCI protection, and overcurrent protection. Proper code compliance helps prevent electrical hazards, supports successful inspections, and ensures the charger installation is compatible with long-term building safety standards. Labels communicating voltage, amperage, and wiring specifications further support inspection and maintenance activities.

Federal, State, and Local Labeling Requirements

Many jurisdictions require specific labels to be placed on or near EV chargers and electrical components. These labels may include voltage and amperage ratings, disconnect location markers, utility interconnection notes, grounding requirements, and warning or caution signage. Labeling standards vary by municipality but serve an important role in ensuring first responders, inspectors, maintenance staff, and residents have clear information about the equipment and its operation.

Cybersecurity and Communication Protocol Certifications

Modern EV chargers increasingly rely on network connectivity and cloud platforms, making cybersecurity and communication protocol certifications essential. Chargers may need to demonstrate compliance with OCPP (Open Charge Point Protocol) for interoperability, demand-response certification for utility integration, and cybersecurity frameworks such as ISO 27001 or SOC 2 for secure data handling when connected to cloud services. These certifications ensure that chargers are protected from cyber threats and function properly within broader EV ecosystems.

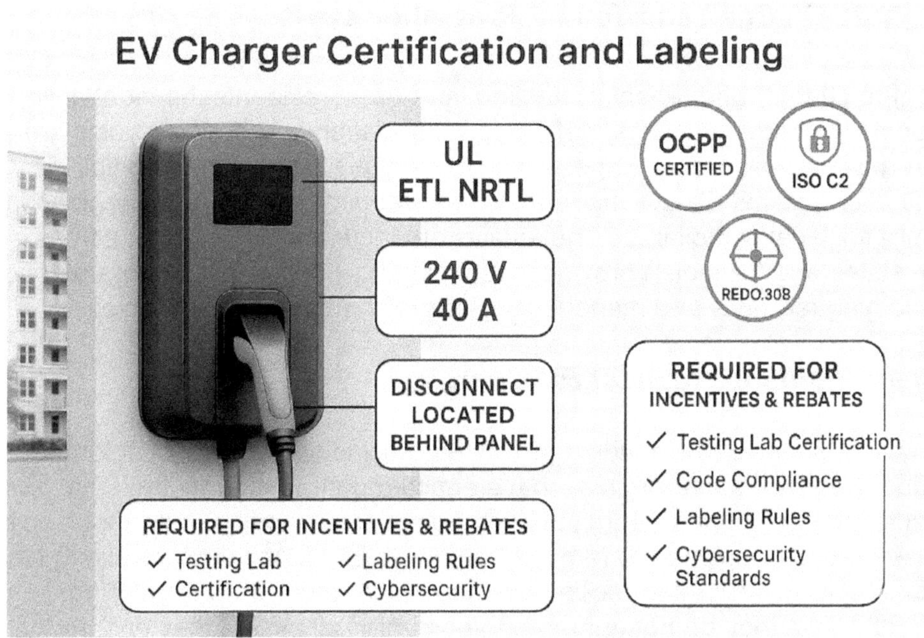

EV Charger Certification and Labeling Regulations

Requirements for Rebates, Grants, and Utility Incentives

Many EV charging incentive programs—including federal tax credits, state rebates, and utility grants—require that chargers meet specific certification and labeling standards to qualify for funding. Programs may mandate NRTL certification, OCPP compliance, Energy Star efficiency, or specific safety labeling as part of eligibility criteria. Meeting these requirements not only ensures compliance but also maximizes the financial benefits available to apartment property owners investing in EV infrastructure.

"Right-to-Charge" and Tenant Protection Laws

"Right-to-charge" and tenant protection laws grant residents the legal ability to request EV charging access, define how installation and ongoing costs are shared, allow landlords to impose only reasonable restrictions, prohibit discrimination against EV-owning tenants, and require detailed documentation to ensure full legal compliance. These laws are increasingly common across U.S. states and Canadian provinces, shaping how apartment owners respond to charging requests and manage long-term EV infrastructure policies.

Tenant Rights to Request EV Charging

Many U.S. states and Canadian provinces—including California, Colorado, Florida, New York, and Virginia—have enacted right-to-charge laws that give tenants the legal right to request EV charging installations at their residence. These laws are designed to remove barriers to EV adoption by requiring landlords to consider charging requests in good faith rather than dismissing them outright. While they do not guarantee approval in all cases, they ensure that tenants have a formal pathway to request and negotiate access to charging infrastructure.

EV Charger Cost Responsibility

Right-to-charge laws typically define how installation, electrical upgrades, maintenance, insurance, electricity usage, and potential removal costs are allocated between tenants and property owners. In many jurisdictions, tenants may be responsible for the cost of installation and additional electrical capacity needed for their charging space, while landlords may need to coordinate access, approvals, or system-wide upgrades that benefit the property long-term. Clear cost allocation rules help prevent disputes and ensure transparent financial expectations.

Reasonable Restrictions Permitted for Property Owners

These regulations allow landlords to impose reasonable restrictions on EV charging installations—so long as the restrictions do not effectively prohibit charging. Acceptable limitations often include compliance with building and fire

EV Charging Right-to-Charge Tenant Protection Laws

codes, restrictions on charger placement to protect safety and aesthetics, requirements for compatible equipment, insurance obligations, and adherence to electrical capacity limits. Reasonable restrictions protect property operations while ensuring tenants can still pursue charging access.

Equal Access and Anti-Discrimination Requirements

Some right-to-charge laws include anti-discrimination provisions that prevent landlords from treating EV-owning tenants differently from other residents. These rules prohibit landlords from denying lease renewals, charging excessive fees, or restricting parking access solely because a tenant owns an electric vehicle or has requested charging infrastructure. Equal access provisions support fair treatment and encourage broader EV adoption across multifamily properties.

Documentation and Legal Compliance Requirements

Compliance with right-to-charge laws requires strict documentation, including written acknowledgment of tenant requests, timelines for approval or denial, conditions for installation, and agreements covering maintenance, insurance, and removal. Property owners must maintain clear records demonstrating compliance with the law, building codes, and reasonable-restriction criteria. Proper documentation protects both parties from disputes and ensures transparency throughout the approval and installation process.

Insurance and Liability Compliance

Insurance and liability compliance for apartment EV charging systems requires property owners to ensure appropriate insurance coverage, conduct fire-risk and electrical assessments, use certified equipment and approved installers, establish clear rules for resident and guest responsibility, and maintain documented inspection and maintenance programs. These requirements protect the property against charger-related incidents, reduce financial exposure, and keep insurance policies valid while supporting safe long-term operation of the charging infrastructure.

Property and Liability Insurance Requirements

Apartment owners must confirm whether their existing property insurance and general liability policies extend coverage to EV charging equipment, electrical upgrades, and potential charging-related incidents. Some insurers require policy updates or endorsements to cover new risks associated with EVSE installations. Carriers may also require owners to disclose project details, provide engineering drawings, or demonstrate compliance with local codes to ensure that new infrastructure is properly insured from day one.

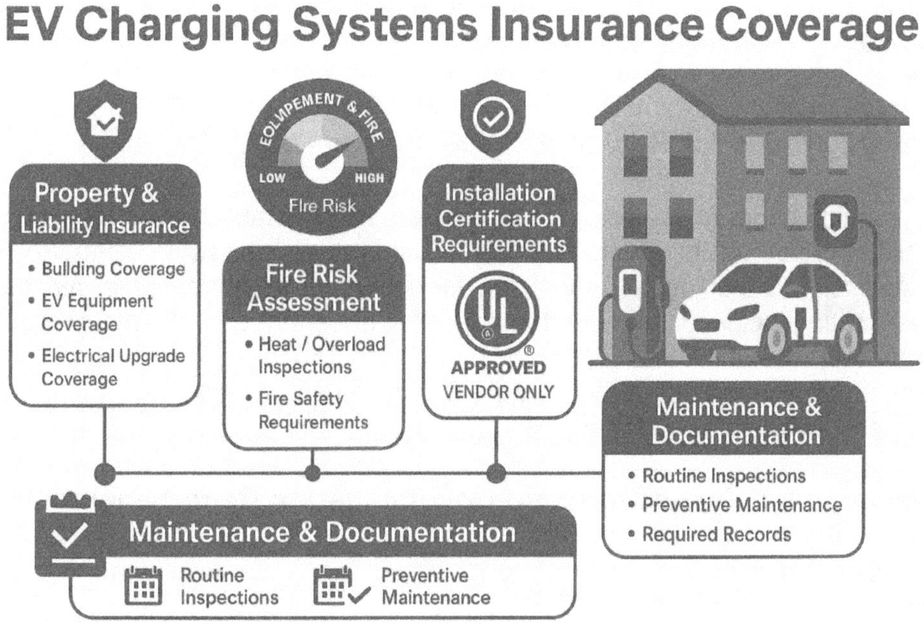

EV Charging Systems Insurance and Liability Compliance

Equipment and Electrical Fire Risk Assessment

EV chargers introduce additional electrical load and potential fire risks, making fire-risk assessments an essential insurance requirement. Carriers may request documentation showing that proper load calculations were performed, circuits are protected according to NEC standards, and ventilation or thermal safeguards are in place. Inspectors may evaluate panel capacity, transformer loading, wiring methods, and charger placement to verify that the installation does not increase the likelihood of electrical faults or overheating.

Installation Standards, Certifications, and Approved Vendors

Insurance coverage may only apply if EV chargers meet recognized national safety standards and are installed by qualified professionals. Many carriers require UL- or ETL-listed chargers, NEC Article 625 compliance, and installation by licensed electricians or certified EVSE contractors. Using non-certified equipment or unapproved installers can void insurance coverage and increase liability exposure, making adherence to certified products and vendors essential.

Liability Rules for Residents, Guests, and Public Users

To limit exposure to claims, property owners must establish clear user-responsibility policies outlining who is liable for damage caused while using the chargers. This includes responsibility for connector damage, cable misuse, overheating incidents, vehicle damage, or injuries that occur in the charging area. Well-defined rules, supported by signage and lease addendums, help reduce ambiguity and protect owners when misuse or negligence leads to property or equipment damage.

Maintenance, Inspection, and Documentation Requirements

Insurance carriers often mandate ongoing maintenance, inspection, and documentation to ensure coverage remains valid. Owners may be required to keep records of preventive maintenance, software updates, electrical inspections, thermal checks, and equipment cleanings. Failure to maintain proper documentation can jeopardize coverage and increase liability. A structured maintenance plan ensures long-term equipment reliability and supports compliance with insurer expectations.

Chapter 10

EV Charging System Energy & Options

EV charging system key options such as smart energy management, solar integration, battery storage, EV wireless charging and vehicle-to-grid (V2G) technology help apartment owners improve energy efficiency, lower operating costs, and enhance long-term sustainability. These advanced technologies not only reduce electrical demand and environmental impact but also enable properties to participate in evolving energy programs and generate new sources of value from their charging infrastructure.

EV Charging Smart Energy Management

EV charging smart energy management helps apartment owners optimize power distribution, reduce peak demand costs, integrate with existing building systems, and qualify for utility incentives. Through intelligent load control, real-time monitoring, and automated energy scheduling, these systems ensure that chargers operate efficiently and cost-effectively while maintaining grid stability and supporting sustainable property operations.

Load Balancing Control

Smart energy management systems use dynamic load balancing to distribute available electrical power across multiple chargers in real time. By preventing individual circuits or panels from being overloaded, these systems allow properties to install more chargers without expensive infrastructure upgrades. Load balancing also helps maintain steady electrical performance, reduces the risk of breaker trips, and ensures reliable service for tenants even during high-demand periods.

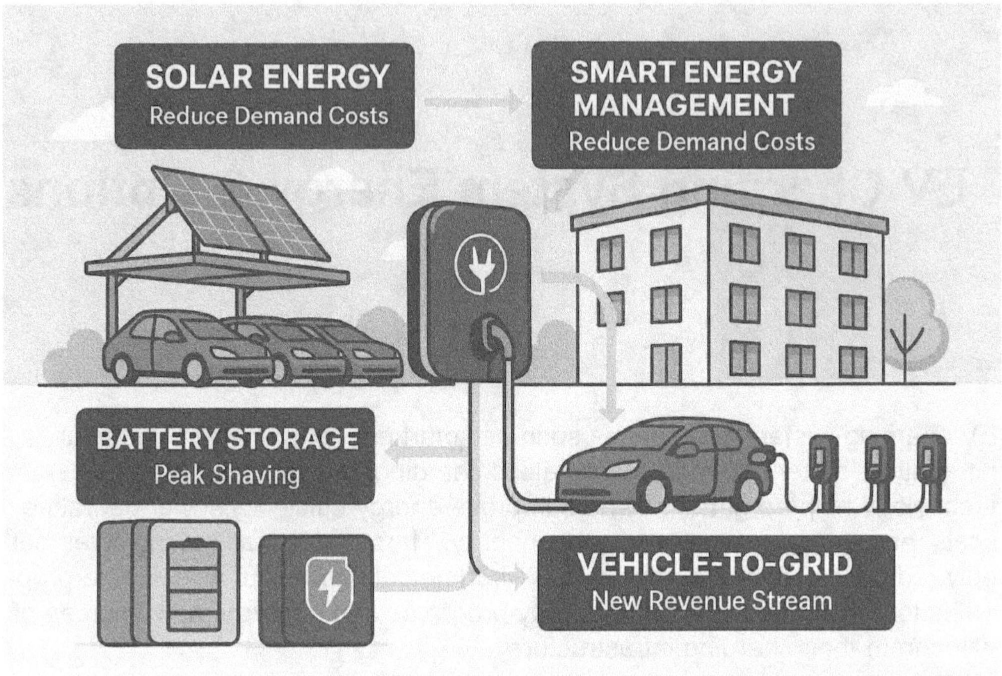

EV Charging System for Apartments Energy Options

Time-of-Use (TOU) Optimization

Many utilities charge different electricity rates depending on the time of day. Smart energy management software can automatically schedule or throttle EV charging during off-peak hours when electricity costs are lowest. This approach can significantly reduce operating expenses—sometimes by 20–40%—while aligning property operations with utility rate structures. TOU optimization also supports grid efficiency by shifting charging loads away from peak demand periods.

Building Energy Systems Integration

Advanced energy management systems can integrate EV charging with broader building energy systems, including HVAC, lighting, and solar generation. This integration gives property owners a unified view of total energy consumption and allows them to prioritize critical loads during high-demand periods. By coordinating charging activity with other building systems, apartment complexes can maximize energy efficiency, reduce overall costs, and support sustainability initiatives.

Utility Incentive Programs

Utilities across the country are increasingly offering incentives, rebates, or rate credits for properties that implement smart charging and load management systems. These programs often reward participation in demand response or grid services, where chargers can automatically adjust usage based on utility signals. By adopting a compliant energy management system, apartment owners not only reduce costs but also gain eligibility for long-term financial benefits that improve project ROI.

Solar Energy

Adding and integrating solar energy with EV charging allows apartment owners to generate clean on-site power, reduce grid dependence, lower operating costs, and enhance sustainability. By designing a coordinated solar-plus-charging system, properties can take advantage of renewable energy incentives, optimize energy flow with storage solutions, and strengthen long-term energy resilience while providing a visible commitment to sustainability that appeals to eco-conscious tenants.

Solar Energy Potential

Evaluating solar potential begins with understanding how much energy your EV charging network will require and how much of that load can be offset through on-site solar generation. Owners should consider factors such as roof or carport surface area, shading conditions, local solar irradiance, and expected daily charging patterns. Proper sizing ensures the solar array's output (measured in kilowatts) aligns with both current and future EV charging demand, helping reduce utility costs while optimizing system efficiency and return on investment.

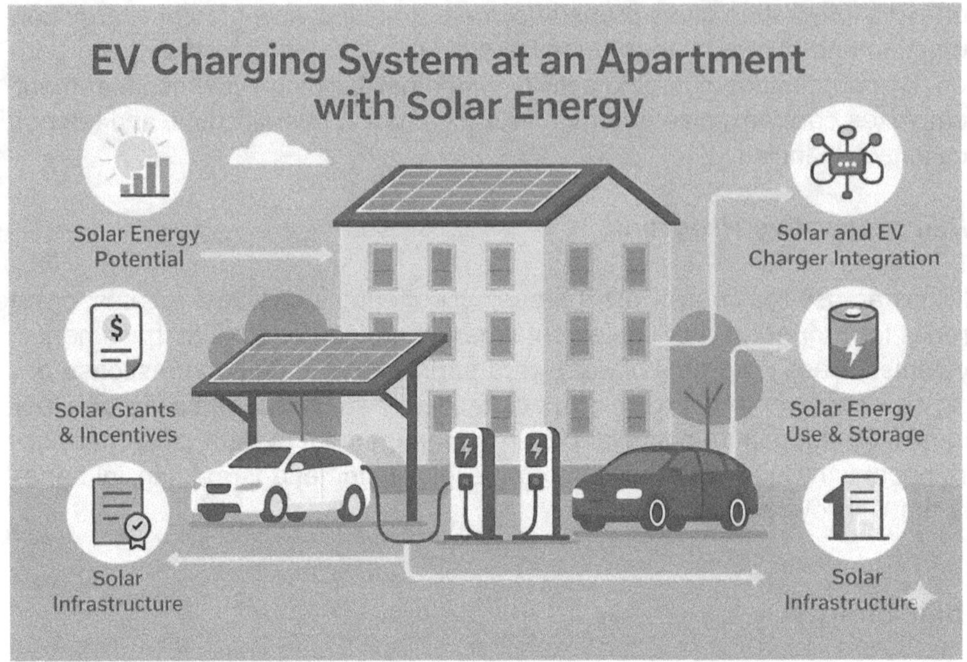

EV Charging System at an Apartment with Solar Energy

Surprising Fact *- In some cases, apartment complexes can use solar powered EV charging stations to avoid the huge expense and disruption of running new wiring or upgrading building electrical service. The solar EV charging kit contains a solar panel, battery, and EV charger. This can turn a remote parking lot into its own off-grid (or grid-light) charging node without trenching, conduit, or transformer upgrades. Because solar-PV + battery EV-charging systems draw power directly from on-site generation and storage - not the building's loaded feeders. This reduces much of the cost and regulatory friction tied to expanding electrical service.*

Solar and EV Charger Integration

Integrating solar panels with EV charging systems allows properties to directly route renewable power to vehicle chargers through advanced energy management platforms. These systems can prioritize solar power for daytime charging, automatically supplement with grid power when necessary, and report usage data for tracking and incentive purposes. The result is a cleaner and more efficient charging process that minimizes grid strain and demonstrates a forward-looking approach to sustainable property management.

Solar Grants and Incentives

Numerous solar-related funding opportunities exist at the federal, state, and utility levels to reduce upfront installation costs. Programs such as the U.S. Investment Tax Credit (ITC), performance-based incentives, and net-metering arrangements allow property owners to recover a significant portion of project expenses while generating long-term energy savings. Apartment owners can also benefit from specialized clean energy grants and financing tools designed to encourage renewable integration with EV charging infrastructure.

Solar Infrastructure

Adding solar energy systems requires careful coordination of electrical design, site layout, and structural integrity. Rooftop and carport systems must account for weight loads, conduit routing, inverter placement, and potential shading from nearby structures or vegetation. Local permitting authorities may require design reviews or inspections to ensure compliance with building codes and safety standards. Early collaboration with engineers and permitting agencies helps avoid delays and ensures an efficient, code-compliant installation.

Solar Energy Use and Storage

Pairing solar with battery energy storage adds flexibility and resilience to the property's energy strategy. Excess daytime solar power can be stored in batteries and used later for evening EV charging or to reduce peak demand charges. This combination also enables participation in demand response or energy market programs, creating new revenue streams while improving grid reliability. Scalable designs allow apartment owners to expand both their charging and solar capacity as tenant demand grows, building a future-ready clean energy ecosystem.

Battery Energy Storage Systems (BESS)

Battery Energy Storage Systems (BESS) help apartment owners lower electricity costs, provide backup power, enhance solar energy integration, and improve the overall efficiency and reliability of their EV charging infrastructure. When properly designed, a BESS can smooth energy demand, protect against outages, and support smarter energy management while meeting strict safety and compliance standards.

Peak Electric Demand Reduction

One of the most valuable benefits of adding a BESS to an EV charging system is the ability to manage and reduce peak electrical demand. Batteries can store power during low-cost, off-peak hours and discharge it during high-demand periods when electricity prices are highest. This strategy not only helps reduce demand charges from utilities but also makes EV charging operations more predictable and financially sustainable. By shaving peak loads, properties can often delay or avoid costly electrical service upgrades while maintaining reliable charging access for residents.

Backup Power

Batteries provide critical backup power that keeps EV chargers and essential building systems running during utility outages or grid disruptions. For apartment complexes, this capability enhances property resilience and ensures uninterrupted service for tenants who rely on EV charging. BESS solutions can also be configured to automatically transition to backup mode during power failures, offering peace of mind and strengthening the property's reputation for reliability and preparedness.

A Battery Energy Storage System and electric vehicles with bidirectional capability can work together to make an apartment community more resilient. When combined with the building's management system, they allow the property to supply its own power during outages, reduce peak energy costs, and maintain essential services even when the grid fails.

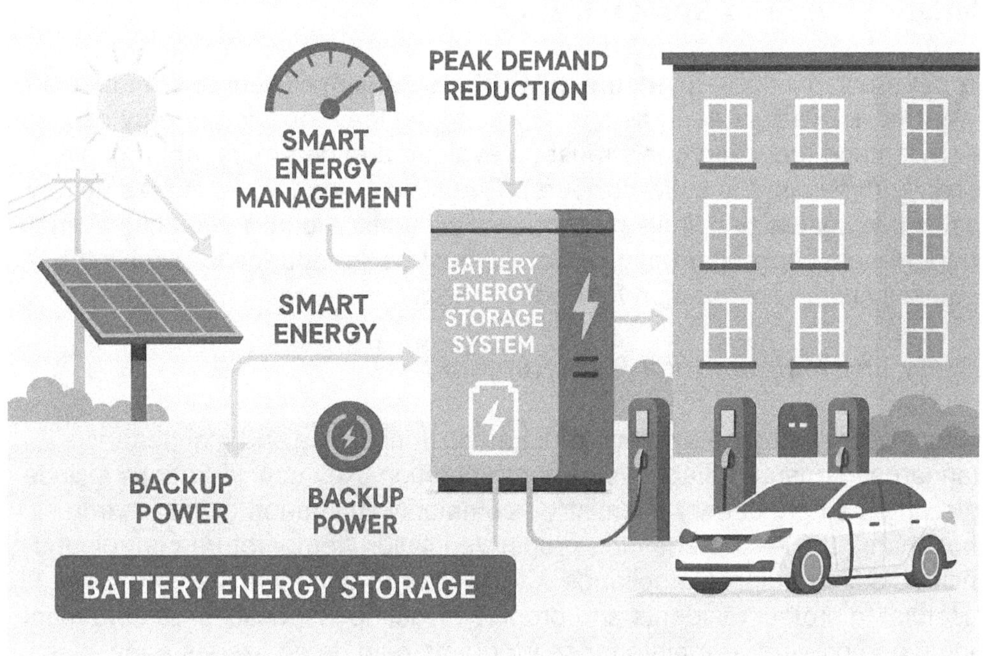

EV Charging System at Apartment with Battery Energy Storage System BESS

Surprising Fact *- An average EV car battery stores enough energy to completely power a typical 4 bedroom home for about 3 to 4 days. Some EVs have vehicle to home (V2H) capability which allows them to provide and control backup home electricity.*

Smart Energy Management Integration

When integrated with smart energy management systems, a BESS becomes a central part of an intelligent, balanced energy network. It can store excess solar energy produced during the day and release it at night when vehicle charging demand rises. This coordination between solar generation, energy storage, and grid interaction optimizes overall energy flow and reduces costs. The result is a self-sustaining energy ecosystem that makes apartment properties more efficient and environmentally responsible.

Battery Sizing and System Design

Proper sizing is critical to ensure a BESS meets both current and future energy demands. Factors such as total EV charging load, building energy use, and peak demand reduction goals must be evaluated to determine appropriate capacity (measured in kilowatt-hours). Oversizing a battery increases upfront cost, while undersizing limits performance benefits. A qualified electrical engineer or energy consultant can model different use scenarios to identify the optimal system configuration for each property.

Safety and Maintenance Requirements

Battery energy storage systems must meet strict safety and maintenance standards to ensure reliable, long-term operation. Key considerations include selecting the right battery chemistry—commonly lithium-ion or lithium iron phosphate (LFP)—and ensuring proper ventilation, temperature control, and enclosure fire ratings. Compliance with NFPA 855 and local fire codes is essential to protect residents and property. Routine inspections, remote monitoring, and preventive maintenance programs help detect issues early, extend battery lifespan, and maintain insurance and warranty eligibility.

EV Wireless Charging

EV wireless charging technology is a game-changing solution for cars, trucks, and other types of vehicles eliminating the cumbersome charging cables and connectors. Surprisingly, wireless charging can achieve up to 95% efficiency—almost identical to traditional wired charging. However, this technology faces key challenges, including the need for precise vehicle alignment, limited compatibility between different charging pad systems, and higher upfront costs compared to wired chargers. In this article, you will learn how EV wireless charging works, the biggest hurdles it must overcome, and real-world examples of how it's being implemented today.

EV Wireless Charging

You want to discover more about EV Wireless Charging? Listen to the podcast session that this article summarizes - EVBusiness.net/102. Also available on Spotify, Pandora, Audible, iHeartRadio & other podcast networks.

EV Wireless Charging Operation

EV wireless charging, also known as inductive charging, relies on electromagnetic fields to transfer energy from a charging pad embedded in the ground to a coil in the vehicle's undercarriage. This technology can be applied in both stationary and dynamic settings. For stationary charging, vehicles park over a designated charging pad, while dynamic charging allows vehicles to charge while moving over embedded road coils.

One of the most surprising aspects of this technology is its efficiency. Wireless charging can achieve up to 95% energy transfer efficiency wiith a distance of 12 inches or more, comparable to wired charging solutions. This dispels the misconception that wireless charging is significantly less efficient and showcases its potential as a viable alternative to traditional plug-in charging.

Benefits of EV Wireless Charging

The primary advantage of EV wireless charging is convenience. Users no longer need to fumble with cables or worry about different plug types and adapters. This seamless charging process is particularly beneficial for fleet operators, where multiple vehicles require efficient overnight charging. Additionally, wireless charging can enhance urban infrastructure by reducing cluttered charging stations and enabling embedded road-based charging systems.

Another significant benefit is improved durability and safety. Traditional charging cables are subject to wear and tear, exposure to harsh weather conditions, and potential vandalism. Wireless charging eliminates these risks by removing the need for physical connectors, thereby enhancing system longevity and reducing maintenance costs.

Challenges of EV Wireless Charging

Despite its promising benefits, EV wireless charging presents several challenges that must be addressed before widespread adoption. For optimal energy transfer, the vehicle's receiving coil must be precisely aligned with the ground-based charging pad. Any misalignment can reduce efficiency and lead to incomplete charging. While modern vehicles are being equipped with alignment assistance systems, this remains a key implementation challenge.

Limited Availability and Compatibility Issues

Currently, only a few automakers, including Mercedes and Tesla, have begun incorporating wireless charging technology into their vehicles. Moreover, different manufacturers may develop proprietary charging solutions, leading to potential compatibility issues between charging pads and vehicles. Industry-wide standardization is needed to ensure seamless adoption across all EV brands.

Higher Installation Costs

Installing a wireless charging system is generally more expensive than traditional wired chargers. While the long-term maintenance costs may be lower due to reduced wear and tear, the initial investment can be a barrier for widespread implementation. Businesses and municipalities must evaluate the cost-benefit ratio before transitioning to wireless charging infrastructure.

Implementing EV Wireless Charging

For successful implementation, wireless charging requires both ground-based infrastructure and vehicle integration. Charging pads must be embedded into parking spaces or roads and connected to a power source, typically operating at 240 volts for efficient energy transfer. Vehicles, on the other hand, need built-in receiving coils and software that allows for alignment and power regulation.

Several features enhance the usability of wireless charging, including automatic coil alignment, obstruction detection, and bidirectional power transfer. Vehicle-to-grid (V2G) capabilities allow EVs to not only receive power but also send excess energy back to the grid, improving overall energy efficiency.

The Future of EV Wireless Charging

While still in its early stages, EV wireless charging is rapidly gaining traction. Tesla has announced plans to integrate wireless charging into its upcoming RoboTaxi fleet, signaling a shift toward autonomous charging solutions. Additionally, various startups and industry leaders, such as Witricity and InductEV, are focusing on commercial applications, particularly for buses and fleet vehicles.

Looking ahead, standardization efforts by organizations such as the Society of Automotive Engineers (SAE) will play a crucial role in making wireless charging a universal solution. As infrastructure expands and costs decrease, EV wireless charging could become a mainstream option, reducing reliance on traditional charging stations and accelerating the global transition to electric mobility.

EV Charging to the Grid (V2G)

Vehicle-to-Grid (V2G) technology enables apartment owners to transform parked electric vehicles into active energy assets that can return stored power to the building or utility grid. This bidirectional energy exchange creates opportunities for new revenue streams, enhances grid stability, and increases overall energy efficiency. As utilities and manufacturers expand V2G pilots and standards, multifamily properties are well-positioned to benefit from this next phase of EV infrastructure innovation.

Vehicle-to-Grid (V2G) Technology Overview

V2G technology allows bidirectional power flow between EVs, chargers, and the electrical grid. Instead of simply drawing power for charging, V2G-enabled vehicles can discharge stored energy back into the grid or building systems when demand is high. This capability turns parked EVs into distributed energy resources, providing valuable support for local energy management and grid balancing. For apartment complexes, this means that shared charging infrastructure can evolve into a flexible energy asset that both serves residents and contributes to overall grid reliability.

Rebates and Selling Energy

One of the most compelling benefits of V2G is the potential for financial return. Properties equipped with V2G systems can sell stored EV energy back to the grid during periods of high demand, participate in demand response programs, or use V2G power to offset internal building loads. This can reduce utility bills and generate new revenue streams while supporting community energy

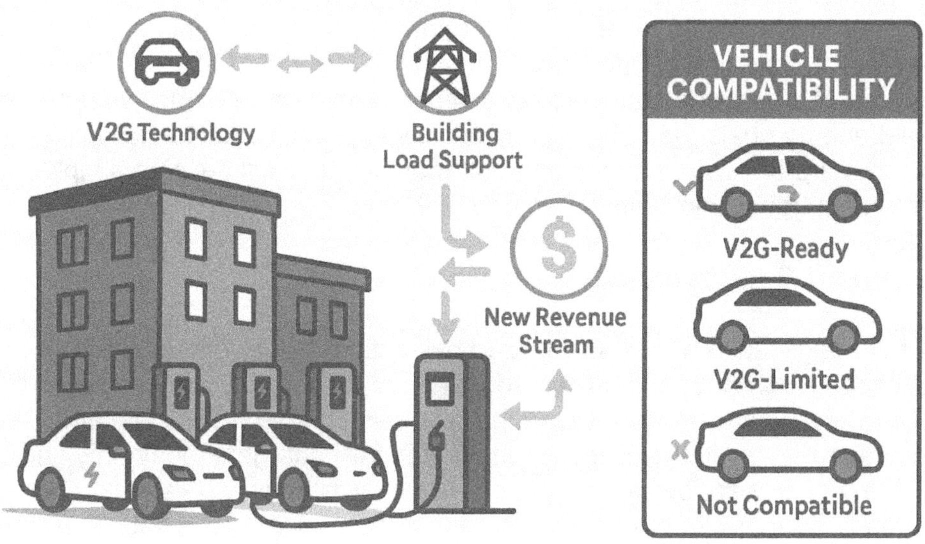

EV Charging at Apartments with Vehicle to Grid V2G Capabilities

resilience. As incentive programs and energy marketplaces expand, properties that integrate V2G will gain a competitive advantage through lower operational costs and added sustainability value.

Surprising Fact *- Apartment tenants with EVs that participate in vehicle to grid (V2G) can serve as on-site, mobile energy storage, allowing apartment complexes to significantly expand EV charging capacity without increasing building electrical service capacity (panels, feeders, transformers). This allows the addition of more EV chargers without triggering costly utility or service-upgrade requirements, because the EVs themselves buffer and supply power.*

Vehicle Compatibility and User Management

Not all EVs currently support V2G functions, and each participating vehicle may have different charging limits, permissions, and user preferences. Property owners should establish clear participation agreements and software controls to ensure that residents can safely opt in or out of energy-sharing programs. Well-defined settings help balance tenant convenience with property-level energy goals. As vehicle compatibility improves and standards become more consistent, managing user participation will become simpler and more automated within property energy platforms.

Equipment Requirements

Implementing V2G requires specialized bidirectional chargers, compatible V2G-capable vehicles, and advanced communication protocols such as ISO 15118 to enable secure data exchange between chargers, vehicles, and energy management systems. Because most standard chargers today only support one-way power flow, apartment owners interested in V2G should plan for pilot-ready or upgradeable infrastructure. Investing in V2G-compatible systems now can future-proof properties for evolving energy markets and ensure readiness as automakers expand V2G support in upcoming EV models.

Utility and Energy Regulations

Participation in V2G programs depends heavily on cooperation with local utilities and compliance with interconnection and metering rules. Regulations are evolving as utilities begin to test compensation models for energy supplied back to the grid from EVs. Apartment owners should engage early with their local utility provider to understand grid requirements, available incentives, and necessary technical approvals. Proactive coordination helps avoid delays and ensures that the V2G system operates safely and within regulatory frameworks.

V2G comes with an additional burden on the utility companies when considering there are regulations that calls upon the utility companies to maintain the power quality within permissible limits for voltage and frequency. By-directional power flow inadvertently adds utility companies to design more resilient power system protection to handle any hazards. Roof-top renewable energy is usually available with bi-directional power flow capabilities with many practical solutions commercially available for apartment owners. However, for V2G solutions, their scalability continues to become a topic of exploration especially for large numbers and dispersed nature at apartments. Therefore, to ensure such adoption at wide scale a deregulated power grid system allowing V2G solutions to directly provide distributed generation at large scale becomes an area of exploration for apartments.

Permission to Operate (PTO) Grid Interconnection

Permission to operate (PTO) is a formal approval from the utility company that allows a distributed energy resource (such as solar panels or EV charging infrastructure) to connect and operate in parallel with the electric grid. The PTO process typically involves inspection, verification of safety and compliance, and confirmation that the system will not adversely affect grid stability. For EV charging infrastructure, obtaining PTO is crucial before activating chargers that may export power (such as bi-directional or V2G systems). The utility may require documentation, testing, and sometimes coordination with local authorities before granting PTO.

Sustainable Solutions with Renewable Energy Integration

An EV charging system for apartments operating to reduce the tail-pipe emissions must derive motivation to further reduce emissions from conventional power generation resources. The on-site renewable energy from roof-top solar comes as an excellent potential for apartments. Published research by the National Renewable Energy Laboratory has validated that almost any region in the United States has enough solar irradiance to generate electricity from on-site solar with positive returns on investment (ROI). Commercialization of roof-top solar comes from awareness and motivations toward a sustainable future. Many developers in the construction industry have implemented large scale roof-top solar photovoltaic solutions for apartments. However, for modern apartment communities, such systems must become part of standard amenities.

Appendix 1 - EV Charging System Resources

If you're looking to dive deeper into the world of EV charging systems at apartments and businesses, we've put together a set of trusted resources that expand on what you've learned in this book. These tools and platforms are designed to help apartment owners & managers, EV equipment distributors and systems integrators, EV charging professionals and others to discover, learn and be able to explain charging equipment, systems and services.

EV Charging System Training – Classroom & Online Formats

This book and expanded versions of its content are available in instructor-led training sessions, both online and in person. You can use these to build foundational knowledge or as part of business and training programs.

Whether you're preparing for EV certification, training new staff, or looking to develop EV charging knowledge and skills, these classroom tools are highly adaptable.

To get more information about EV Charging for Apartments Training course, go to: EVBusiness.net/evcacourse

EV Business Magazine

Do you want to keep up with EV industry news, technology, business and solutions?

EV Business Magazine is a go-to publication for staying ahead of industry trends.

You will find key industry news stories, articles on EV industry technologies and solutions, lists of upcoming EV industry events and more.

To view or subscribe to EV Business Magazine, go to EVBusiness.net/magazine

EV Business Podcast

EVBusiness podcast brings you insider conversations with experts who are shaping the EV industry.

EV Business podcast episodes provide:

Quick Learning Sessions – Ideal for sales agents and techs looking to absorb info during commutes or lunch breaks.

Explainer Interviews – Topics like over-the-air updates, fleet monitoring, or remote diagnostics, made clear and relevant.

Emerging Trend Alerts – Stay on top of what's next with insights into policies, software rollouts, and consumer behavior.

To tune in to stay sharp and informed, go to EVBusiness.net/podcast

EVs Charging for Apartments and Businesses Group

Do you want to get questions answered and interact with industry experts?

Join the EV Charging for Apartments and MDUs Discussion Group.

This discussion group is your charging stop for asking questions, sharing ideas and networking with EV professionals and experts.

To start interacting with EV industry people, go to EVBusiness.net/evcm

EV Industry Directory

Do you want to find an EV tool, supplier, or electric vehicle specific service?

The EV Industry Directory is your directory guide.

It helps you quickly locate: EV-Ready Tools and Software – From diagnostic equipment to dealer apps.

Verified Service Providers – Charging networks, installers, battery recovery services, and more.

OEM and Supplier Listings – Contact info and service outlines for hundreds of EV ecosystem companies.

Save time, find what you need, and work smarter with this curated directory.

The directory is open for anyone to use and for companies to be listed at no cost.

To find your EV industry tools and solutions, go to EVDirectory.org

www.ingramcontent.com/pod-product-compliance
Lightning Source LLC
LaVergne TN
LVHW080309110826
845155LV00023B/98